I0161233

WHAT PEOPLE ARE SAYING ABOUT
FOOD ADDICTION: PROBLEMS AND SOLUTIONS
AND THE CARYL EHRLICH PROGRAM

"This is it! You finally found it – a way to lose weight and maintain a healthy weight without dieting. You can follow this plan at home, in restaurants, and at friends' homes.

Caryl Ehrlich has developed and perfected a way, The Program way, to show you how to take control of your eating, and how to distinguish between when you are hungry and when you are eating for some other reason. She helps you see the habits that made you overweight, and helps you overcome them with her behavioral approach.

Food just becomes less important as you work your way through The Program. You'll be surprised at how simple it is. And you will lose weight with so much less effort than with any diet you have ever been on. The Program encourages you to try new foods and savor the things you choose to put in your mouth. It works because it makes sense, and is lasting unlike other weight loss experiences. This way of eating becomes a normal way of life in a short time.

I saw a friend who looked – smaller, healthier, and happier. He told me about Caryl. I learned The Program and became smaller, healthier and happier myself. This book brings the brilliance of this method of managing food to a wider audience, who can now also look forward to being smaller, healthier and happier themselves."

— **Susan Dwyer, New York City**

"I am a totally happy alumnus of The Caryl Ehrlich Program. The uniqueness of the plan — and the reason it succeeds over the years — is that it is not a diet in the classic sense of the word; rather it is behavioral modification program that offers simple "rules" of how to eat, not so much what to eat. To this day, tips like weighing yourself twice a day, counting the number of items consumed every day, keeping portion sizes the size of a deck of cards, and slowing down when I eat, keep my weight under control."

— **Elkan Abramowitz, New York City**

"The Caryl Ehrlich Program has given me the tools first to lose the weight I needed to lose and then to keep it off. It really is not a 'diet' in the traditional sense because it's something you can live by and do the rest of your life and be totally happy. As Caryl says, 'There's nothing you cannot eat!' You just have to stay within the Program guidelines in terms of how you eat, when you eat, and her famous 'Skipping and Scattering' of types of food throughout the day and week. It works.

"Daily weighing morning and bedtime has become a ritual for me; it provides immediate feedback as to what I've been doing. With my food log, I can go back and diagnose exactly why the scale has moved up a pound or so and adjust.

For a while, I thought the travel scale idea was crazy, but when I went on long trips, it became hard not to have the daily feedback.

I enjoy the things I do eat so much more now vs. just wolfing them down and not even noticing.

"Because of my lower weight and lesser body fat, I feel more energetic; I've gone back to the gym twice a week with a trainer, and I play tennis every weekend. Thanks, Caryl!"

— **Bill D., New York City**

"The Caryl Ehrlich Program is not a diet. It is a reprogramming of many habits I picked up over the years that had led to me overeating and not being able to maintain the weight that I wanted to be. The Program helped me break the cycle of the habits I had, introduce new habits and learn how to act appropriately around food in social settings. The Program is miraculous as it doesn't stop you eating all the things that you love. Yet its results are definitive. More importantly, it is a lifelong Program. It was a complete success for me."

— **Patrick LH, New York City**

"I'm very results oriented, and Caryl knows that all of us need to set a target to shoot for and a weight number is that objective 'end game.'

The best part about the program is a more proactive approach to taking ownership of your eating habits…."

— **Price from Texas**

"The Program changed my life. Before I'd always been in the Yo-Yo weight mode, constantly going up and down and usually ending up higher than when I started. With The Program, for the first time I was given a strategy about how to eat, not just what (and what not) to eat. Now I eat anything I want to, I just don't do it all the time and without structure the way I did before. Caryl taught me that if I change my behavior, the food I eat will follow and weight loss will be the natural result. It was almost easy — twenty-five pounds lost in three months and I felt fabulous and not deprived. The Program changed my whole approach to food, which makes it possible for me to cope with any situation — a buffet, a big dessert table, an opulent cocktail party — and come away satisfied and comfortable. All my life, whenever I've been on a diet (which has been most of the time), I've always intoned the mantra — "I'm not on a diet, I'm pursuing a way of life" — but it was never true before now. Before my diets were all about controlling my eating, instead of being about structuring my eating. The first is all about deprivation, the second is all about organization — have whatever you want to, but have it at the right time, in the right way and in the right amount."

— **Warren K., Dallas, TX**

"I was introduced to Caryl Ehrlich and The Program and I freed myself from the shackles of dieting and changed my behavior and relationship with food!"

— **Joanne Savino, New Jersey**

"I did The Caryl Ehrlich Program over twenty years ago. While I was not a lot overweight, I felt I had this seven-pound weight fluctuation I had no control over. What I learned was not only how to control my weight even to the one-half pound, but how to enjoy eating without worry or diet. I learned that choosing what you eat is a lifelong project, a lifestyle choice, so to speak. I learned to trust myself; that if I gain a few pounds, I can go back to my new regular way of eating (The Program way), and bring the weight right back to my desired weight. The Program has trained me for a life of satisfying worry-free eating."

— **Joan Lefkowitz, New York City**

"The Program is the best thing I ever did in my life. It changed me forever. I am so lucky I met Caryl. The Program is not a diet; it is a way of life. You never think of food in the same way again. The Program is simple. You can maintain a normal life and still keep your weight in check. More important than weight loss, Caryl helps you to understand yourself better and the reasons why you eat. She knows the pain of not being able to "take off your jacket" or "the fear of a summer party invitation" and "what to wear." The Program gives you the confidence to know that you can do it."

— **Brian J. New York City**

"After gaining weight during my son's diagnosis of cancer and his death, I struggled with the stress weight and it served as a reminder daily of the battle we waged on behalf of him. I wanted this off and wanted it off in a healthy way. Caryl's Program was the answer I was looking for. It worked well beyond my expectations because she coached me through it and encouraged me as well.

"The first time I heard of a soup meal, I balked and fought back. I thought, 'How crazy. I need protein and lots of it. Soup! For a meal! Boring, not filling. Not enough protein and not manly.' How wrong was I? I look forward to soup and enjoy it so much more now after The Program. The Program has made me enjoy food and its flavors and a variety of combinations even more."

— **Tait, Dallas, Texas**

"The Caryl Ehrlich Program is unlike any other program because I could eat everything prepared any way. The only exclusion is that no diet foods are allowed. The Program is very doable. I could eat anywhere and no one would know that I was doing anything special. I think this worked for me because The Program is a solid behavioral approach with suggestions for many different food-related situations from which I could choose what specifically worked for me.

Caryl offers strategies, encouragement, applause; she's always following up and counts the smallest victory to highlight how far I've come. She corrects my negative thinking, puts a positive spin on it and then my actions improve. The food-log evaluation is an invaluable tool to show me what works and what needs work. Caryl's Program is not about deprivation with lists of what not to eat. The difference with me now is that I've learned how to get that weight back to the exact number I like it to be. The bottom line: I lost the weight twenty years ago and have kept it off through numerous eating challenges."

— **Lana J., New York City**

"My Program . . . yes. I continue to stick with it, and now I am twenty-five pounds thinner than when I started a few months ago. I am very pleased with my results and the scale continues slowly to inch down. I have another eight or so pounds to lose to meet my goal, but I know I will get there.

"The best thing, besides the compliments and feeling great, is that I keep telling people I am NOT on a diet. I have just made a life adjustment in how I eat. It happens to be true. I eat everything I want, just less, and I use many of your techniques. I think my chances for keeping it off are better than any 'diet' I have ever been on. So you are my hero (and yes, you can quote me).

"P.S. I was a bit below my goal weight on 11/19/15, my wedding day. Thanks."

— **Diane, New York City**

"In the middle of August 2008, I visited my doctor complaining of malaise, stomach pains, and overall fatigue. Following a perfect physical report, my doctor forced me to step on the scale. It had been years since I dared to weigh myself, only acknowledging weight gain through the fit of my clothing. Much to my shock, I was at least thirty pounds over my goal weight! My doctor gave me the name of Caryl Ehrlich, who ten years ago helped the doctor's wife lose twenty pounds which to this day she kept off. Caryl's program just made sense!

Caryl taught me how to eat smarter without ever having to deprive myself of any of my favorite foods. By learning how to eat slower and confronting my addiction, I changed my eating patterns! In only a few months, I'm thirty pounds lighter and feel confident, attractive, and am enjoying my new life. Instead of dreading getting dressed in the morning, I relish it. I can now wear a belt, button down blouses, even my "skinny" jeans. I can't thank Caryl enough for helping me change my life."

— **Felicia M., New York City**

"Thank you so much for giving me the tools in thought and action to maintain a comfortable weight! I am still at my goal and have made it through the holidays...wahoooooooooooo!!!"

— **Renee, Milwaukee, Wisconsin**

CARYL EHRLICH

FOOD ADDICTION:

PROBLEMS AND SOLUTIONS

Food Addiction: Problems and Solutions
Copyright © 2018 by Caryl Ehrlich

All Rights Reserved. No part of this book may be used or reproduced in any manner whatsoever without the expressed written consent of the author, except in the case of brief quotations with credit embodied in articles, books, and reviews.

Address all inquiries to:
Caryl Ehrlich
Caryl@ConquerFood.com
www.ConquerFood.com

ISBN: 978-1-940984-87-2
Library of Congress Control Number: 2017902333

Editor: www.superiorbookproductions.com
Interior Design: Fusion Creative Works, fusioncw.com
Cover Design: Mercantile Media, mediamercantile.com
Cover: 2001 Collage, "Person Filled with Reasons to Eat" by Caryl Ehrlich

Published by:

AVIVA
PUBLISHING
New York

Aviva Publishing
Lake Placid, NY
www.avivapubs.com

Every attempt has been made to source properly all quotes.

Printed in the USA
First Edition

". . .the idea that addiction is simply a consequence of willfulness still permeates the profession."

— Journal of the American Medical Association (JAMA)

I dedicate this book to Joan Lefkowitz
who kept kicking the box.

The book is not intended to replace medical advice or to be a substitute for a physician. Always seek the advice of a physician before beginning any weight-loss or exercise program. The author and publisher specifically disclaim any and all liability arising from the use of any information contained in this book. If you are under a physician's care for any condition, he or she can advise you about information described in this book.

CONTENTS

DEAR READER

Dear Reader,

What is Food Addiction? Do you have it? There's a little quiz in the book that might give you the answer.

This book is about "compulsive eating," "overeating," and "I can't stop once I start eating" behavior, i.e., Food Addiction. It is about feeling out of control around food, and how to regain your control by learning new behavioral techniques.

When I wrote my first book, I couldn't think of a name for it. I even hosted a party of ten friends whom I gathered so each one could come up with ten names for the book. Other than *Fifty Ways to Lose Your Blubber* (which was not used), there was not one name that appealed to me. My publisher named it *Conquer Your Food Addiction*. It was based on The Caryl Ehrlich Program (The Program), a behavioral approach to weight loss I'd been teaching since 1981.

When I excitedly called my best friend to tell her the publisher had named the book *Conquer Your Food Addiction*, there was a long silence.

"It IS an addiction," I said into the phone.

"I know," she said resignedly. "But did they have to put it on the cover?"

It's hard to think of yourself as an "addict" if you are not mis-using traditional substances like cigarettes, alcohol, and drugs, or if your addiction is not related to a substance, like being a workaholic or shopaholic. But a foodaholic? How could that be? Food is good and healthy, and life-sustaining, right?

You may be thinking, "I eat well. I could lose a few pounds, though. I don't have much to lose but I feel out of control around food. The last time I weighed my goal weight was when I was in my late teens and early twenties. And to top it off, I seem to gain a few pounds every year." That's part of the definition of addic-tion: continuing to do whatever you are doing even though there are negative consequences.

No one sets out to weigh five, ten, or sixty pounds more than their best weight. I didn't set a goal that would have me weighing fifty pounds more than I wanted to by the time I was in my thir-ties. Did you? No, of course not. It was the dutiful child in you that finished everything on your plate. And that ritual became more and more frequent. Another example of ritual behavior that leads to weight gain is how you eat a black & white cookie, a chocolate chip cookie, or an entire box of cookies. The way you stir your coffee or mix your drink. All rituals. And rituals have a way of increasing in frequency and volume. One small cup of coffee becomes a medium, then a large, and then an XLarge, just like clothing sizes. Daily consumption of a particular food or beverage increases to twice daily or more.

My original goal years ago was to be able to eat real food in the real world prepared any way I wanted, with no one knowing that I was trying to lose weight. I succeeded. You can too.

Go ahead. Put the butter on your baked potato because it's not about the food you eat. It's about your identifying your inappropriate use of food – like eating when you are lonely, bored, anxious, sleepy, and grumpy. Or you're eating because it's your birthday, my birthday, our anniversary, graduation day, or the 4th of July and you're thinking, "I'll never pass this way again." It's about finding the right way to change your habits and replace your "Addict" voice with your "Program" voice.

My focus is to help you identify your entrenched patterns and figure out how to best interrupt each cycle to create a new pattern – a new behavior that will eventually be as comfortable as the old way. Eventually it will be the default setting. The preferred way.

Over the years, I collected email conversations (participants' incoming emails and my email responses) because I thought they might help others. Many of those verbatim emails are included in this book with fictional names to protect people's privacy. I included these stories because I believe they speak to many situations, perhaps even yours.

In our fast-paced world when instant gratification isn't instant enough, the thought of stopping to smell the roses, or to take 20 minutes to eat a meal, is a foreign language worth learning.

Onward and downward,
Caryl

If you have any questions, comments, or inquiries:
Caryl@ConquerFood.com
www.ConquerFood.com

THE PROGRAM WAY

The Program is a shortened way of saying **The Caryl Ehrlich Program**, which is a comprehensive behavioral approach to weight loss. One of the first questions people ask is: What can I eat? The answer is: anything; you just can't eat it all in the same meal.

The problem is that many of you who are watching your weight are so used to limiting what you can or cannot eat based on a mass of misinformation — ill-informed, over-hyped weight-control messages in the marketplace — that you simply don't get enough variety or satisfaction from what you do eat. Or someone else is deciding what you should eat. The Program shows you interesting possibilities of how to enjoy what you're eating and still lose weight.

The more important dimension of **The Program** concerns your inappropriate, ritualized use of food. You may have unconsciously created actions and thoughts containing food, to distract yourself from feeling things you don't want to feel. The Program contains many components. Food is just one of them.

The other parts of food addiction are the behavioral ritual blanket you've woven to self-medicate, and zone out. Then your mood, situation, and circumstance dictate when, what, and how much you're going to eat. Before you know it, you're eating just because it's there, or you're bored, or it's the only thing you could find, or the stock market went down (or up). It doesn't matter. That web of distraction comprises the things you say (*I can't eat that; I can't stop once I start; I can't eat in that restaurant*), what you wear (*I only wear dark colors; I can't wear belts; I can't shop in that store; all the clothes in my closet are tight*), finding the right recipes (*This is fat-free; this is sugar-free; this is taste-free*).

Another part of your web of distraction might be how you buy and keep clothes you've never worn. Or discussing with friends every up and down of how "good" and "bad" you are with your weight-loss plan. One of the most popular distractions is to avoid getting on the scale. If you don't know what you weigh, you don't have to do anything about it.

You might be avoiding the beach for fear of walking around in shorts or a bathing suit. When it comes to distracting ritual behavior, it is just as seductive as the smell of a cup of coffee, the texture of a roll, the flavor of sirloin steak, the crunch of a French fried potato. *This is how I eat in a Chinese restaurant, an Italian restaurant, Sunday brunch, when I celebrate, when I grieve.* These ritual behaviors are familiar and comfortable. If the ritual has many components, it can distract you from always thinking about the reason you eat when you are not hungry in the first place.

The Program will lead you from your old way of thinking — The Addict Pea Brain way of thinking — to a new way of thinking — The Program Brain way of thinking. And then cheer you on to the finish line as you choose to weigh _____ pounds.

The way to unravel the snarl of ritualized behavior you've created is to rewrite, in your own handwriting, the foundation of The Program. Then read and reread those sections. Or highlight them with a colored marker as you read. You learn by speaking and hearing, writing and reading. You want to use all four barrels to quell the power of the entrenched habits that seem cemented to your psyche.

Practice the new way, and your new way of thinking and acting will become comfortable, automatic, and preferred.

HOW DO YOU KNOW WHETHER YOU ARE A FOOD ADDICT

Food Addiction is a chronic, progressive disease.

Three components of food-addiction you should know about are:

- Resistance to Change
- Frequency Patterns
- Portion Sizes

Let's look at each one now in more detail.

FOOD ADDICTION COMPONENT ONE: RESISTANCE TO CHANGE

Though you might be unhappy with your weight, it doesn't mean that you want to relinquish all your old habits, which are oh so comfortable that you don't even realize you were not born this way. Even though you want to weigh _____ pounds, you'll resist change. Resistance to change is very prominent in most addictions but particularly potent when it comes to your behavior with food.

The fantasy thinking is, "I do want to reach my goal, but I don't want to change anything."

In the first meeting, people will tell me they'll do anything to reach their weight goal. The next week they tell me: "I kept my log for a few days and then stopped. I got on the scale in the morning but couldn't manage it in the evening." Rather than a wide variety of food, you continue eating the same thing every day. You might think it is the food that comforts, but in reality, it is the ritual that makes you comfortable. From the first step to the last, it is the ritual or the cycle of addiction. From the first sighting to the last moment of remorse, the cycle takes hold.

Maybe you think you can handle extra food in your refrigerator when you've never been able to handle it before. Not admitting you have a problem is a problem. It is resistance to change. There may be a thousand ways you might be resisting: By letting others decide when you eat, what you eat, and how much you eat. You might leave it to others to shop for food for you and prepare it; many people tell me, "My husband (or wife) does all the cooking. I hate to ask for special dishes." Resisting change might be when friends want to eat after (rather than before) the theater or a movie and you say, "Okay." Which ways do you sabotage your weight loss goals by saying, "Okay," just to please a friend.

If you are so hooked on a particular item (like coffee, alcohol, or sugar) that stopping causes withdrawal, you've built a tolerance and are not feeling the hyped-up feeling you want to feel. Because you use a particular food (or foods) so often, the escalated frequency and portion feels normal.

FOOD ADDICTION COMPONENT TWO: FREQUENCY

How often do you have a cup of coffee (or more) at breakfast? Do you drink coffee throughout the day? Do you buy it at a certain place where they know you want double cream and double sugar? You are reinforcing a frequency pattern. And once the barista knows how you drink your beverage, he/she takes over the task of mindfulness. You become mindless. You don't have to think about anything. That's why you keep going back. Everyone knows your name. Well maybe not your given name, but they know you as "Medium-coffee-with-double-cream-and-sugar." It's now automatic for you. It's automatic for the server. We are all creatures of habit.

Is bread a part of every restaurant meal? Do you always partake of appetizers in a restaurant when they are available? How often do you say yes to sharing a dessert. Your friends don't need you to say yes. If they really want it, they will order it. It may not seem like a lot — a little coffee here, a drink there, some bread and dessert on Saturday night, a little more at a client lunch.

Do you always eat toast, coffee, and orange juice with your omelet on Sunday morning? Whatever you're doing once a week, you're doing fifty-two times a year. Twice a week? That's one 104 times a year.

One or more coffees a day is gallons by year's end. Two pieces of bread every single day, after 365 days, is counted in loaves. A cocktail every night is barrels of brew by year's end. Five times a week might be that extra twenty or thirty pounds you're hiding behind a vest.

At year's end, you've had lots of bread, two slices at a time, vats of coffee, and cases of alcohol in addition to bags and boxes full of candy, popcorn, potato chips, pretzels, cookies, ice cream bars, and other similar finger foods.

The frequency increases. The once-a-day becomes twice-a-day. Having a drink on the weekend becomes having a drink every time you're in a restaurant. You're in a restaurant many times each week for business and personal reasons. That all adds up.

What foods are you consuming so frequently that you've lost count?

There is water, and everything else is food. A Program participant told me she sipped tea all day long and didn't know how to count it so she didn't write it down. "It has no calories," she said, pleading her case. She'd forgotten my mantra: If it's not water, it's food.

Another participant made a pot of soup every few days and kept dipping her cup into the simmering concoction until it was gone. Then she'd make another pot.

If you're eating one item of food every day, you're consuming it 365 days a year. If you're having multiples of any item (two pieces of bread, two cups of coffee, and multiple glasses of wine), you do the math.

Skipping and Scattering is to counter the daily consumption of any food. If you have any item today, whether salad or steak, coffee or cake, Skip at least one day before ordering that same item again. Every other day of one item would be 182 times a year. It also helps you unravel some of your entrenched, ritualized behaviors. It makes you think about whether or not you had the same item yesterday or would prefer to have it tomorrow. Getting out of denial and into mindfulness is half the battle. The woman who helped organize materials for this book became aware that she was stopping off every day (five days a week) to get a free sample from a candy store on Fifth Avenue. When she realized how frequently she was doing that, she started walking on Sixth Avenue (Avenue of the Americas) in New York City.

Purchasing and consuming these foods has become so ritualized, automatized, and comfortable that you can't recall your habits not being a big part of your life. The question isn't always about what you are eating. The question is: How often are you eating the same item(s) of food(s) throughout each day?

FOOD ADDICTION COMPONENT THREE: PORTION SIZE.

A cup is 8 ounces. Yet most of the cups/mugs/glasses I see are masquerading as a cup but are really oversized beverage containers. Not only has the size of a cup increased to mug size, but there is a now a venti (24 ounces or in Program jargon, three cups of coffee), and a trenta (31 ounces. Do you not see that is almost a quart of beverage?!) One fast food restaurant has a 42-ounce beverage container.

Bagels have grown from 3-4 ounces to 6 or 7 ounces in the last twenty years. Rolls and muffins have muffin-tops of their own. A glass of wine used to be poured into an 8-12 ounce goblet. Now a goblet in a restaurant might be 18-22 ounces. If you have one drink in a restaurant and you are served a 5-ounce portion in an 18-ounce glass, visually it looks like a very small amount of wine. It might prompt you to order a second drink. Has that happened to you?

Even more troublesome is when you're at a party with the 18-ounce glass and people pour far more wine into a bigger goblet than they would into a smaller one. For liquids, 8 ounces or less is a portion of coffee or tea. Alcohol is 5 ounces or less of wine. And beer should be poured into a glass so you can see how much there is while you're sipping along with food and water.

A friend who collects cookbooks told me that the portion per person has increased in recipes dramatically over the past fifty years.

People are totally confused with soup container sizes, each different from the next. Another reason for spooning things into a bowl or putting other foods onto flat plates: You'll be much more aware of amounts.

Your portions have increased, the frequency has increased. And you've increased.

You might say you'll do anything to change, yet you resist doing the new things. When learning how to change habits of thought and habits of action, your Addict Pea Brain (the mindless, reptilian, instinctive, unthinking, habituated part of your conscious brain), may have other ideas. The old habits are deeply ingrained and entrenched from years of repetition. It's not that the old way is so wonderful, but it is familiar and comfortable, which is why you hold onto it with such passion.

If you do the new way enough times, it becomes familiar and comfortable too. It becomes the default setting. But so far, the old way is still compelling.

You may think: If I do something different, I won't feel as comfortable as I do with my old habits. Of course you don't know that to be true. So you continue to do the old way, reinforcing it once more, keeping it chronic. You eat because something looks good or smells good or just because it's there, or to distract yourself from stressful decision-making, or boredom. Your resistance to change is clear. You want to change your weight, but you may not want to change your habits.

By the time you find The Program, you've most likely tried every popular weight loss method-of-the-day. You might tell me you'll do anything. Yet when you review your progress on The Program, you realize that you are marking "could do better" or "seldom or never accomplish" next to the statement that asks whether you are keeping a log of all consumed foods, which is a critical part of The Program.

You kept a log for a few days and then the weekend arrived. You wrote down everything except what you ate at a party. The same happened with the assignment to weigh first thing in the morning and the last thing at night. There's a conscious and unconscious resistance to change.

Yet you do change. Just this morning, a woman from Canada told me that when she first heard no-diet soda or diet-crap in the first meeting of The Program, she couldn't believe that two months later her beverage of choice would be water. But she sure did resist in the beginning.

CHAPTER 1

PITFALLS

REASONS I EAT/POSSIBLE PITFALLS

You may think you eat when you're hungry, but most likely, you don't even know what hunger feels like. Do you know what hunger feels like? Or are you eating because someone said that dinner was on the table? Are you eating because a basket filled with bread just arrived?

I remember waking up a few weeks into my own Program years ago with an uncomfortable feeling. *What was that?* I thought. I finally figured out I was hungry. I remembered that feeling when I was a child. I woke up hungry and could not go to school without eating something. When I started overeating years later, I ate so much in the evening, I was not hungry for breakfast. Sometimes, I was not hungry until late in the afternoon. I should have been.

There are thousands of reasons that trigger your overeating — and overeating doesn't necessarily mean large quantities of food consumed at the same time. It could be that during the day you have a bite of something you found in the refrigerator, or you drink a cold beverage because it's hot outside. Maybe the candy bar at 4 p.m. was helping you quell anxiety. For a moment. But then you need more and more (portion size increases), and you gotta get your fix more and more frequently.

Are you eating more in the evening than during the day?

During the day you have places to go, people to see, people to call, and there are numerous things to do: to buy, to shop, to chop, to clean, to create, to cook whew! There are hours to go before you sleep. Television may not to be to your liking, so you may have, in the past, browsed among the foods in the kitchen that are instant, quick, and require no preparation. Maybe microwavable.

Or you're out with friends and listening to their often-told story that was boring to begin with. You might order an un-planned dessert.

Perhaps it is broken-hearted eating. You've all been there. Did the other person ever come back and say, "Stop eating. I won't leave"?

Which one (or more) of the following habits or rituals pertain to you? Circle or highlight the ones that you relate to.

Boredom. Boredom is one of the most popular of all the Pitfalls or Reasons Why You Eat.

Keeping busy during the day is a comfortable part of life. You get up, shower, shave, dress, get the kids off to school or yourself to work. There are numerous distractions from coworkers, bosses, and subordinates. There are phone calls to make, meetings to attend, texts to send, e-mails to edit, and so many projects to complete that there never seems to be enough hours in each day.

Then the workday is over. The evening arrives. Boredom sets in. The eating begins! Television might be boring, cleaning doesn't hold your interest, and compared to the daytime hours of places to go and people to see, evenings are slower paced.

Boredom is not a reason to eat. If you are eating to kill time, find another hobby. Numerous courses are offered to please the most discerning person. There are books to read, concerts to attend, and places to visit. Can't leave your home? Learn to play bridge, mah jong, or Scrabble. One family member got into coin collecting. His wife loved her garden.

Stress. Another Possible Pitfall is Stress. It ties with Boredom in popularity, as a reason you eat.

There's obvious stress caused by anxiety, pressure, and constant worry. It may be deadlines in a business setting, tension, and strain in a personal or professional situation. Stress might be related to financial or health worries, or it could be trying to find a balance between family, friends, and coworkers. All these situations are stressful. It's not a reason to eat.

Is it unplanned food that is proffered, pushed, and purveyed in a restaurant? Is it the bread in a basket, celery and olives on a tray, and the cookies that come with the check? It's stressful when you want to weigh _____ pounds, and you are given free food. Your Program Brain is thinking: I do want to weigh _____ pounds. And your Addict Pea Brain is thinking: Should I? Shouldn't I? I want it. It looks good. It smells good. It's free and it's here. This is stressful.

Eating instead of doing a chore. As I'm sitting here writing, I'm also editing other chapters. As things occur to me, I go from one chapter to another. In the past when I couldn't think of one more thing to write, I might have detoured into the kitchen, an old habit. Now I realize that writing is not always a straight line. It is not always comfortable. When writing, many pauses, evaluations, and creative battles occur before the words reach the page or stay on the page. None of it is a reason to eat.

Instead of eating, I turn off the computer and get comfortable reading or watching television. In that way, the moment passes and I got some rest. My break might be five minutes, or more, depending on what is needed. It's not a reason to eat.

Do you eat to avoid doing something else? When I am thinking of food, and I know I'm not hungry, I know I need a break.

It was there. Another reason people eat is simply the presence and availability of food. It might be in a restaurant where a salad and a beverage come with a meal. It could be at a dinner party where the host(ess) puts platters of cheese, crackers, chips, and dips on all the side tables in case someone is hungry before dinner is served.

Are you eating things so they won't spoil? Do you think "it's" so small it can't possibly count?

Leaving food in the freezer makes the perfect barrier of inconvenience — you have to defrost it (or cook it) before you can eat it. If it is sitting in your refrigerator in its edible incarnation, and you're looking for something to avoid boredom or stress, you'll eat it because it is there.

Prepared food in your refrigerator is too instant, quick, and easily available.

Forming a bond. Perhaps you think you're forming a bond with someone, so you share popcorn when at a movie or dessert in a restaurant. Perhaps the other person has ordered dessert with two forks and an expensive bottle of wine to enjoy as the sun sets. One of the most popular reasons people overeat in a restaurant or at a party is to please someone else.

This book's editor wrote me the following comment after reading that above paragraph. He said, "Exactly. I went to lunch yesterday and I never order dessert, but my companion ordered dessert so I did too, even though I knew I didn't need it or want it, but I wanted to please him, not make him feel guilty about eating his. I didn't really consciously realize all that until later when I came home and went back to editing your book!"

You might eat during food preparation and put-away. Perhaps once you start, you can't stop. You might think, *What difference does it make? I blew it anyway.* Maybe you use food as a reward because you did something wonderful or as a punishment because you already overate and you're thinking, *It won't make a difference.*

When you smell the coffee in your office, or the popcorn in a movie, or fresh doughnuts in a bakery, do you queue up? Do you use food as a meal extender? You're having such a nice time and don't want the evening to end, so you order another cup of coffee, a cocktail, a dessert. You're entertaining guests. There is an abundance of extra food and all those leftovers.

Going home to family is tricky for some. You may feel guilty that your friends and family have been cooking since last Thursday, and you have to taste and comment on everything that is offered. Does the cook get offended if you don't have seconds and thirds?

Are you too tired to cook so you *pick pick pick* and convince yourself you didn't eat anything?

You eat differently with men, women, and children. You eat when you're up or down, alone or with others.

Fatigue is often mistaken for hunger; so when you're tired you get the urge to eat.

In order for the lost weight to remain lost, you want to identify your Pitfalls.

Whether you overeat because of genetics, ethnicity, religion, circumstance, situation, or emotion doesn't matter. Perhaps you eat for some of those reasons or all of these reasons. Each of you gets into the habit of using food inappropriately by eating even if you're not hungry. Having followed these habits for such a long time — sometimes decades — they've become involuntary conditioned responses. Everything you highlight or circle is what your extra pounds looks like. In one ten-minute period of time, you could get a phone call, feel stressed, be having company, and be unable to find your car keys. That's life. And none of it is a reason to eat. The only reason to eat? Hunger. And it's not even on the page.

IS YOUR PARTNER A COMPASSIONATE COLLABORATOR OR A SECRET SABOTEUR?

Two can shed those unwanted and unhealthy pounds as easily as one.

Regardless of what month it is — February, December, June, or September — it's always a good time for spouses, lovers, roommates, and even office friends to begin to offer the moral support that makes it easier for everyone to learn better eating habits. Under the best circumstances, it's not easy to lose weight. But when a partner is offering unplanned food instead of moral support, it's doubly difficult. And even if he or she insists, "I love you just the way you are," you'd like to lose those extra pounds just the same for yourself.

If your partner is a Secret Saboteur, he or she might tell you how great you look, but still ask you to taste the cookies that were just baked. One woman told me her husband kept offering her "ippsy pippsies," a euphemism for "It's such a small amount it couldn't possibly count." Your partner needs to be told, "If you really love me, keep my water glass filled." Or better yet, "Buy me jewelry; I can get food myself!"

A Compassionate Collaborator is someone who will smooth the eating road before you, lead you not into food temptation, and support whatever method works for you.

When I ask participants whom I'm teaching in person, out of all the Pitfalls, which ones occur most frequently, across all ages, sexes, and ethnicities, it is unstructured time, and boredom, usually evenings and weekends that is a big eating trigger. And a close second and third are stress and anxiety.

Here are some tips to help you set goals with the people you often eat with, to identify destructive eating habits (Pitfalls), and create constructive habits together:

- Whether just dating or living with a significant other, or your college roommates, discuss the foods you bring into the house. Have rules about putting all food behind closed cabinets. If you don't see it, you're less likely to eat it.

- Ask, "May I get you something" rather than trying to whet the other's appetite by describing all available food in the house. You might be eating to please someone else, not because you're hungry. Ask the other person to give you the same courtesy.

- Don't offer unplanned food to one another.

- Acknowledge that your partner has a weight problem. Even though you may love your wife, husband, or friend just the way he or she is, don't fight your partner's desire to change his or her eating habits. Your partner wouldn't be telling you this personal truth if it were not important.

- Prior to eating, decide on meal content together. You're more likely to stick to your meal plan if you discuss it with each other. Even deciding which restaurant to go to is helpful.

- Plan your food consumption in the morning. This way, you won't have hamburger for lunch if your partner will be cooking meatloaf for supper. A lack of variety can quickly push you off your plan.

- Look for opportunities to offer each other encouraging remarks. For example, rather than focusing on problems and shortcomings, say something like, "Your new way of eating seems to be working. I can see the difference in the way your clothes fit."

- If your partner has to work late, eat first even though convention keeps encouraging you to eat together. Then when the late-working partner arrives, drink water and make conversation while your partner eats dinner. If you both have extremely busy schedules, you might make a date to have dinner together at least one night each weekend and one night each weekday.

- Finally, never infer that love or friendship will be withdrawn if food is refused.

Amanda T. had a weight problem for the better part of her life, which became worse after her daughter's birth. At times, she suffered bouts of depression and loneliness. She lived with a man who liked to cook heavy meals all day long. He expected her to eat whatever and whenever he cooked.

I suggested she have a discussion with her boyfriend about what she needed food-wise, number of items, and the correct portion and to tell him she needed a hug rather than food. Often, when someone is trying to control what you eat, they are trying to control you.

TEN TELLTALE SIGNS THAT YOU'RE OUT-OF-CONTROL WITH FOOD

You may be overweight — ten, fifteen, twenty-five pounds or more. Each of you have habits and rituals you've repeated over a lifetime of eating. My habits might have been different than yours. Your habits may be different from those of relatives or coworkers. Whatever each of you are doing yields your current weight. The number of habits and the frequency of each habit dictates how many pounds you can gain in a given period of time. The more habits you have, the more weight you'll gain.

Being aware of your Possible Pitfalls will help you plan ahead so you won't be always falling into the same hole.

When I was at my heaviest (fifty pounds ago), one of my habits was that I'd have a daily large cup of coffee with double cream and double sugar. One more habit among many was to have an alcoholic beverage before every restaurant dinner. Or I always had a decaf cappuccino at the end of every meal. I was often in a restaurant in the evening.

You may be having a business breakfast with others in your industry, going to lunch with a coworker, or taking a client out for dinner. Add to that the number of times you, your spouse, and children are celebrating something with food.

These are all rituals that involve habits that may need to be identified in order to reach your goal weight and keep it off. An example might be to have an item every other day rather than the every single day or twice a day ritual you've created. Your ritual has likely increased from your younger years of having a drink every time you're in a restaurant.

As you work on identifying some of your habits, you also want to think about what you could do next time. What could you say or do or think that would make a difference. Create a new, more constructive habit and you will see your weight loss become more significant.

One day you might work on the soda with every lunch habit. Perhaps it is having a sandwich (two pieces of bread) every day too.

Another day, it might be working on the basket of bread on a table or eating the cookies that come free with the check. Just today I saw a food log with tuna fish/white bread for three meals this week. The man admitted that tuna fish and white bread was his favorite and that the three times he had it was down from his usual five times a week. I'm not saying not to eat tuna fish. What I'm saying is that if you have anything three days in a row, you're not trying to find a wide variety of food that is out there and delicious. And after the first bite of the tuna fish sandwich, you're most likely back to mindless.

Do you fit into the *all-or-nothing* category? Are you on your Program during the week only to be off your Program on a weekend? Or do you eat moderately at each meal only to eat compulsively from after dinner until bedtime? That was me. So friends who ate dinner with me always commented they didn't know why I'd gained weight; when I was with them, I barely ate. They hadn't seen me eat from when I got home to bedtime. I was a secret eater. Of course my weight wasn't a secret.

If you are binge eating or compulsively eating when you're not hungry, and feeling out of control around food, you want to create some new patterns you can incorporate into your current rituals around food. The nature of habit-making is that it is progressive; you eventually cannot get enough food frequently enough (once a day becomes twice a day or more), and the portion size of the food increases as well. Two cookies become three cookies, and before you know it, you're eating the whole bag or boxful.

To see whether you are consistently overeating, only to feel remorse afterwards, ask yourself whether any of the following statements pertains to you. Check the boxes that pertain to you so you can review them from time to time so you don't drift back into mindless eating again:

- ☐ You need food to change your mood.
- ☐ You think food makes you happy.
- ☐ Food is your entertainment.
- ☐ You go for hours without eating, but once you start eating, you can't stop.

- ❏ You watch television and run back and forth to the kitchen all evening.

- ❏ You eat moderately in public (or in front of friends) only to eat in a frenzy when alone.

- ❏ You never eat bread at home, only to finish an entire basket of bread when in a restaurant.

- ❏ You eat when you're angry, anxious, depressed, or bored.

- ❏ You stock up on certain foods, such as buying two boxes of cookies or the super-sized soda; you never allow yourself to run out of favorite foods.

- ❏ You purchase food in various stores so no one but you knows how often you buy things and how much you're buying.

- ❏ After you've overeaten, you feel remorse.

If you answered, "Yes" to most of the above, whether or not you are overweight by obvious standards, you may have an eating behavioral problem that needs attention.

When it comes to tell-tale signs, the questions might change. I've written these lists before, and my questions are slanted depending on how I feel and what I've heard that day. It's all the same. You are compulsive or obsessive about food. Your eating habits are out of balance in comparison to other things in your life.

Ursula A.: I have battled with food all of my life: dieted obsessively in my teens, gained weight in my early twenties, and was considerably overweight; I dieted at one time and lost seventy pounds. This has been a pattern for years — overweight, dieting, and gaining it all again. In short, I am obsessed with food.

I noticed this morning, when I was scarcely awake, that I was thinking about chocolate! I have noticed a few times that in a sort of semi-conscious state, I am dreaming about eating. I am constantly ravenous. I don't know why. Even after I have eaten, I can't carry on. I feel awful being overweight; it makes me depressed and very unhappy. I try and counteract the binges with making myself sick. I have done this for years. I know eating is emotional, but I also wonder whether there is a biological aspect to it. On one diet, I noticed I wasn't constantly ravenous all the time, although I found the diet very limiting. Also, a lot of the food I enjoyed eating wasn't allowed. I am currently 5' 10" and weigh nearly 196 pounds, and I hate myself. I hate being fat and I hate being out of control. I've done all the diets, even psychotherapy (am still there), but I have the same problems. I don't know where to go or what else to do.

Caryl: The next step is to figure out why you are so upset that you need distraction from your emotional discomfort. Eventually you'll create new ways to cope, to fill up the time where you used to eat. And clean out your kitchen cupboards.

Throw out everything you're used to bingeing on. If you keep the food in your home, you're basically telling yourself "I can handle it." You cannot handle it. If you could have handled it, you wouldn't be looking up "food addiction" on the Internet.

Cindy G. was thirty-nine years old and married with two young children, ages three and six when she came to me for help. Her family owned several candy stores in Hawaii, so she was regularly surrounded by chocolate. She was thin until her twenty-fifth birthday. She weighed 175 pounds after her second child was born and couldn't lose the pregnancy weight. Cindy started with a popular weight-loss method, but consistently failed because she found it too difficult to limit her food intake in the recommended daily amounts.

Cindy G.: It seems I'm okay on and off. I guess I am more off The Program than on The Program. Why does it seem like I want myself to fail?

Caryl: You don't want yourself to fail. You've turned your pro-action entity over to your Addict Pea Brain. This is the mind-less, never-thinking-about-consequences sort of brain. It doesn't know good or bad. It just wants to be told what to do so it can mindlessly help you achieve your most dominant thought. In the past, if your senses were heightened around sweets, for example, you used to act on that prompt. The automatic, non-thinking mind does what it's always done. It reinforces an eating pattern you have created and reinforces it for weeks, months, or years. If you change your old behaviors to new behaviors (The Program way of thinking) and create new patterns by repatterning, even-tually the new way will become your preferred way. The new automatic response.

Fran S.: I took home my leftovers of steak, baked potato, and creamed spinach and put them in the freezer. Two hours later, I defrosted and ate them. I'm trying to understand what happens and how to avoid feeling addiction remorse. I think what triggers the eating is anxiety about finding work. I go through periods of distress and self-attack. I think I eat to not allow myself to be worried by money. I also had a thought yesterday that I'm rather bored. I eat to avoid the obvious concern that I should be looking for another job.

Caryl: And it's not a reason to eat. Eating becomes the prob-lem when you use it to distract yourself from larger problems. You feel ambivalent about your work, so you give yourself some-thing else to worry about. You feed your addiction cycle, feel addiction remorse, and then beat yourself up at the end. All you have done is avoided dealing with your work worries. You know, for sure, that eating isn't the answer either.

Bethany L.: I am following The Program. I just wish I felt happier about not eating as much as I want to. Will I ever feel free from wishing I could eat everything? Do people with this problem ever find that they don't care about food so much? Or will it always be a struggle?

Caryl: You ask whether you will ever feel free from wishing you could eat everything. That is an unrealistic expectation and fanciful thinking. You and others often believe they would be happy if they could eat everything in the world as often as they want, in an unlimited portion size. But big portions equal big people. Eating more items than you need will increase your weight. That is a fact of life.

What you are feeling and thinking is part of the addiction. Think of it as an entity in your mind that keeps telling you to eat (The Addict Pea Brain). Think of The Program (all of its concepts) as The Program Voice. By rewriting Program notes into a separate book of your own, you'll begin to internalize the new concepts. By reviewing them daily, or more, The Program Voice (and you) will be reminding yourself of all the things you're trying to accomplish.

Eventually, you'll slow down the eighteen-wheeler.

The opposite of loving all this stuff is not hate but indifference. That comes with time. You are still holding on to a food connection. You connect volume and food and *eating everything* with happiness. Real happiness is waking up without feeling the bondage of food addiction. Happiness is being calmer around food or fitting into your smaller clothes. Happiness is going to dinner with a friend and getting so involved in the conversation you almost forget to eat. Happiness is being in control and indifferent to food. Just the other night I kept cutting food from my favorite food and giving it to my dear friend. I would have never been able to do that years ago. And it was fine. It was effortless.

Will it always be a struggle? No. You may still be lonely, tired, bored, frustrated, and angry. But you won't be acting on it with food. However, if you repattern with verve and passion to conquer your food addiction, and really create new coping strategies, food will take up a smaller, more balanced, more appropriate space in your life. It becomes less and less important. Fill up your life, not your belly.

The more you think about the things you're reading here, the more you will have little clicks of recognition along the way. The moments pass. They always do.

Charla M.: I usually would bring tons of diet soda to a party knowing most people don't think about providing it. I had a bad habit with it and was dehydrated most of the time because of it. Last night I brought bottled water as my back up. Water is my new drink of choice and I feel better, my skin looks better, and I'm less tired.

Caryl: Perfect. I have not one more thing to add. You planned, executed, and succeeded. Brava.

Jane C.: My biggest problem is the drive home from work. I am alone and stressed out from teaching all day. My monster-binger drives me to any store for a giant bag of whatever. I have tried some snacks like broccoli. I have tried driving a different way. I have tried eating lunch a little later so I don't feel hungry, but to no avail. It's not every day, but often enough that the days I make it home feel like miracles.

The nighttime is worse. No matter how much I plan, I can manage one or two nights of healthy eating per week. The other nights I wake up in the middle of the night and go make oatmeal or pancakes!

Caryl: Regarding your food detours, if you stop off for a bag of something, buy a smaller portion or container of that item. That's a good first step. Try weaning yourself from these items.

Take a different path on the way home. Listen to an audio book during your drive home or a mixed CD that puts you in a different mood. Record some Program thoughts onto a CD and listen to that on the way home. What you're trying to do is learn how to relax and enjoy the ride home. Create some no-food techniques to reduce stress and make you feel good.

Any slight change of each step of the trip will pay off. This is the part of your day that needs repatterning. Since all the places you buy these things are part of the addiction too, try traveling without money. There are options. I used to take evening walks without any cash or change so I couldn't pick up those little somethings I would buy compulsively. Most local stores around my home have an $8 minimum purchase when using a credit card.

It's unrealistic to think you can change a lifetime of doing what you've been doing by doing the new way one or two times. You are making it home on certain days. Try for additional days. Maybe you'll increase that total. And remember, the things you mentioned as things you *have to have* (giant bagsful of whatever) weren't even in existence when you were born and life went on. Over the years, food has been beautified, fancified, and glorified. It has become entertainment. It is not. And none of it is a reason to eat if you're not hungry enough to commit to a meal by Program standards: food on a plate. Fork down between nickel-sized bites of food, among other things you're learning about.

You might feel anxious or tired or be suffering numerous physical and emotional discomforts by going from working at school or an office to a different kind of work when you get home. In the past, you've used food to quell your anxiety or distract you from the annoyance or anger you feel because of what you have to do for your growing family. Keep working on finding ways to cope with life that don't involve stuffing down feelings or distracting yourself with food.

Also, recognize that many of your attempts may not succeed at the start. "Once you learn to quit trying, it becomes a habit," said legendary football coach Vince Lombardi. I take that to mean that when you are doing something so automatically, you've stopped "trying" to do it because you are doing it naturally without effort. It becomes a learned behavior, a new default setting.

Acknowledge your accomplishments. Find relief in knowing that the moments do indeed pass. You will get better at all of this, and then, when you go off your Program, the question won't be about what you've done, but what you could do next time. Make a left turn instead of a right one. Point of Purchase needs a bit of work; delaying techniques need polish.

Take a deep breath. Pro-actively create new behaviors of thought, word, and action to replace the old automatic urges. Food addiction is a progressive disease, but patience along with perseverance help to turn it around. You not only have to learn a new way to eat (which seems to be working for you), but you also need to work on repatterning your old automatic responses. Find strategies to cope with the ups and downs of life. You can do it!

Alicia L.: I have binged two days in a row and couldn't even get on the scale this morning. I feel helpless. Then I started thinking about all the things I could change, and I decided to start with having two-item meals. I thought, "If I want different results, I have to do things differently."

Caryl: Nice job. Had you not been thinking about the problems, you wouldn't have come up with a solution. Think about your cycles of eating as something like links hooked together, where one link is connected to another link, and so on. Each step of the cycle of addiction is connected to the next and the next. So the compulsion is not toward the substance (it could be just as easily drugs or alcohol or shopping), but to the nervous system having a need to complete the cycle.

The cycle begins with thinking of buying food, to the actual buying, to how you open a package, to how eating one food leads to the next, and the next, until you're completely narcotized and exhausted, to when you finally stop. The next thing you feel is the remorse and helplessness — all parts of the addiction cycle.

Interrupt (via repatterning) any part of the process. It can shorten these episodes. Little by little, the small steps, efforts, and attempts will accumulate and add up. The choice to do nothing is still a choice to do nothing. Keep working on it. You're going in the right direction. Persistence pays off.

Kitty Dukakis, a recovering alcoholic, said, "A user does whatever they have to do, so they don't have to stop using."

COMPULSIVE OVEREATING UMBRELLA

You might be thinking that you're addicted to food. I've found that the foods most often used and abused are bread, beverage, dessert, and alcohol. They are all instant and quick and require little or no preparation. Quite often they are portable and/or can be eaten without utensils.

Some people eat large quantities of red meat and cheese. Others pile on the pasta. Some of us are cross-addicted, giving equal attention to several different foods.

Then there are the behaviors:
  a. The speed of your eating
  b. The volume of food with which you've become comfortable
  c. Incorrect thinking

These three things: speed eating, volume eating, and mindless eating, along with the foods themselves, combine to create the habits and rituals of the food addict/compulsive overeater that might be you.

None of these episodes need contain a lot of food if you are doing these actions frequently enough. Find out which items influence you the most and how you might make small little changes in your behavior to yield bigger results.

One man who was having three cups of coffee each day, first Skipped and Scattered. He achieved some weight loss from that one step. When he got smaller, he made the portion smaller and recently told me he was drinking a regular-size cup rather than the larger one he had purchased in the past. And it was okay.

Start reading *A Compulsive Overeating Umbrella* and identify some of the instant foods on your trigger food list.

Give thought to how your bagel and coffee (flour and caffeine) breakfast has remained steady all these years. See whether you always have an alcoholic drink and eat bread while reading a menu. How many nights a week do you sit on the couch and watch television with a bowl of something in your lap? Once you see which foods you choose the most, you can buy them (or not) with more thought.

When reading Rapid Eating, say the words *I'm compulsively overeating if* before each phrase starting with I eat too fast. When you're finished reading, go back and check all the statements that pertain.

Do the same with Volume. Think about the words as you read them slowly. It helps to identify the problem so the solution will emerge.

Do the same with Thinking Incorrect Thoughts. You'll see what needs your attention. They are all part of the habits, patterns, and rituals that are compulsive overeating.

Rapid eating (now countered by nickel-size bites, fork down between bites); Volume (now countered by a more appropriate portion size); And Thinking Incorrect Thoughts (now countered by Repatterning your thoughts, words, and actions).

After seeing a few logs this week I've added to the Volume section *I'm compulsively overeating if I eat so much I can't recall it enough to write it down.*

A COMPULSIVE OVEREATING UMBRELLA
(A DISEASE)

If you're following the MEAL PLAN The Caryl Ehrlich Program suggests, and still have difficulty reaching or maintaining your weight loss goal, please consider working on, some or all of the following problem areas.

TRIGGER FOODS

_____   flour (all bread: crackers, rolls, muffins, bagels, breadsticks, pita, croissants, matzo, croutons, crust of quiche or pizza, pasta, wraps)

_____   sugar (desserts containing sugar, fructose and sucrose) including fruit, fruit juice and yogurt

_____   caffeine (coffee, cappuccino, tea, soda, and chocolate)

_____   alcohol (wine, beer, and hard liquor cause lack of resolve and may possibly trigger overeating of other food categories)
            (to a lesser degree the following)

_____   fatty foods (all beef, lamb, hard cheese, cottage cheese, fried foods, cookies, cakes, salty food such as chips and popcorn, plus mayonnaise, butter, and sour cream all contain a relatively high percentage of fat)

_____   salty/crunchy (potato chips, popcorn, nachos, nuts, seeds, pretzels i.e. finger foods)

NOTE: Foods in this column all have an instant-requires-little-or-no-preparation quality. They trigger voluminous, ferocious, and "I can't stop once I start" eating behavior.

RAPID EATING

(I'm compulsively overeating if)

_____ I eat too fast
_____ I don't savour my food
_____ I don't taste my food
_____ I don't chew each bite before swallowing
_____ I don't put utensils down between bites
_____ I'm not present at mealtime
_____ I don't take drinks of water between bites
_____ If I eat a second helping

VOLUME

(I'm compulsively overeating if)

_____ I eat portion-sizes too big for the smaller person I want to be
_____ I drink unlimited quantities of beverages such as coffee,
        tea, and soda
_____ I order, buy, prepare, or serve too much food
_____ I eat too many items at each meal
_____ I eat more food each day, containing more calories, than
        I can burn
_____ I eat too much, too fast, too late
_____ I eat so much I can't recall it enough to write it down
_____ I always take second portions
_____ I do not leave food over
_____ I plan to overeat:
        a) By not planning otherwise
        b) By not planning ahead in detail
        c) By not planning alternative behavior

BY THINKING INCORRECT THOUGHTS

(I'm compulsively overeating if)

I think:
_____ I've got it made
_____ I can stop at any time

_____   I don't have to do this anymore
_____   I don't have a problem
_____   I can get away with it
_____   One bite won't hurt
_____   I can eat unlimited amounts of food if they are low in calorie
_____   The amount of food is so small, it won't count
_____   I'm not a compulsive overeater
_____   I'm on vacation and don't have to do anything until
      I get home

OUT OF CONTROL — YOU ARE NOT ALONE

The following people told me their stories of their out-of-control behavior in one-on-one sessions. The stories are told in their own words, and there is a tone of amazement, confusion, and embarrassment in them. The stories are included here so you realize you're not alone. Although I discussed "next time" plans with these program participants, I did not include those parts of the discussions. Here are their stories:

Ray R. recounted her story of being out-of-control. As she spoke, she looked confused and humored by her own story, and she only smiled when I told her she was not alone.

"It's 105 degrees where I'm at. I'm walking around in minimal covering except for shorts, a tank top, and my silver bedroom slippers. My hair is held on top of my head with the aid of a barrette. I'm cleaning out closets. This is messy, sweaty work to begin with. I walk into the kitchen with thoughts of drinking out of the omnipresent water glass always sitting on the counter to the left side of my kitchen sink. My eye notices a little white object in front of the refrigerator. I bend down to pick it up. It is a piece of candy from a package I bought the day before. It was dropped last night when I was walking back and forth from watching television to the kitchen to take a piece of candy at a time, always eating it until it's gone. At the time it dropped, I looked for it but couldn't find it. Then I forgot about it until just now. I brush it with a finger to make sure nothing on the ground is still on the candy. I put it into my mouth. I feel so out of control, but I put it into my mouth anyway. It tastes fine, and I don't see anything wrong with that. But there is. Isn't there? Why do I do that? And why don't I think it is strange?"

Another participant tells this story: "You're not going to believe this," Sarah H. began, while laughing. "You know, between me and my husband, we receive a lot of gift liquor and candy during the holidays. I seldom drink. That's not the problem. The problem is the gobs of chocolate that get delivered to my home and office and his office. Everyone seems to know my favorite because two out of three are things I would buy anyway — no, I don't tell anyone the details of my candy preferences," she laughs. "We give tons of it away to friends and coworkers, but some of it does find its way back to our apartment." She smiled. "Here's the: *I can't believe I did that* moment. You ready?"

"I'm ready," I replied.

"I came home and had a satisfying dinner. I wasn't hungry. There were several chores I wanted to complete before I went to sleep. It was kind of late, around midnight, and my husband had gone to sleep a few minutes earlier. When I knew he was in bed and sleeping — I actually listened at the door to hear him breathing regularly — I got up from the dining room table where I'd been sorting the mail and bills and walked into the kitchen. And here's the fun part. There was a huge bar of candy in the freezer that had remained unopened for more than two weeks, and I felt so proud I didn't open it. I know. I know. I was in denial. But at the time, all I could think was look how *good* I've been. If I want a piece of candy, I can have a piece of candy. I can handle it."

"Sort of zombie-like?"

"Exactly, zombie-like.

"It was hard to open the package at first, so I got a knife from a drawer and cut the package neatly so if someone casually peeked into the freezer, that person wouldn't notice the package had already been opened. I thought, 'I'll just reach my hand under the foil wrap, pull out a piece and that will be that.' But I couldn't pull out one piece because it had all melted together into one huge block before it had been put into the freezer. So I did the only thing a sane person would do: I grabbed that knife and started hacking away at the unyielding chocolate bar.

"If there had been a musical accompaniment, it would have been the hacking violin sounds of the slasher scene in the movie, *Psycho*. That's what I felt like, a psycho. I was so out-of-control, I had to laugh. Here I am in my expensive, pretty nightgown and robe, living high up in a building on Manhattan's Upper East Side, with a river view no less, and I'm hacking away at a piece of chocolate with a huge knife while my husband is sleeping in another room. You can't write this stuff."

"Did you finish it?"

"Yes. I kept going back and forth to the kitchen. Once the package was open, I'd do a little paperwork, then make a trip back to the freezer until it was gone. I clearly cannot stop once I start.

"When I was finished — not satisfied because when I am in that state of mind I can never get enough; I always want more and more and more — I wrapped up the candy wrapper and tossed it into the trashcan. Then I took a few paper towels and crumbled them on top of the candy bar. 'Leave no evidence,' I thought."

Linda M: When I quit smoking five years ago, I substituted sweets for cigarettes after meals, trading one addiction for another. I gained some weight at first (metabolism shift plus extra calories), but I'm an active/athletic person, so it wasn't too bad. But now I need to kick my sweets habit! I crave some kind of end-of-meal satisfaction, and I usually turn to sugar. I rarely snack or eat sweets otherwise. I'm a vegetarian and eat sensible meal portions.

I started with big desserts like cookies, ice cream, or cake — and it really did help me stay away from the cigarettes! Now, I try to keep portions reasonable and have a favorite chocolate. (By the way, I must eat chocolate, nothing fruity will do!). I only have big desserts on special occasions.

Needless to say, my weight is still an issue (I'm about 25-30 pounds overweight) and, as I get older, it's getting worse. How can I kick my 300-calorie-a-day sweet habit? I have a hard time stopping with just one favorite cookie or piece of candy — I need to eat six. Of course, my thin husband doesn't understand why I don't have more willpower.

Caryl: Basically, you exchanged one habit, cigarette smoking, for another habit of putting something — in your case, candy — into your mouth whenever you're feeling powerful emotions. It could be anxiety, stress, depression, or boredom, to name a few.

One thing to learn is to feel unexpressed feelings, such as frustration, anger, and resentment, rather than using food to continue to repress those feelings when you're not hungry. Many people find that writing down their feelings is the most effective way to express them.

Venting your unexpressed feelings allows you to get them up and out rather than continuing to stuff them down. Find ways to feel feelings. Fill your time with newly created coping strategies. Try to identify the situations or emotions that triggered your past cigarette smoking and current sweet tooth. From a smoking cessation program, I learned the smokeless inhale and still use that technique decades later.

You stopped smoking five years ago. Smoking took up a lot of time, from purchasing the cigarettes, to opening the cigarette package, to lighting the cigarette, to inhaling, exhaling, and extinguishing . . . a whole gamut of steps. Instead of using up time with your smoking and eating habits, you need some creative solutions.

Experiment with hobbies, write in a journal, start a jigsaw puzzle, walk in your neighborhood, take a course, brush your teeth, call a friend. Find which actions work best for you. Use it again. You can always return to the table for a lovely cup of hot water. This is a pleasant hot beverage you can choose rather than remaining addicted to choosing tea or coffee in essence, eating when you're not hungry. One attempt at repatterning does not a habit make.

Your eating day is open-ended. Think about where the food/fuel needs to take you for each leg of the day. Work on the place where you look around for something familiar to purchase. I used to think I had a *compulsion to purchase* when I'd go into a store where I used to buy candy; even though I wasn't still buying the candy, I felt a compulsion to buy something. So I used to buy those little packages of tissues.

Before rolling your cart to the check-out counter, see whether your purchases match your plan. Once you're out the door, you're home free. If you buy less, you'll eat less. "There is no way to gain control of your life, if you are controlled by an addiction," says author Susan Forward.

Aaron E. was a twenty-three-year-old, aspiring writer when he began The Program. He worked part-time at a bookstore. He often got up late, skipped breakfast, ate lunch and dinner, and then binged for the rest of the night as he concentrated on his writing. He ate whatever he happened to find in his cabinets or refrigerator. Often, his girlfriend would also come over to bring some late-night snacks for him.

Aaron E.: How do I know if I have a food addiction? I love food, but so does everyone I know.

Caryl: If you're eating food on a plate with utensils because you're hungry, and it lasts twenty relaxing minutes (or more), and it tastes good, you're most likely fine. However, eating something because you happen to find it in your cabinets or refrigerator, or because your girlfriend brings you late night snacks, or just because it's there, is not a reason to eat.

If you are eating because you're bored, anxious, frustrated, or lonely, you may have a behavioral addiction — eating to diffuse discomfort. Continually going into the kitchen to raid your cabinets or refrigerator could just be you trying to walk away from the discomfort of writing. You're not looking for a particular food, just whatever is there. It will distract nicely for the moment, but it won't change anything. If you think now about what you'll do next time, you can pre-plan your thoughts, words, and actions for a better outcome. Then the next time you will have a better outcome.

I purchase 100 seven-ounce plastic cups at a time and leave water wherever I am. There's a cup on the desk while I type, one near the television, one in the kitchen, bathroom, and bedroom. If you see it, you will drink it. There's also evidence that if the glass or cup is clear and you can see the water, you most likely will drink it more often than when the glass is opaque.

Maybe you're using food to procrastinate rather than because you're physically hungry. These things are progressive. In the beginning, before a substance is being abused, it appears as if you're handling it. It appears as if you are making a choice to overeat — eating more than you need. There's a line you cross when you're not handling it. The frequency and portion size spirals upward.

You may not realize the upward progression until the scale goes up or your clothes become tight. (They must have shrunk at the cleaners.) If the frequency and portion of any item increases, your weight will increase as well. Maybe not right away. It takes time for your actions to accumulate and end up in a weight gain.

Diet foods usually have a low-calorie or no-calorie component. The weight loss industry has forever used calories as a component of weight loss. "If I eat fewer calories, I'll lose weight." It is so much more than that.

If you're eating something just because it is low in calories, you might be thinking you can eat an unlimited amount of this food. What happens is that often you feel stuffed, bloated, and uncomfortable after eating gargantuan portions of salad, for example, because you perceive it to be "low in calories." When you are eating foods that are not so low in calories, you expect to feel full, stuffed, and bloated. And remember, if you're eating a trough of vegetables or salad all the time, then there is nothing low-calorie about them.

If you can take it or leave it, you don't have a problem. But if you *gotta have it*, and feel anxiety when you don't eat (or drink coffee, or have sweets way after dinner), you most likely have a substance abuse problem and the substance is food.

Jane B. was thirty-nine years old, divorced, and the mother of two teenage daughters. She was 5' 2", and according to health charts, her weight was on target at 110 pounds. She was worried about the weights of her daughters who were about her height but weighed 20-30 pounds more than she did. As a teenager, she had struggled with an eating disorder and still felt guilty about eating.

Jane B.: Whenever I eat something fattening or simply not healthy, I feel guilty. I have been battling this feeling for most of my adult life. I have two daughters who are teenagers, and I am constantly watching what they eat. From time to time, I will make comments to them.

Caryl: The guilt you feel is part of the cycle of addiction, as is monitoring your daughters' weights. I know it is tempting to try and help someone else, but if you have eating issues, chances are, that is what you are teaching your children, either verbally or with body language. It's challenging enough to change your own habits, and almost impossible to change other people's, especially if those people don't want to be changed. Unless they ask for help, leave them alone.

You've most likely been sending unconscious signals to them since birth. My dad was a smoker, and although he never sat me down and taught me to inhale, I learned to smoke by watching. My mom ate sweets after dinner, and I learned those skills from her. When I saw those actions were hurting me, I eventually learned to *stop* smoking and how to eat only when hungry. You can learn these things too.

Once you make a commitment to be in control of your own eating, every thought and action should reflect that goal. As tempting as it is, don't offer your opinion to your daughters unless they ask for it. Let their doctor evaluate the possible problems and perhaps help find a solution. They may be fine just the way they are. You can prepare and provide good foods in healthy portions. Show, don't tell. Healthy portions does not mean big portions but the correct portion. If you make a big deal about what your daughters are eating, they might become secret eaters. The question isn't what they are eating, but why are they eating.

Regarding feeling guilty about eating something you deem improper — nothing is improper. Get the widest variety of foods and food preparations. Enjoy a new vegetable, a uniquely prepared protein, or delicious dessert, but do Skip a day before eating the same item again. It will help you interrupt the Frequency pattern you've created. And Scatter every item between breakfast, lunch, and dinner. That also helps to lessen the hold your old patterns have on you. Enjoy it when you have it. You are worth it.

Artist Sol LeWitt said, "Most ideas that are successful are ludicrously simple. Successful ideas generally have the appearance of simplicity because they seem inevitable."

DENIAL

One component of addiction is denial. (Denial is a state of mind marked by a refusal or an inability to recognize and deal with a serious personal problem.) You might travel from thinking, *I'm okay, I'm okay, I'm okay around food* to *I'm not okay.* Consistently eating more than you need, even though there are negative consequences, is part of the addiction, too.

I am a food addict. No matter how many years I practice the new, mindful way of eating, the new habits will always be less substantive than the old habits and patterns I have practiced over a lifetime of mindless eating. The old way will always have more practice, heft, weight, and power than the new way.

From years of pushing the envelope myself — that's what addicts do — I know for sure I don't have willpower or self-control; they were both surgically removed at birth. You can, however, learn to buy a little less, order a little less, prepare and serve a little less. By the time food is presented, you'll eat a little less. Ultimately, you'll weigh a little less.

It is the times when you've gone off your Program by leaving food lying around in a too instant, quick, and available form that you're most likely thinking: *I can handle it,* or *one won't hurt.* (That's denial.)

It is not one of anything that causes a weight gain. It is that the old way has a ritual, frequency, and portion-size that has been established over a lifetime. And, if the item you choose happens to be one of the current foods you use to distract yourself, then it is not one of anything because you can't stop once you've started. You're gonna eat it 'til it's gone.

Do you believe you should be able to leave junk food lying around your home and office and not eat it? (That's denial.) A young, overweight father of two tells me, "I know I can lose all the weight (75 pounds) if I can get to the gym regularly." (That's denial.) If you're using a food or beverage to distract yourself from feeling angry, lonely, tired, stressed, and bored, and you've received some temporary relief from your emotional discomfort, why should you stop going into the kitchen to get that food — that distraction? When you get there, you always get what you want: something with which to self-medicate.

Even if you go to the gym, you're not going to lose weight (and keep it off) unless you start eating in a way that affects the amount of food (less often, smaller in portion) than what you have been eating. You're eating more than you can burn.

When you create a new automatic response to replace your old automatic response (repatterning), then when you go to the kitchen, the food isn't there. You'll find something else (less destructive) with which to distract yourself. Eventually, you'll stop going into the kitchen. It's a process.

The few moments of comfort you receive from drugging with food are totally disproportionate to the quantity of drugs (food, portion size, and frequency of usage) you need to achieve those few moments of emotional relief. Because you build a tolerance to drugs (you cannot ever get it big enough and you can't get it frequently enough), you're never satisfied.

If you still think you're handling your out-of-control eating because you only overeat once a week, you're in denial. Because that one overeating episode will become two overeating episodes, and if you say you can handle it, I'd say you may be in denial.

CHAPTER 2

THE BONDAGE OF ADDICTION

EATING IS ONE OF THE SNEAKIEST OF ADDICTIONS

You know you have issues with food, but maybe you're in denial that you have an addiction. Ask yourself, "Do I ever hide food? Do I pay cash for food so my bookkeeper (husband, wife, friend, or relative) doesn't see how frequently I'm purchasing a particular item (cookies, candy, cheese, alcohol, chips)?" One woman I know pays cash for many things so her husband doesn't know how much she spends on candy, ice cream, and chips that are never there when he goes looking. You might even be buying the same item in several different places so the person at the checkout counter doesn't realize how many times a week you're purchasing said item. Does this behavior sound familiar? If a child buys that much candy for his mother, he might find it amusing. But if she were buying alcohol that many times a week you'd be alarmed.

And one reader wrote: When I was a kid, my mom would drive me to the corner store and send me in to buy her candy bars because she was too embarrassed to go in herself.

Another Program participant laughed embarrassingly. "Wow, yes, I used to buy wine in several different stores. I didn't want any one of those cashiers judging me. Frankly, I didn't want to know myself. That's why writing it down is so sobering."

Before I stopped smoking — another very ritualized behavioral addiction — I recall buying three cartons of cigarettes at a time and carrying two packs in my purse. I was so afraid I'd run out. Are you afraid of running out of food? Do you always replace it before you run out?

You buy extra items so you won't run out. Though, for me, I don't know why I was so worried. It wasn't like I was living in the middle of nowhere. I live in the middle of Manhattan. You can get food twenty-four hours a day.

Buying extra dishwashing liquid when it is on sale, filling up the tank of gas in your car so you visit the gas station less frequently, or stocking up on toothpaste when there is a two-for-one sale are all great ideas. They provide a possible saving of time and/or money.

But when you buy extra food, you'll keep chipping away — taking two grapes, part of a cracker, a bite of salad from your kid's plate, a taste of your husband's entrée. It all adds up. It's like grating a little cheese on some of your meals; eventually, you'll have to buy another block of cheese.

Learn to buy one dessert or one roll or one of whatever for the meal you're planning. Eat it with a meal, and then it's gone. If you buy a box of something, you're planning to eat a box of something. Maybe not in the same meal or even the same day, but eventually, you'll eat the whole box.

Are you afraid of running out of food, cigarettes, anything? Careful — it may be the start of addictive behavior.

Beware of habituation: the need for more and more of one item to get the same hit when less of that item was previously needed.

There is disagreement in the medical and scientific communities about whether a behavioral addiction is the same category as substance addictions like alcohol and prescription drugs. But other than the drugs in caffeine and alcohol, most addictions are marked by repetitive use. And the frustration at being unable to change the outcome of food consumption (or gambling or shopping) is just as frustrating for a person out of control with food as someone else who is out of control with drugs.

You can stop drinking and drugging and smoking. But you can never stop eating. You not only have to learn new eating habits, but you have to let go of old, destructive, entrenched, and familiar eating habits as well.

ADDICT PEA BRAIN OR PROGRAM BRAIN? THE CHOICE IS YOURS

Why do you continue to reinforce old, destructive behavior when you'd feel better if you reinforced new more constructive behavior? Say hello to your Addict Pea Brain.

Your Addict Pea Brain is a reptilian, instinctual, mindless, automatic, unthinking, follow-the-Yellow-Brick-Road part of your brain. It thinks in terms of all-or-nothing, black-and-white, good-and-bad, and helps you achieve your most dominant thought no matter how illogical that thought happens to be.

You learn a habit — a thought, word, or action — by repeating each step of the habit until it becomes familiar, comfortable, and automatic. Washing dishes, typing, and driving are examples of practiced habits. An actor rehearsing is practicing the words and the actions so by the time he appears in front of an audience, the performance is fluid. The actor has become the character.

The Addict Pea Brain's only goal is to take all the same steps to reinforce all the same behavior (whether constructive or destructive) to yield the same old result. If the habit you've created has a food component, as soon as you build a tolerance, the frequency and portion size will automatically increase. Each old step also takes time. As addiction takes over, you'll spend more time feeding it.

When the thought or word or action is about brushing your teeth or taking a shower, it is counterproductive to have to think each morning "Crest or Colgate? Mint or regular? Do I condition or shampoo my hair first?"

When the sequence is routinized, it easily becomes automatic. It frees your mind to be creative about something more important, like what you'd like to accomplish today, food-wise or otherwise, whether you need an umbrella or not, where you parked your car. When the sequence is counter to your weight-loss goal, you want to be aware and awake so you can create a more productive, rather than destructive, new path.

When you walk into the same restaurant or food emporium you've visited numerous times before, your Addict Pea Brain takes over. Each eating encounter has a ritual all its own. Each encounter has solutions all its own. In this way you will stay at your goal month after month and year after year. There are always thin people at the business meetings and family gatherings. You can be one of those people yourself. Your hand automatically reaches out for the foods known in that particular restaurant. It might be the chips or bread or pickles that are served while you're waiting for even more food to arrive. Dozens of practiced behaviors crocheted into a daisy chain of polished actions and reactions are what lead to ultimate and inevitable remorse.

You can reach your weight goal in a relatively short period of time. But you still need to attend weddings, business breakfasts (lunches and dinners), cocktail parties, meetings with your children's school, rehearsal nights, and kids' ball games (whew!), and navigate the food at each function. You have different habits and rituals in place. You have to attend all these and more while you are trying to reinforce the newer way of thinking and eating.

If you evaluate each progressive step (this takes just a few seconds), you'll see the exact moment when you think I'm okay to the moment when you realize you're not okay. You want to stop eating. You can't. The old finish everything on your plate habit is compelled to complete the cycle up to the point of feeling remorse. That is the moment of addiction where you're straddling the wire. Reinforce the old way and you keep it chronic. Reinforce the new way, The Program way, and you feel like Rocky in the movies. Thanks, Mr. Stallone, for that wonderful character who kept getting up.

Planning now for the next time might seem futile, but the brain somehow files away the new plan so it will be there the next time you are in a similar situation. Your brain might signal: "Alert! Alert! Chips in the area!" Then your Addict Pea Brain begins deferring to another part of your brain —The Program Brain. The Program Brain is thinking, *I wasn't thinking about the chips two minutes before I saw them*, and keeps walking.

Eventually, you can go into that restaurant or grocery store and the choice isn't whether or not to eat the pickles or the chips. The choice is do you want to weigh your current weight or do you want to weigh your goal weight? The choice is yours.

Each of you needs to go through this process of identifying your usuals and automatics. I remember the first time I ate Szechuan Chinese food. Having grown up eating Cantonese Chinese food in restaurants, I looked forward to the habit of eating dry noodles with duck sauce served gratis at the beginning of each meal. The waiter had to explain to me that Szechuan-style cooking is from a different province in China, and they didn't serve dry noodles there. I expected something. It didn't come. Hearing the information caused a *momentary* discomfort.

It passed. It was not a reason to overeat later, though the reptilian brain may think it is.

It's at that very small moment that you need to learn to calm yourself with breathing or envisioning. If you let that moment live by calming yourself with food, it might distract you for a moment. But then you'll keep the entire sequence chronic.

By thinking now about what you could do next time — and next time could be two days, two weeks, two years from now — that planning in the present for something in the future pays off.

When your Addict Pea Brain kicks in and you reach out for the chips (or celery sticks, protein bars, a few grapes), the newly Programmed brain will think, "Last time, I ate when I wasn't hungry enough to commit to a meal, and it wasn't worth it." This time you can step back, take a deep breath, and tell others you're *looking forward to dinner* or you *had a late lunch*. Assure them you're fine just sitting and relaxing.

With more awareness of your Addict Pea Brain, you can think of the healthier sequence of thoughts so that next time you can correct the behavior with the information garnered from the previous food encounter. For example:

- Plan ahead and convey that information to the person in charge of meals. I found that unless I do so, no one seems to care when you eat, where you eat, or what you eat. You need to know the following things before you put your hand on the restaurant door:

   - You need a Plan "A": Content — is it to be an All-Vegetable Meal? A Soup or Egg Meal? A chicken/fish or veal Meal?

     The number of items: Is it a one item, two item, or three item meal?
     Bread, Beverage, Dessert, or Alcohol, one of four or none. If so, which one. None is a choice too.

- You also need a Plan "B": What to do, say, or think if Plan A isn't working. Practice your thoughts, words, and actions until they are automatic. Then when you need them, you'll have them.

I used to walk down the street and every time I'd pass a place that had food for sale, I'd say no thank you to the storefront. Or I'd be listening to an old sitcom or movie, and if food were offered, I'd lean in to hear how the character handled unplanned food. They all seemed to be saying, "No thank you" in a fluid way. The last one I saw was a male character in an old movie saying "maybe later" to the offer of a drink. "I'd love some water" is always a good choice for a response.

You may have noticed the phrase, the choice is yours. Ultimately, you want one thing more than another. It's like a process of elimination. You want this more than that. And that more than another. Be thoughtful about what you eat as much as you are thoughtful about what you wear or why you shop in one place over another.

Aria C.: It's hard for me to discern whether I am eating because I am stressed or eating because I am physically hungry. I tend to eat when I am stressed, and believe me when I say I can eat like I've been starved for weeks. I find myself at times just wanting to give up. Then I go back and look at my goals and realize they are all still valid.

Caryl: In the beginning, you're getting comfortable by evaluating each behavior and incorporating it into your life. Your goal is to integrate The Program deeply and comfortably into your life so it will seem familiar and comfortable; it will become the way you do things.

Relatively speaking, you've done the new way about a minute and a half compared to the habits you previously reinforced for decades. It took tennis champion Serena Williams decades to perfect herself and her tennis game to become the role model, businesswoman, and wonderful athlete she is.

As you continue on The Program, The Program voice will be louder and stronger, and you will realize that eating more than you need does not change your stress level — if anything, it will worsen it.

Aria C.: What I am learning is how easy it is to return to old habits.

Caryl: A habit is something you can do without thinking — which is why most of us have so many of them.

Your old eating habits have an established portion size and an established frequency pattern. So when you dip into the old habits, you're not merely having one cookie, one No-Meal Meal, or one of anything. You're pulling up the connected links of a chain of established portions, frequency, actions, and reactions to specific foods that you practiced and made automatic in the past.

The old habits are quite deep. The Addict Voice is strong. Even though you create new habits, they are not as solid, practiced, and perfected as the old ones.

Where there is a *once*, there will always be a *twice*.

When I teach people to stop smoking and they do stop, I always remind them: You're a puff away from a pack a day. It's the same thing with eating.

You buy a box of something with the intention of eating one every other day. It works fine until you have two in one day, or one two days in a row. Then you finish the entire box. It happens quickly because the rituals are mindlessly automatic from years of reinforcement. By following one ritual — and there are dozens, maybe hundreds — you keep the behavior reinforced and locked it in one more time.

If you're thinking *I can handle it*, you're in denial.

If you could have handled it, you and I wouldn't be chatting. You can't handle it. I can't handle it. So when you dip your hand into one of this or that, it's already attached to a whole snarl of frequency and portion that you established and reinforced and polished for years. That's what keeps all your habits locked in. The one cracker becomes two, three, a handful, a boxful. Repeat. Where there is a once, there will always be a twice.

Alicia P.: Two things: (1) I feel like I have had a complete paradigm shift when it comes to cheese. I've given up all dairy products before (for allergy reasons), but saw no discernible difference, so I went back to them. Two days before I saw you, I got a health e-mail where a doctor said he thinks the increase in cardiac deaths among women, ages forty to fifty, is due to excessive cheese consumption. Then I saw you and you mentioned cheese sticking to the arteries. I know all this. I've read so many nutrition books I'm almost an authority. But there was something about receiving that message two times over the course of two days that made me think, "I'd better pay attention." And I have. I will not be eating cheese.

Caryl: We hear these things. It's all out there, but we sort and dismiss and don't listen — so determined is your system to protect the addiction, the perceived comfort zone. Then one day Bing Bang Boom! A light flickers in your Program Brain. You see the power of repetition.

The repetition of hearing information from many sources (some making more sense than others, some making the point in a more humorous way than others), finally reaches the inner recesses of your Addict Pea Brain and change begins. That's why it's so helpful to review and review your notes. Eventually, the information takes hold.

Reaching these conclusions about cheese shows you the importance of reviewing your notes when you don't think you need to. And one day you're in the right place at the right time. The Program voice is strong and clear and replaces the frantic I-gotta-have-it (whatever it is for you) old mantra.

REASONS YOU EAT

When it comes to reaching your weight-loss goal, it is helpful to pinpoint the reasons you eat, how often you eat, and the circumstances under which you eat. Often, it is not one upset or lousy day that causes you to eat, but an accumulation of things throughout the day or week — just waiting for the straw that breaks the camel's back.

When you "tough out" a difficult moment, remember, you're trying to complete a previously entrenched cycle of ritualized steps. If you try to ride the discomfort, you might perceive that you have won. The next time, however, you'll be a little more lonely, tired, bored, frustrated, or angry, and you will eat.

You want to pro-actively create a new way of thinking and acting. When followed consistently, the new way becomes the comfortable way.

One habit you'll want to practice is eating only when you're hungry. As you read about some of the Possible Pitfalls that justify a reason to eat, circle or highlight the ones that pertain to you and your eating habits. If a reason to eat that is personal to you does not appear, make note of it at the end of this section.

QUESTIONS TO FURTHER PINPOINT YOUR HABITS AND RITUALS

(Underline or circle as you relate to some of the following.)

Do you eat because food looks good, smells good, or tastes good? If you eat because you're hungry, and coincidentally, your food choice tastes, looks, or smells good, it's a bonus. However, keep in mind that just because something tastes, looks, or smells good (many foods fit that criterion), it is not a reason to eat.

Do you eat because of emotional hunger, such as unexpressed anger and rage? Do you stuff down feelings with food and drink? Are you self-silencing? I think fatigue, tiredness, and exhaustion are different in depth of feeling. If I had one to choose it would be fatigue, which can be physical as well as mental and you think food will give you energy. You know it won't, but it's such an old, comfortable habit.

Do you eat because of peer pressure? Maybe it's a Sunday barbecue at your brother's. Or maybe it's business pressure. How many days each week do you have to take a client to a restaurant? Is it peer group pressure that causes you to say, "Yes" to more food than you need or even want? "Come with us," says a colleague. "We're going to Happy Hour and everyone is coming." Or the other people at the table are ordering everything on the menu, and you don't want to be left out. Wanting to belong.

Do you think of eating food at a specific time of the day? It might be breakfast, lunch, or dinner, late afternoon, late in the evening, or after dinner but before bedtime. When do you eat?

Or maybe you use food to procrastinate? Are you eating to avoid working, cleaning, nurturing, being nurtured, or having sex? Do you eat to avoid intimacy?

When on vacation, are you eating because you think you'll never pass this way again? Do dessert and coffee end every meal?

Are you having such a nice time that you don't want the evening to end so you order unplanned food or beverages? I call it a meal extender. Do you think, "What the hell? I'm on vacation!"?

Or perhaps you're eating because food is part of the package? Maybe you're eating food that is included with your room, your plane ticket, your business meeting. Often, food is eaten because it came with a meal, it came with the airplane ride, it came with the room — those little chocolate candies on the pillow or the over-stuffed mini-bar. It's everywhere. A high-end department store in New York displays candy for sale next to each cash register.

Are you eating certain food combinations because that's how you always ate them? For example, toast with coffee; cottage cheese with fruit; a hamburger, French fries, and a cola all together simply because that combination is how you always ate them? Are you saying, "Yes" to baskets of bread in a restaurant? Or is it the dry noodles in a Chinese restaurant that cause you to reach out and touch some?

Do you eat to escape your life? Are you eating when you're down, depressed, sad, lonely, grieving, anxious or just plain bored? Are you eating to escape, to zone out, to narcotize, to numb yourself? Are you eating to comfort yourself or are you using food as a companion, a friend? If you weigh more than you want, you are not comfortable. Food is not a comfort.

Are you eating to celebrate your birthday, my birthday, our anniversary, Fourth of July weekend? One-day eating festivities have turned into four-day-weekend eating contests! Joey Chestnut scarfed down seventy hot dogs (with buns) in twelve minutes on Memorial Day (2016) at Nathan's Hot Dog Eating Contest in Coney Island, New York. Do you think food is the entertainment?

Do you eat because someone else is picking up the check or because of your own money problems or personal problems? Are you eating because something came free with what you did order? Even eating a vegetable or salad that came with the meal, you've been taught to think that is a good thing. But what if a fried octopus eyeball was put on your plate; wouldn't you figure out a way to say, "No thanks. I'm good."

There is the deli-man who always slices more of whatever I'm ordering. I tell him a quarter of a pound of turkey, for example (.25 of a pound). I see on the scale it is .33, a third of a pound. It might seem inconsequential, but it is very important if you look at the bigger picture. How many times a week does the deli-man do you a favor?

So I mention the overage of turkey on the scale. He lifted the extra amount and printed the price sticker. I was charged for a quarter pound. In a split second, he returned the extra turkey he'd removed before the weighing, wrapped up the package, and handed it to me. I think he thought it was a money thing. It wasn't.

I want all the food in my kitchen to reflect the correct portion. That way, I can identify it across a crowded plate, a crowded buffet table, or a deli-man's scale when I'm out.

Do you have an overeating episode because you can't stop eating once you start? Do you think you blew it anyway so you say, "To hell with it" and eat some more? If you hurt your knee, would you amputate the whole leg? No. Of course not. But you trip with a little overeating and forget to praise yourself for all you have done. That is also addictive thinking.

Are you unable to say, "No" to an appetizer when everyone else is eating one? Are you thinking, "What will I do while they are eating?" Are you eating because it was there?

Have you given yourself permission to eat for good news, bad news, or no news? One man admitted he eats *during* the news.

Do you eat something because you heard it was the best? With today's media bringing you a review of a restaurant before the paint on the wall of a new place is dry, everything seems to be the best.

The description of food, the look of it, the plating, the atmosphere is all pulled apart by professionals to convince you it was the best, the most unusual, the classiest food, the most creative combining of foods you'd never even heard of. Was it? Was it the best?

Are there any foods you automatically think about when reading, going to the movies, or watching television? Popcorn popped into my head as soon as I typed the word movies. I haven't acted on that thought for decades, but it's still a little combo many people reinforce. Whether it's a cup of tea or a piece of fruit, it accumulates. When you're reading, you can eat as long as it is food on a plate eaten with utensils and lasts twenty minutes or more and the tea or fruit is (or is not) a part of the meal.

There's the completion of the pleasurable cycle. When you start pulling apart these food combos, the craving diminishes too. Though I like potatoes, yams, and corn, I was never a big rice fan. Yet every time I ate Asian food and the dish came with rice (there's that "came with the dinner" pitfall), I would eat it and at times asked for more. Once I tried a no-starch day because I'd eaten mashed potatoes the night before. Rice seemed to soak into the sauce never to be missed when I chose not to eat it automatically.

Sometimes I take home the brown rice which I do like, but I'll put it with a vegetable meal, or not. It's never automatic as it used to be when I ate everything that was served to me, everything that came with a meal. I don't take the rice every time.

Is an abundance of extra food available in your home and office? I once conducted a workshop at a round-the-clock business. While waiting for someone to escort me from the waiting room to the presentation room, I peeked around a corner only to come head on to a wall-to-wall, floor-to-ceiling bookcase of cubbyholes, each filled to the brim with bags and boxes of potato chips, popcorn, pretzels, and general categories of junk food, though I hate to call it food of any kind.

Further into that room were numerous vending machines containing endless bottles of every brand and variety of soda, tea, and other sweetened and caffeinated beverages. On the other wall was a long counter with vats of steaming coffee, tea, and hot chocolate. And it was all free! Do some of the assistants in your office keep bowls of candy on their desks, free for a smile or a hello?

During food preparation, do you nibble? Do you mindlessly put food into your mouth during food preparation and put away? Are you eating off of your kid's plate before you put the plate into the sink?

One man laughingly told me he "ate from his kid's plate to save her from childhood obesity."

So you threw yourself on a chicken nugget for your kid, I asked.

"Yes. I did," he said. "And I'd do it again. For the kid."

Do you use food as a reward? Fitting into pants that have been hanging in your closet for four years is a reward. But if something makes you feel stuffed, bloated, and bad about yourself, it's not a reward. Food is not a reward. Weighing what you want to weigh is the reward.

Do you believe it's wrong to waste food? Yes? Then buy less. Prepare less. Serve less. There'll be less to throw away. Do you hate to waste food so you eat it before it spoils? If you eat food you do not need, it too, is wasted.

You may think everything will be fine once you reach your weight-loss goal. The truth is that you will still feel lonely, tired, bored, and angry again. That's a fact of life. It's just not a reason to eat. You need to find other things on which to spend your time, money, and energy. Develop new ways to deal with the ups and downs of life so you'll feel comfortable feeding the smaller person you want to be.

It's important to be mindful about who, what, or where you are more likely to eat. Being aware helps you make conscious choices, which are always more successful than winging it. Write down all the reasons you've circled or highlighted. Write down other personal reasons you did not find above. Add as many pages as you need.

_____

_____

_____

Fern S.: Many things have happened in my past that I am trying to deal with. But I hate thinking about my childhood, and I eat to avoid confronting my past.

Caryl: Traumas get buried and are kept alive by not confronting them. It is hard to change if you don't know what you want to change. Open the curtains and bring the sunlight onto the page by writing about it. You've lived through the worst of it. You've gone through the trauma and lived to tell the tale. It will be helpful to remember it with the guidance of a therapist. If you keep it buried, it will continue to define you. Start planning to be the person you want to be. Confront the past so you can plan the future. Whether physical or emotional abuse, it is abuse. Stuffing down feelings with food only distracts you for a moment. Then those stuffed feelings become the beginnings of an eating disorder.

It might be misdirected anger. You hurt yourself not the person with whom you are angry.

Camelia C.: I have other issues in my life, as everyone does. I come from an exceedingly abusive background, including sexual abuse that started in infancy and carried on until adolescence. I have dealt with these issues and always thought my weight was a safety net because of the extreme sexual abuse that started before I had words or language. I also thought I'd dealt with that in therapy and moved on long ago.

Caryl: When you use any drug, in your case food, it becomes familiar and comfortable. It is scary to eat only when you are hungry after you've used food for so many other reasons in the past. But rather than getting angry at the person who hurt you, you are hurting yourself. That is misdirected anger. You're hurting yourself; self-silencing once again.

Regarding dealing with these issues in therapy, you are a different person than you were even a week or month ago. When reviewing the same material, you'll have new or different insights. It is painful. I've heard therapy discussed as being like a spiral staircase; you go up it and down it over a lifetime. Eventually, you'll figure it out to your satisfaction and move on. The time frame is different for every person. Eating doesn't help. Find other ways to comfort and/or distract yourself instead of eating.

Carrie C.: I've been having a tough time lately — pushed way too far over the emotional edge. But that is life. I just have to learn how to stay on The Program and eat sanely, despite emotions. Need to read notes and read your book. I tend to get into heavy denial when I am in the middle of stressing out. I think I do so well on The Program, keeping my life in some kind of order, and then it just seems to blow apart.

Caryl: All you're describing is life. In the past, you may have hidden under, behind, and around your addiction, hoping these moments would work out. Everything worked out, but they would have anyway, whether you ate or not. Welcome the frustration of dealing with it directly. Welcome the discomfort and find pride in thwarting it. Food won't help. These are the things you will learn in the first year. After a while, the same emotional thing will happen again and you'll begin to think, "Last time I overate and it didn't change anything."

What part of The Program did you stop doing? The log? Weighing in the evening? Which area needs shoring up? Find the right coping strategy and practice it. This, too, requires trial and error. When these things happen again, and they will, you'll have new automatic responses of thoughts, words, deep exhalations, and possibly even a walk or a nap to replace your old, automatic response of eating.

I read an article in *The New York Times* about a woman named Rita Gomez who works for the Getty Museum and is in charge of packing up great works of art for transport to other museums and galleries.

"Sometimes it takes months to calculate the best way to crate and pack masterpieces," she says. "I think when you have a more complicated project, you wake up thinking about it and you go to bed thinking about it. You're modeling in your head. I'm padding it, cutting it, and so on."

Are you modeling your eating in your head? Are you thinking about your eating-encounters-to-come before you go to sleep? Are you taking time to calculate the best way to achieve your goals? Keep working on it. No matter what you did, wasn't it still less food or less frequent than in the past? Yes?

Selma C.: I am medium height yet overweight, and so very frustrated at not being able to lose 7-10 pounds. I weigh the same I did a few days ago and feel sad about it. I just feel like eating and forgetting about the last 7-10 pounds. Any advice?

Caryl: Sorry you're not feeling great, but eating won't make you less sad, and being sad is not a reason to eat! It will merely distract you for a bit of time. Eventually, the feeling will emerge again, and if you use food to distract yourself each time, you'll need more food at each encounter and the encounters will become more frequent. If you always do what you've always done you'll get what you always got.

If you're trying to reach your weight-loss goal and the scale isn't moving, you're eating more than you're able to burn. Whatever food your body cannot burn (utilize) gets converted to fat and gets stored. You don't want to create more fat-inventory. You have a warehouse of fat already. You want to have a sale and get rid of the fat-inventory.

Yvonne: I read and reread your first book. I read it twice because I find it really intelligent and healthy. I am struggling with my weight and have been since twelve years old. My parents cook really healthy food, but I am a bulimic overeater, a binge eater — so food is my drug. It has been two years since I seriously realized it, and I'm working on it. I tend always to think about food — I always need to eat.

I'm so used to the old patterns, and I always go back to them because it's so easy and gives me that (temporary) amazing feeling — my high. Sometimes, I also feel that I have no friends and that makes me feel depressed or anxious. It's really hard, and I often turn to food for comfort. Meanwhile, I'm trying to gain control over my life, and I want to go to the next step and win the fight with my addictions.

Caryl: If you feel uncomfortable and need food to calm yourself, your goal is to learn how to feel comfortable with the ups and downs of life without putting food into your mouth — to find alternative behaviors that comfort.

Little children suck their thumbs. That's how they cope. Others wear themselves out with physical activity. Still others get lost in books and articles. I create collages and assemblages. I also like jigsaw puzzles. How about knitting? That is so trendy now. And it's impossible to eat while you're knitting. You need to experiment until you find a handful of food-free strategies that work for you. Perhaps it is a little bit of many things. Keep searching.

It seems as if you want to make a commitment to yourself. It is called the "no-matter-what" pledge. As you continue to follow The Program, you want to hang in there no matter what. And, if you are doing some of the assignments, this is working. It takes time to form a new habit. You'll reach your goal. It is the person who thinks all-or-nothing, black-or-white, who loses focus. Do the very best you can do, at that particular time, and under those particular circumstances. You'll get to your destination.

Gloria S.: Not only do I make up reasons to eat, but I also justify them when I am not hungry — because I paid for it, because there are starving people in other places, because I won't have time to eat later, so that it won't go to waste, but mainly to please my boyfriend.

Caryl: Realize you've become comfortable eating for all the wrong reasons. You've ended up feeling bloated, your clothes are tight, and you're not feeling great about yourself. And you're eating to please someone else.

When you do the new way, The Program way, enough times you'll be eating for all the right reasons and your clothes will be loose and you'll feel good about yourself. What is the new way? It is eating when you are physically hungry. Nickel-sized bites. Food on a plate. Knife, fork, spoon. Sip water before and after each bite of food or sip of beverage. And each meal lasts for twenty minutes or more. Interspersed with bites of food and sips of water is conversation. Ask questions and wait for answers. Learn how to be with someone who is eating when you're not hungry.

When changing your behaviors, the carefully composed use and inappropriate use of food starts to change a little bit at a time. All the feelings (frustration, boredom, anger, among other feelings) that you used to hold down by eating, now float to the surface. Rather than surrendering to the old, comfortable, and familiar way of eating — which keeps the whole cycle habitual — start working on the new habits. If you work on them enough, they'll eventually be familiar and comfortable, habitual. It's about changing your inappropriate overreaction to food and having a different reaction to the same subject.

You may feel a bit of anxiety until it is comfortable, but it's *still not a reason to eat.* Try to find other ways to calm yourself without putting something into your mouth. Learn to deal with problems more directly rather than using food to distract yourself. Eventually, you'll become used to the new way (you get used to anything) so you won't feel anxious around food. It doesn't mean you won't be lonely or tired or bored or angry. You will come across those emotions. That's life, but still it's not a reason to eat. By using food, you don't escape the problems. You merely delay them.

WHY ARE YOU CRYING?

"Why are you crying?" I asked a woman who came to my office.

"I don't know," she replied.

"What is it that is so painful?"

The pain is different for everyone, but people trying to conquer a food addiction share common themes of varying degrees of loneliness, isolation, abandonment, sadness, and neglect. Or not.

It could be an old hurt resurfacing where someone criticized your shape or brains or fashion sense. Those feelings of sadness, resentment, anger, frustration, and anxiety have been seared into your brain so they affect the way you feel about yourself. They are the reasons why you continue to eat rather than address the real problem; unfortunately, overeating doesn't change much of anything except your waistline and how you feel about yourself.

You're trying to fill an emotional hunger with a physical substance — in this case: food. It can't be done. You build a tolerance to whatever you've chosen to eat or drink. The incorrect use of food is very progressive. Frequency increases as do portion sizes.

Discomfort from withdrawal of your usual behavior is what causes the most discomfort. That discomfort could be frustration at not getting what you want in life when you want it. It could be anxiety; Worrying about the future.

Use a deep-breathing delay technique to calm yourself. Many people find solace in meditation, yoga, stretching, and walking, among other things.

Each person is different. Search for the perfect techniques that will help you proactively help a difficult moment to pass.

If hunger is not the problem, then eating is not the solution.

What causes your discomfort?

Irene P. was a thirty-nine-year-old, divorced mother of a teenage girl when she came to see me. She worked as a curator for a museum in New York. Her father had abandoned her and her mother when she was two. All her life, she'd had to cope with various problems, including depression and alcoholism.

Irene P.: If you have depression and have anxiety attacks along with being an alcoholic (sober for almost seven years), there's nothing else to do but eat. So help! How do you deal with this?

Caryl: Eating to distract yourself from drinking, depression, or anxiety is just one more compulsive behavior designed to keep you from feeling the good as well as the bad emotions. It takes plans, attempts, efforts, and cajoling to change such an entrenched habit. Once you talk about these things, you'll most likely be able to let them go.

Make a commitment to yourself to continue trying until you succeed. Sometimes it takes a lot of thoughts, a lot of actions, a lot of days until the new way kicks in. Pick one thing you can try to do one day. You might write about your sadness, put the writings in a balloon, and send it into the cosmos. Learn to express feelings. Feel the feelings. By continuing to use food to escape reality, you keep your inappropriate food usage habitual.

Many men and women resist keeping a feelings journal, but once they've tried everything else, they try the journal and admit it is amazingly helpful. Journaling forces you to follow a thread of thoughts to its natural conclusion, which would have evaporated into thin air if you were merely thinking about it.

A key component to conquering errant behavior is to identify clearly obvious patterns and habits. Be aware though, that part of the tenacious addiction is "resistance to change". Admit you want to change. Then you can work on finding solutions that work. Work little by little toward that solution, and applaud any and all of the smallest of efforts.

Sometimes the patterns are connected to the actual food, or a pattern might emerge in the type of restaurant in which you dine. Also look for patterns of thought. What are you thinking when you think it might be a good idea to fill up your body with food when you are not hungry? How can you change those thoughts to better align with the _____ pounds you want to weigh.

Jayne D.: I cannot stop eating. I eat when I'm not hungry. It's horrible. It's come to the point where I disgust myself. People tell me that I am not fat (I'm a size 6/8). But I feel totally out of control around food. This can't be healthy. Any advice?

Caryl: Feeling out of control with food has many reasons. Some women are small by most standards. They come to me not just to lose weight, but to gain control around certain food and food encounters. Although you're managing to burn-off the food from your "I cannot stop eating" episodes, this compulsive overeating will get worse. Feeling disgust is part of addiction remorse. You are worth creating new automatic, food-free reactions to replace the old, food-filled reactions. Even if you cannot figure out the *why* you eat, you can figure out the *what to do* when not hungry. You try it once, and then you keep trying.

FOOD ANXIETY

Food Anxiety is an emotional discomfort you experience when anticipating a challenging food situation — one in which you may previously have used food to calm yourself. Food anxiety occurs when you haven't even yet gone to a function where there will be lots of food, but you're already anticipating. Just thinking about it makes you anxious. You're worried about something upcoming, something that has not yet happened.

What causes anxiety? For everyone it's different. Fear is common. Fear of meeting someone new, fear that someone won't like you, or fear of not meeting deadlines can cause anxiety. Anxiety might be caused by a fashion insecurity or negative self-image and low self-esteem. Perhaps you fear your choice of restaurant or your favorite food will be judged by someone. You're worried about something that might or might not happen.

I was anxious about telling my office landlord that I would not be renewing my lease. When I finally spoke to him, it was a non-issue. He thanked me for calling and that was that. But until I called, I anticipated every possible scenario, except what actually happened.

Food anxiety might happen, for example, at a culinary arts trade show, where every booth has something edible with which to entice every passerby to the booth. You might have been thinking about this problem before you arrived at the trade show. You have already established eating habits at every booth at previous trade shows.

But before you mindlessly start grabbing food once again, ask yourself, "Was I thinking about this particular food two minutes before I saw it? No? Then why am I thinking of eating it now? Is not fitting in so debilitating that I'd rather eat than feel uncomfortable? Am I eating to relieve the discomfort of not eating?"

Why eat these vast quantities of finger foods at a trade show when you could purchase these things for yourself twenty-four hours a day, 365 days a year and don't? It's a conditioned response to the situation and circumstance. You attended, and you overate. Now, every time you go back to that setting, you feel the need to complete some connection you made (however subconscious it is) between attending and eating. If you do that enough times, those two actions — attending the trade show and eating food — will be forever connected.

It's not about the food. It's about anxiety that comes to the fore when something is bothering you. You may be using food as a distraction because it is easily available and socially acceptable. You might be eating because you've made a habit of eating at a trade show or other weekly, monthly, or yearly function from the first time you attended. Anxiety and unfamiliarity set in without the expected food consumption.

Anxiety occurs many times during the day. You may have unconsciously created your eating habits to calm yourself. You could just as easily have created some other habit, but you didn't. You now have a second chance, a third chance — another chance to change your habits.

Perhaps your anxiety is a reaction to discomfort caused by having dinner with your company's salespeople — the ones who are not selling enough. Your old way was to drown your sorrows by eating and drinking more than you would have if you were home alone, just so you wouldn't have to tell your coworkers they are not living up to your sales figure expectations. Maybe you're feeling anxious about being the salesperson who is not living up to your company's expectations.

How do you overcome this anxiety? By realizing your feelings need to be expressed. Write about those feelings in a journal — perhaps a page or two of your logbook. Journaling is an exercise to get the feelings off your chest (hips). Talk about a problem with others who are *not* in your industry. When you finally do speak to your employees/employer, you'll have a better understanding about what is really important and how to express it. Your eating will not make it better.

Sally P.: I find an intense amount of anxiety surrounding weight loss. I am often left behind to watch jackets and purses because I am too tired or too slow to participate in sports like swimming, basketball, and baseball. I try to tell myself that my whole family will benefit from a more fit and healthy me. But that just increases the pressure.

Caryl: Anxiety may be caused by changing from familiar behavior to unfamiliar behavior. Being faced with fear of the unknown is a perfect time to find new ways to cope. Some habits take a few days to create, some a few weeks, some a few months. Repatterning by deep breathing, changing locations, learning how to calm yourself, or reading your notes may help you through the transition period until you become comfortable with the new habits.

Deep breathing works for me when the situation I'm in makes it impossible for me to move. Consciously relaxing body parts from head to toe works, too. Thinking of relaxing my hair, forehead, eyebrows, eyes, nose, and so on all the way down to my toes keeps me conscious of how tense I am. It helps enormously to relax. Try that simple exercise. Find ways to calm yourself with easy-to-do motions or thoughts.

Take a deep breath. Exhale. Do some stretching of your neck, shoulders, arms, and legs. This will distract you from the bit of discomfort you are feeling. And just as you are used to doing what you are doing and you don't like the outcome, if you do the new way enough times, you'll get used to the new habit and you will like the outcome. The anxiety will pass.

Ken R.: Last night, I was anxious and kept thinking about eating. I didn't do much in the way of repatterning, but the moments passed anyway and I got through it okay. I watch what I bring into the house, so there wasn't much food that was quick or instant. I'm also leaving on a trip tomorrow, and I packed my scale first like you suggested. I never would have done that before.

Caryl: You may have been thinking of eating to distract yourself from something else. Isn't it interesting to see that the moment passed? It's a good thing you don't have much food in the house. Keep working on the reason why you are anxious and/ or looking for something with which to occupy your time, your mind, and your mouth. You're shopping better and dealing with the old habits at the Point of Purchase so there isn't all that extra food in the house. You're confronting denial; you acknowledged the moments did pass, and it was okay. Focus on the fact that you are down eleven pounds and have not gained any of that back. You're doing fine. Enjoy your trip. Enjoy that you packed your scale first. Be proud.

UNREALISTIC EXPECTATIONS CAN CAUSE FAILURE

Weight gain is an evolutionary process. Some people call it creeping weight. The scale turtles inexorably upward — a tight skirt, a belt notch, a can't-zip-up-my-pants inch at a time. Yet you expect the scale to go down as rapidly as a high-speed elevator. This erroneous thought pattern — practiced and perfected as with any bad habit — is an unrealistic expectation. It is dangerous to be sure with any endeavor, but deadly when it comes to weight reduction.

I could have, I should have, I didn't, I wanted to are the loud laments of the perfectionist. Perfection is an illusion, however. Since you'll never be perfect, in your mind, you don't ever succeed. Then you think: *I failed, I blew it, I'm weak* (or bad), or whatever you say to beat yourself up, and you stop trying altogether.

Why not acknowledge small, incremental improvements — times when you did better at one meal, one day, or one event than you might have? Focus only on what you did, not on what you thought you should have done. The inclination to focus on the negative is part of the all-or-nothing addict mind. You think that if you can't do it perfectly for an entire week (even though it is unrealistic to think you can), you won't do it at all. It would be more pleasurable to look for the positive and see that list grow.

All-or-nothing thinking is far more destructive to your weight-loss goal than a friend baking brownies and leaving them on your desk. If you eat even one brownie but manage to give the rest to coworkers and friends, you think you've blown it. A better way of thinking would be to realize you ate only one, when in the past you probably would have eaten several, or maybe all.

Unrealistic expectations give substance, heft, and power to an unrealized goal. They quash the budding crocus of success as it pushes through the thick asphalt of failure. Unrealistic expectations kill the flowering of dreams because you become so disappointed that you give up hope.

Thomas Edison never stopped trying. "I have not failed 10,000 times," he said. "I have successfully found 10,000 ways that will not work."

The only reality is where you are today — perhaps 190 pounds — and where you were a week ago — perhaps 195 pounds. And even if your weight remains the same, there are other questions to ask: Did you keep a food log of everything you ate? Did you drink the requisite amount of water? Did you do better with your eating at an industry function than you might have? Did you eat less than usual at your mother's? Yes? Then you're ahead of the game.

Marcia S., an unrealistic thinker, lost seven pounds in two weeks. The third week she lost one pound. When I asked for a positive story, she said, "Nothing good happened." She was miserable.

"But you lost eight pounds," I reminded her.

"Yeah, but," she continued, "I was so good all week, and the scale didn't move."

"You lost one pound this week," I reminded her, "and you didn't gain back the previous seven."

"Yeah but . . . " she repeated. "I lost that pound at the beginning of the week and didn't lose anything the rest of the week." She was unable to acknowledge anything positive. So great were her unrealistic expectations that it was impossible for her to feel joy or satisfaction in what she had accomplished.

Ignoring these fragile buds — by not watering, nurturing, and turning them to sunlight — they turn to dust. You're used to seeking out the imperfect, and because you're not yet in the habit of recognizing the fruits of your labor, they dwindle on the vine. What remains are the weeds of destructive, negative, unrealistic thinking. These thoughts can and do take over your mind and your heart. Unrealistic expectations make you believe you'll never succeed, every effort is for naught, and you are forever destined to fail.

If you give too much credence to your real or imagined failures and not enough to your attempts, your interim successes, and your accomplishments, you will become the failure you think you are.

Were your parents critical and judgmental? Are you too hard on yourself? You may have internalized their voices.

Create your own positive voice. Think of the reasons you want to reach your weight-loss goal (or any other goal), not the reasons you don't want to remain at your present weight.

Tell friends how good you feel rather than reliving your less-than perfect efforts. Give importance to the good stuff. Let everything else go.

Try to monitor your negative, unrealistic thinking. See how many times you give yourself credit for doing something positive — "I only ate when I was hungry the entire week . . ." — only to take it away by adding, ". . . except for Thursday night when I worked late and had three slices of pizza." It is not a good habit of thought to give one evening of pizza the same weight as six days of staying on your Program.

Thinking realistically and positively may be tricky at the beginning because you've been thinking unrealistically and negatively for a long time. It takes practice and perseverance to change your attitude, but you will succeed. Perhaps not immediately, perhaps one baby-step at a time, perhaps 10,000 attempts later. But, as the artist, Georgia O'Keeffe said, "You musn't even think you won't succeed."

I COULDN'T DO IT PERFECTLY SO I DIDN'T DO IT AT ALL

I sent an e-mail on a Thursday to a participant who began The Program on a Monday, four days before. *Awaiting your morning weight and a positive story*, I typed.

Coming back by return e-mail several hours later, I read, *I couldn't do it perfectly, so I didn't do it at all.*

All-or-nothing. Small efforts don't count. Black-or-white. I can go for days without eating, but once I start, I can't stop. That type of thinking is destructive and demoralizing.

Since perfection is an illusion, you'll never get it perfect. Even if you achieve this status once, you most likely won't be able to sustain your behavior on a consistent basis. If you continue thinking all-or-nothing, you'll miss all your improvements, advancements, and successes you get by inching slowly forward.

You may be thinking of a weight problem or eating disorder as one big all-encompassing entity. So when you attempt one assignment on The Program and have not yet made the thought-word-action combo your own for that one food encounter, you think you've failed.

Yes, you might have found one way that did not yet work during one particular eating encounter. You might feel defeated, stop, and do nothing. Or you allow your efforts to add up to weight loss even in all their imperfections. Remember, you've concocted tens of thousands of eating rituals over decades of holidays, celebrations, and day-to-day eating. Your old habits did not happen overnight. Show up for yourself. Keep trying. You don't have to be perfect. Just be present.

Marina A.: My work is very intense (not an excuse for anything, just a little reality). My eating is out of control again. And it doesn't feel good. I keep starting off my days well and deteriorate toward late afternoon. And when that happens, I just feel like I already messed up for the day, eat whatever I want, and comfort myself by saying there's always tomorrow.

Caryl: Perhaps I can guide you to what is important rather than you trying to get all of it going again at the same time. The Addict Pea Brain thinks in terms of all-or-nothing.

There is a middle ground. So even though you may not have gotten on the scale, you could still have a one-item soup meal for dinner. You can still keep a log. Review your notes for five minutes. Did you ask yourself whether you're hungry? You might count the number of items each meal, each day. It is not all-or-nothing. It is little attempts and baby steps that add up.

Even one successful attempt connects to some other successful attempts. You will get to where you want to be. If you stop trying, it will stop working.

My success is not because I am perfect and did everything perfectly 100 percent of the time. My success is because I never stopped thinking about what I was doing and tried to do something about it. I think about the next meal, about how many items are needed, what they would be, what the difficulties in the situation might be — all this while showering, dressing, and living longer.

> *"It does not matter how slowly you go*
> *so long as you do not stop."*
>
> **— Confucius**

Taryn S.: I came home the other night from catching up with some girlfriends. During dinner, they commented on how great I looked. Feeling comfortable, I proceeded to gorge myself on various appetizers, my entrée, a couple of drinks, and even a slice of cheesecake. I felt justified eating all this food because I had worked so hard to look so great. One night couldn't hurt. But I felt the addiction remorse set in as soon as I got home. Instead of planning out my meals for the next day (my Program Brain was really urging me to), I raided my cupboards for snacks and sweets. Again, I justified my actions by telling myself that this day was already a lost cause, and I don't care anymore.

Caryl: You're in your addiction when you say, "I don't care." Your old practiced behavior was to think you'd blown it when you had all that food for dinner, and you reinforced your old, out-of-control behavior by continuing to eat even though you weren't hungry. Work on finding ways to cope with disappointment and frustration. Attempts count, too. Nothing need be perfect. And clean out your cabinets so the next time you're in the same state of mind, there will be nothing to find in the cupboards. If there's nothing there, you'll do something else. You'll find a new way to cope. If you're keeping instant foods in your home for spouse or children and you're eating it, they're not eating it.

If getting food delivered until midnight is a reality of your neighborhood (as it is mine) tear up and toss those takeout menus. If you want food that much, get dressed, go outside, and get it. Few do.

Keep reviewing bread or beverage or dessert or alcohol — one of four or none.

It's okay you forgot. And I believe you do care. You just resorted to an old habit in a moment filled with lots of old habits. By continuing to eat off The Program, you are reinforcing the eat-when-I-am-feeling-up-or-down pitfalls. Talk to yourself. You can do it. Think of all this in advance of each encounter. Take a deep breath and exhale. Let the moment pass. It will. It always does.

Afterthought: I now recommend that everyone, no matter what they are doing, should stand once an hour wherever they are and do some stretching. From your neck, to shoulders, and back. Standing at your desk and typing is a recent reality in offices all over the world. And walking on a treadmill while working on your computer is here to stay.

CHAPTER 3

THE BASICS

THE BASICS

You can do a few things to start changing habits. The Basics are a synopsis of the concepts covered in The Program. They include lots of things you can do that'll help you remain mindful, conscious, and present about where you are (weight-wise), where you want to be, and how to keep the weight off. If you do The Program, it works. If you stop doing it, it stops working. And by "it" I mean all of the concepts. So if, for example, you cannot write for twenty-four hours enough to keep your food log, you can still weigh yourself, eat slowly, and sip water.

And as one participant told me, "It worked so well I stopped doing it."

The Program Basics are used throughout the book to give you structures to learn. The Basics are your minimum daily requirement so you'll be thinking about food (and your behavior around food) in a new way — The Program way.

You might be asked to keep a daily log of food; if you swallow it, you ate it. It all adds up. Or to ask yourself a question before any eating such as "Am I Hungry, or What?"

1. **Workbook.** Go out (or search online for) and buy an attractive three-ring binder that is easy to access. I found that an 8½ x 11" is a good size for most. You might want to keep your food log and other information in your computer and/or cell phone. Or perhaps you want to be able to look at The Basics when waiting for your car, or listening to it as a recorded announcement on your phone. Press a button and you'll find the pieces of The Program that prompt Program behavior.

   Enter your weight-loss goals, as well as your food consumption and twice daily weight into the book. You'll need more blank pages as you continue to read. Personalize your book. Put an old photo of yourself at your goal weight, on the inside cover so you'll be looking at the person you were and can be again. If you like, you can clip clothing illustrations from magazines and newspapers; something to strive for. I wanted an snakeskin belt to show off my smaller waistline. It was fuchsia. I wore it until it fell off the buckle.

   Some people want to look great at a wedding (when they go to school, when meeting others). The journey should be as enjoyable as the destination. Create your own book for evidence of your journey — how you got from there to here.

2. **Set a Goal.** I want to weigh _____ pounds because: Then write a paragraph or two describing what you want to improve and how, including any physical, emotional, spiritual, sexual, social, financial, fashionable, and healthy components to your goal. You want to set and write out your goals because that will help to make them real. As baseball player Yogi Berra said, "If you don't know where you're going, you could end up someplace else." Setting goals helps get you out of denial so you can face the truth of what you want.

One man's goal was to wear white jeans in the summer. I knew he'd reached his goal when he sent a photo of himself in Italy wearing white jeans. You want to be clear about why you want to reach your goal. When you can envision the goal, you can also envision all the steps you'll take to achieve that goal. Make it real.

Gloria C., a late twenties executive in an Internet company, wrote, "I was thinking about the kind of person I want to be. I have in my mind a girl I used to be a long time ago before life beat me up. I was energetic and loved how my body moved and felt. I loved to look at myself in the mirror and admire my muscles and how strong I was. On the inside, I was happy and calm. I could do anything. I want to find her again at this age where I know more and can add wisdom to her. I want to make this happen. I'm ready."

Laurence J., a thirty-seven-year-old married executive at a TV station, told me he wanted to be the person he only dreamt about. That person, he said, "is in control around food, is calm when daily pressures accrue, and clear-minded. I want food to be a small, normal component of my life."

You can write something as simple as: "I want to weigh _____ pounds. I want to look better in clothes, feel calmer around food, reach my weight-loss goal, keep the weight off, learn how to eat, feel better, look better, and be healthier and happier, and easily stay at my goal weight." Write from the heart.

It's best to review your goal each morning to see whether your goals need to be embellished, clarified, or reduced. Being at my goal weight wasn't as important for me as having the new way become my default setting, my preferred way, a comfortable way. Once the new habits were in place, I practiced all of them until they became mine.

3. **Envision your success.** If you have a photograph of yourself when you looked or felt your best, put that in your log book or around your home or office.

   Imagine a neon sign spelling out the goal weight of _____ pounds. Pick your favorite neon color and let it sway above your head all day long wherever you are whenever you are near food.

   A New York Greenwich Village mother e-mailed her positive story: "Last night I imagined the neon 121 over my head as you'd suggested, with the glow on my face — and it helped me act elegantly: not picking at leftovers from my young daughter's plate." She further wrote, "I'm feeling better: calmer, more optimistic, more joy in my eating."

4. **Keep a Food Log. If it's not water, it's food. Write it down.** A log should contain the day, date, morning weight (plus evening weight), and what food you ate. It's worth repeating: If it's not water, it's food.

   Write everything down, without judgment. Write down two bites of food from your companion's plate, the pickles and coleslaw on the table that you had not ordered, a sip of this and a teensy bite of that. Write it down.

   A log will help you see frequency patterns of food consumption. You may be eating moderately at each meal only to overeat from after dinner to bedtime. Is that you? A food log will reveal that habit. Or maybe you're in control Monday through Thursday, only to overeat Friday, Saturday, and Sunday. A log will show that, too. Once you acknowledge and admit, "Yes, I do that," it will help you learn to do something else, the next time. That's the thing about eating; there's always a next time.

You'll see all of these things in your log. Then next time, you'll learn to do something else instead.

The something else could be a thought, a word, an action. That is a form of repatterning.

You've created and reinforced old habits of eating for reasons other than hunger, just because it's there, or maybe because you're bored. The following is an example of a Food Log:

	SUN	MON	TUES	WED	THURS	FRI	SAT
Date							
A.M. Weight							
Breakfast							
Lunch							
Dinner							
P.M. Weight							

Free download of this form at www.ConquerFood.com

5. **Weigh Yourself Twice Daily.** I recommend you weigh yourself first thing in the morning as well as the last thing in the evening. It doesn't matter whether you weigh yourself after dinner or right before bedtime. Be consistent.

You might want to weigh yourself after your morning elimination and then again, the last thing at night. You'll start to see an a.m./p.m. differential. Usually when there is two pounds or less of a difference, you'll have a weight loss the next day. If the difference is more than two pounds, you'll most likely either stay the same weight or even gain weight the following morning.

Travel with a scale. There may be a scale everywhere you go, but it's not your scale. You want to weigh _____ pounds

365 days a year, not just when it's convenient. If you pack the scale first, it will fit. If you pack it last, it won't.

One of the reasons why I travel with a scale stems from a behavior learned one summer vacation when friends I was going to visit told me they had a scale. While I was visiting, I found it difficult to weigh myself twice daily because their scale was in their bedroom and they went to bed early. It was inconvenient to enter their bedroom, undress, weigh myself, re-dress, and repeat. And more importantly, it wasn't my scale. The next year, I brought along my own scale. Be consistent with any newly formed behavior until it takes hold.

A friend I once traveled with told everyone we visited that I had packed a scale. They all wanted to use it, too.

When you drift away from doing your Program, the first thing you stop doing is keeping a log. The second thing you stop doing is weighing yourself, perhaps first at night, then in the morning. Eventually, you neglect your scale altogether and choose not to travel with your scale.

Not weighing? That's how the two pounds become five, then ten, then twenty. Not weighing means not knowing. Not knowing means mindless eating.

Even if the scale goes up one morning, you have an opportunity to reverse that behavior right away before the old habits take hold and proceed to replicate the frequency and portion you'd created earlier in your life.

6. **Ask: "Am I Hungry, or What?"** Before consuming any food, ask yourself, "Am I hungry, or what?" Am I lonely or bored, anxious or depressed, happy or sad? When even contemplating food, ask the question: Was I thinking about food before

I saw it? Did the shape or color of the container beckon? Did the aroma turn your head?

Most people do not eat because they're actually hungry — few people can even identify real hunger. More than likely, you may be eating for reasons that have nothing to do with physical hunger — but because you're happy, having fun, celebrating a special occasion, and everyone else is eating. Or you eat because it was there. The reality is that food is here, there, and everywhere.

Whatever your habit, it has been practiced by you year in and year out and has turned your use of food into abuse of food.

6a. If hungry, put food on a plate to be eaten with utensils (not fingers) and make it last for twenty minutes or more. Choose nutrient dense foods prepared anyway you like them. Get the widest variety of grains, greens, starches, lean protein, as well as seasonings, and a variety of preparations. Then occasionally choose (or not) Bread or Beverage or Dessert or Alcohol — one of four or none.

7. **Bread or Beverage or Dessert or Alcohol — one of four or none:** These four items appear to be offered at many meals. Even breakfast contains bread, coffee, and orange juice (bread, beverage, and dessert on The Program). Alcohol is usually available at lunch and dinner meals. These items have little or no nutrition.

8. **Skip and Scatter:** At the beginning of this book, you read about the Frequency Pattern. Skip and Scatter is the antidote to the Frequency Pattern. The Skip part is for you to Skip a Day before choosing the same item again. So if you have a drink with friends at dinner on Friday night, Skip at least one Day before ordering a drink the next time you're having dinner.

I realized that I never drank alcohol while alone but drank only when I went to dinner with others who were drinking. And I did it every single time.

Skipping having alcohol (or bread, or coffee, or dessert) every time I was in a restaurant or eating with friends resulted in me sometimes saying yes and sometimes saying no and it's all okay.

The Scatter Part: Rather than having coffee and toast at every breakfast, why not have the coffee sometimes at breakfast and sometimes at lunch.

You might want to put the toast (or bread) with soup one evening. Scatter most items throughout various meals. In this way, you're interrupting the ritual set up so religiously followed for a long time.

9. **The Fillers.** Fillers are foods that fill you up but don't nourish your body. If you have more bread, beverage, dessert, and alcohol combined than you have others foods, you will not be getting enough nutrition. Your goal is to find the right balance.

10. **It's a Numbers Game — The Number of Items in a Day.** If you're eating too many items at each meal, the extra fuel converts to fat and stores it. How many items feed the smaller person you want to be, and are becoming. Check your dinner meal to see how out of balance it might be compared to your other meals. Quite often, people eat more at dinner than breakfast and lunch combined.

11. **Portion Size.** A consistent portion is helpful, so when you start to eat someone else's portion based on how much he or she wanted to charge you for it (or serve you), you'll have a clear vision of your portion on a crowded plate.

12. **Ask whether you're still hungry.** It is also additionally helpful for you to put down your utensils between bites and pause for a moment while you ask yourself mid-meal (perhaps after 15-20 minutes) whether you're still hungry. If you're eating slowly enough, chances are the answer is "No, I'm not hungry anymore."

If you're thinking of eating after dinner, then ask yourself: Am I hungry enough to make a meal, eat with utensils, take nickel-sized bites, and to make it last for twenty minutes or more? No? Then you're not hungry. Do something else instead.

13. **Make a Plan.** Plan what you're going to eat and put it in your agenda book (cellphone, PDA, calendar). Much of the food you presently eat may be unplanned. You feel lonely so you buy something at the grocery store. Or maybe you hear bad news and soothe yourself with food. Or are you sampling free food though you'd never buy it if you had to pay for it.

At the beginning of The Program, use the Suggested Meal Plans in the book. As you move along, you can be more adventuresome and write your own Plan. If you make a plan of what you're going to eat, you can at least realize that in-between eating is something you thought of doing to distract yourself from feelings, thoughts, and work you didn't want to feel, think, or do, and not because you were physically hungry.

Sometimes, it's the visual stimuli that becomes the catalyst for why you reach out and touch some food, even though you were not thinking of that specific item before you saw it. When this happens, ask yourself whether you were thinking of eating the object of your affection two minutes before you saw it. No? Then keep walking. Nothing here for you to see.

14. A Suggested Meal Plan is a mix of a wide variety of Protein and No-Protein meals. Note that while items like eggs do contain protein, in The Program, only animal protein (poultry, fish, veal, and the like) are defined as protein. Consider an egg a bonus protein. It is a protein but never enough for the entire day.

Whenever you have an egg at any meal, you additionally want to add an animal protein at lunch or dinner that day. Variety includes food preparation and seasonings, too. Identify and circle meals without animal protein. You should end up with three circles at lunch and four circles at dinner.

Breakfast is hot cereal, cold cereal, egg. Within those three categories, try to get as much variety as possible. Oatmeal, farina, grits, and cream of wheat, for example, for the hot cereals and miniature Shredded Wheat and Grape Nuts for the cold cereals. While cooking I sometimes sprinkle the Grape Nuts into my oatmeal for a little crunch.

A protein portion is four ounces. An egg is not four ounces, so every time you have an egg, it is not enough for the entire day; more protein in the form of chicken, fish, or veal is needed each day to ensure you have the amount of protein you need. Eat whole eggs rather than egg whites unless specifically told by your doctor not to.

Eggs are nutrient-dense. One large egg has fifteen essential vitamins and minerals, including iron and calcium, protein, and antioxidants.

What about cholesterol? Eggs do have a lot of cholesterol but saturated and trans fats are much worse for your heart and cholesterol levels than the cholesterol found in an egg.

If you want to write your own meal plan, which I suggest you do, there follows a blank form.

BLANK MEAL PLAN

	SUN	MON	TUES	WED	THURS	FRI	SAT
Date							
A.M. Weight							
Breakfast							
Lunch							
Dinner							
P.M. Weight							

Free download of this form at www.ConquerFood.com

However, if you'd rather not write your own food plan, I provided one for you:

SUGGESTED MEAL PLAN

	SUN	MON	TUES	WED	THURS	FRI	SAT
Breakfast	Hot Cereal	Egg	Cold Cereal	Hot Cereal	Cold Cereal	Egg	Hot Cereal
Lunch	Chicken Tomato Potato Salad	Soup	Tuna Cole Slaw	Broccoli Omelete	Veal Rice	All Vegetable	Turkey Cucumber Macaroni Salad
Dinner	All Vegetable	Veal Asparagus	All Vegetable Yam	Chicken Creamed Spinach Carrots	Soup Side Salad	Shrimp Peas	Onion Mushroom Egg
# of Items							

www.ConquerFood.com for additional Suggested Meal Plans.

15. Smaller Bites for a Smaller You — Repeat Daily At Every Meal

I
Every bite should be the size of a nickel.
Not a shoe or a pickle, but simply a nickel.

II
Put utensils down between bites of food and sips of beverage,
To achieve a needed and wanted leverage.

III
Even bread should be a nickel-sized bite.
Then knife and fork for what's left, is what's right.

IV
Sip water between sips of beverage and bites of food.
No spearing or shoveling; get in the mood.

V
Make sure mouth is empty before eating more.
You're slowing down, it's The Program's core.

VI
The most important of all is certainly when,
You achieve one through five, and then do it again.

16. **Flat Plate Rule. Eat with utensils.** Put all food (including a salad) on your own flat plate. Yes. Take things out of containers and put them a spoonful at a time onto a plate.

Cereal and soup are the only two exceptions to the Flat-Plate Rule. In these cases, use a bowl. If foods other than liquid are put in bowls, the amounts seem far smaller than they are. Most portions are about a handful each and are always on a flat plate.

Danny F. from New Jersey purchased a plastic bag containing "Caesar Salad for 2." His wife put half of the bag in each of two large bowls. Being a Program participant, he asked his wife for a flat plate which he put over the bowl and turned it upside down. When he removed the bowl, there was so much salad that it slipped off the plate and fell all over the table. Both he and his wife got it at the same time. A portion is more clear when on a flat plate. The amount in the bag was clearly for more than two people.

17. **Water:** Water is the best thirst quencher and the best bargain: tap water is free. Even if you prefer designer water, it's cheaper than liquor, better for you than wine.

Water brings nutrients to where they are needed. It flushes toxins out of the system. It helps in elimination. It moisturizes the skin. And it helps regulate temperature. It's a wonderful repatterning tool in that you have to get it to drink it.

18. **Eat with Utensils**. If you eat food out of a bag or box with your fingers, you won't realize the amount you are eating. You'll most likely eat it until the bag or box is empty. The whole process becomes mindless.

Eating with utensils requires you to be more mindful of what you are eating and how much of it you are eating. Using utensils keeps you mindful lest you mindlessly stab your cheek with a fork.

Make sure your brain is in motion before your fork is in mouth.

Suzannah I. called me from Albuquerque, New Mexico and said, "You're going to crack up with this one about eating with utensils. I'd ordered a burrito from a local place and brought it back to my desk for lunch. There was no fork in the bag so I went looking around my office for a fork. Finally, someone asked what I was eating; why did I need a fork? 'It's to eat my burrito,' I said. A small crowd gathered. No one could believe it.

'Pick it up with your fingers,' one coworker suggested. Per my being on The Program for years, I told them: 'I eat everything with utensils.' They looked at me as if I were nuts. Since I seldom order sandwiches anymore, this had never come up.

I finally asked them if they remembered the television show *Seinfeld* where the character Elaine's boss eats a candy bar with a knife and fork. I told them: 'I'm the female version of him.' I never could have done that ten years ago."

When New York's Mayor DiBlasio was photographed eating pizza with a knife and fork, participants of The Program asked if he'd ever been through The Program. The answer is no. He eats the way he was taught. And it's okay. During the 2016 primaries, two presidential candidates have been seen eating pizza with a knife and fork, too. Sometimes, I might eat the grilled veggies/cheese topping. I like thin-crust pizza so if it is thick, I won't enjoy it anyway. It won't be missed.

19. **Twenty-Minute Meals**. It takes about 20-30 minutes for your brain to receive signals of satiation. If you eat too rapidly, chances are you'll eat beyond your hunger and eat far more food than you require. Then later you're thinking: I ate too much.

   Food/fuel need only take you from where you are to the next meal; for example, breakfast fuel needs to take you to lunch, lunch fuel to dinner, and dinner fuel to bedtime. When you are sleeping, your body only requires enough fuel to keep your heart and lungs functioning. The burning of stored fat does that fine.

   How do you slow down your own eating when everyone around you is scarfing down their food?

   To find out where you are, time your meals for about a week. When I did this, I found that I sped through all my meals and that the more food that was on my plate, the more quickly I ate. Twenty-minute meals became my goal.

   Since this type of slow and easy eating was not part of my experience, I had to give serious thought about not only what I wanted to do but how to do it. By the time it was mealtime, I'd be so hungry I wanted to clean my plate as quickly as possible. "Slow eating," as I came to think of it, seemed foreign or odd.

First, I set a kitchen timer and began eating. I watched the hands on the timer ratchet toward the twenty-minute bell, even though I was done in nine minutes flat. I then made myself wait patiently in my chair until the twenty minutes were up. It felt like twenty hours.

I forced myself to put utensils down between little bites of food, count twenty seconds before allowing myself to pick up the utensil (fork, spoon, chopsticks), and take a deep breath before continuing to eat. During a twenty-second rest break, I would take a sip of water before picking up the fork again. Sometimes I needed two or three sips of water to kill enough time between bites. I began to taste food. It wasn't just running through my mouth for a few seconds; it hung around long enough for me to distinguish subtle differences.

Instead of spearing several pieces of food at a time, I tried to eat a little bite of a single item so I could taste the food and feel the texture. Then I'd take a bite from the next category until I'd gone around the plate as the clock continued to tick.

It is unrealistic — not to mention demoralizing — to expect yourself to go from a four-minute meal to a twenty-minute meal with the snap of a napkin. Like everything else, it is a process.

My two-minute or non-existent breakfasts became eagerly awaited, enjoyable meals. The variety of my food choices enhanced each meal. I was not only slowing down; I was looking forward to eating a meal I'd never before considered important. Brenda G. challenged me, "I can't make a hard-boiled egg last more than ten minutes. How do you do it?" It is a good and necessary challenge because anyone can make a large meal last for twenty minutes. Making a one-item meal last for twenty minutes is a skill worth achieving. It's an art form! Let's say you are eating alone. Here's how to do it:

- Get a kitchen timer and set for twenty minutes.
- Read a newspaper article, magazine, or book.
- Cut nickel-sized bites.
- Sip water between bites of food and sips of beverage.
- Finish reading a paragraph, page, or chapter before taking the next bite.
- Take several sips of water before picking up the utensils again.
- Make sure mouth is empty before consuming more food.
- If you're with other people, ask them questions.
- Wait for the answer before resuming your meal.
- And, take little bites, little bites, little bites.

Two minutes became five, five became ten, and finally, about a week after I'd begun putting on the brakes, I set my timer for twenty minutes. When the bell sounded, there was enough food left on my plate for another meal. It felt great!

I then practiced making my lunches and dinners last twenty minutes. In a restaurant, I observed the paintings on the wall and the candles and flowers on the table. I listened to the cacophony of other diners conversing. I gorged on ambiance, not food. If alone, I practiced eating more slowly. In that way, I'd be completely comfortable eating slowly when I was with others.

A 20-Minute Meal will not be handed to you, but it is a luxury worth attempting. Four or five days can pass, during which every meal is relaxing and pleasant. Then your schedule could shift and you might not be able to eat a leisurely lunch. Dinner is rushed because you need to eat it on the way to a meeting. Though life inevitably gets in the way, try to create as many relaxing 20-Minute Meals as possible.

Breakfast, lunch, and dinner can become an oasis in the middle of your busy schedule. You're entitled to three 20-Minute Meals (one hour a day) when you're doing something special for yourself. You are worth it.

When I eat slowly, the meal is peaceful, and I often leave food on my plate. I'm filling up sooner because I am smaller. Eating slowly enables me to identify the feeling of satiation and to leave something on my plate when appropriate. When I take the time to slow down, I feel stress falling from my shoulders and inches falling from my waist.

You are worth taking care of.

Most people are up at dawn and working until late in the evening whether on business or around the house. You are entitled to twenty minutes (or more) for each meal to sit and rejuvenate and relax and get ready for the next leg of the day. That's one hour a day (out of twenty-four) that you do something special for yourself.

The new way is now my comfortable and preferred way. Now, if I eat too rapidly, I feel unsatisfied, cheated, distressed, deprived, out-of-control, and physically uncomfortable. This reinforces how important it is for me to slow down when I eat.

I used to be the first person at the table to finish everything on my plate. Because I ate so rapidly, I did not give my body time to process the food or to send signals of satiation to my brain. It took many weeks of concentrated effort to achieve my slowest-fork-on-the-block status. I am no longer the one looking for second or third helpings, nor do I always look for dessert. Yay me.

20. **Repatterning.** There are a certain number of cuts and bites and sips and swallows of food that will yield the weight you want to weigh. Your goal is to create a comfortable way to

eat the same amount of food in each meal (and each day) only with the new slow way of eating so you will reach your goal. It's a new rhythm of certain amounts of bites of food, sips of water that will equal your goal of wanting to weigh _____ pounds. The rhythm you now have equals the higher weight you weigh.

When you eat slowly, you're changing your inappropriate overreaction to food. It's worth achieving.

THE 20 – MINUTE MEAL INSTRUCTION SHEET

Before Meal	During Meal	After Meal
• Stretch before every meal and one item meals.	• Be present at mealtime.	• End of meal by putting the utensils down.
• Say to yourself: It's going to be okay. I'm fine. It will be enough. I really want to weigh _____ pounds.	• Cut small bites. • Eat food individually. • Don't shovel a spoonful of anything. Take human bites.	• Push the plate one or two inches away from you. • Push your chair back an inch or two.
• Deep breathe once or twice until completely relaxed.	• Put utensils down between bites.	• Either remove plate or have someone else remove it for you.
• Re-Commit to your goal.	• Sip water between bites.	• Acknowledge that what you ate was enough.
• Acknowledge that speed eating does not work.	• Ask questions of your companions, and stop eating while they answer. • If alone, count to 20 or 30 before picking up your utensils again.	• Feel the satisfaction. • Leave the table. • Brush your teeth if possible.

BEFORE MEAL	DURING MEAL	AFTER MEAL
• Plan in advance the category of food you're going to order out or prepare at home. • Plan in advance the *Number of Items* you're going to order. • Plan in advance whether to have a Filler or not. • Plan the re-patterning techniques you're going to use if your original plan is not working. • When eating, wear tight clothes. • Buckle your belt on "snug."	• Make sure your mouth is empty before inserting more food. • Chew thoughtfully. • Taste food. • Leave food on plate. • Ask yourself during this meal if you're still hungry • Leave the table if you're eating too much, too late, too fast.	• Go for a walk if possible. • Reward yourself with a food free present if you achieved your mealtime goals. • Give thought to the next meal plan. • Rewrite this sheet into your logbook and read it during meals when you are alone. If eating with others, read prior to mealtime.

MISTAKING HUNGER

You are not hungry most of the time. You are not always hungry when something smells good, looks good, or tastes good, whether or not you think you are. All food is prepared to tempt your taste buds, even though you're not hungry.

You are also not hungry because there is stress, a deadline, pressure, a personal or business problem, anxiety, tension, it's morning, afternoon, evening, when alone, with friends, week-days, weekends, daytime, nighttime, money problems, it rained, it didn't, came with the dinner, it was there. You are not hungry twenty-four hours a day, though you might think you are.

There are many daily food encounters: friends offering food, a *maitre d'* describing dessert, the smell of popcorn in a movie the-ater, to name but a few. Acknowledging the visual and emotional blitz helps interrupt the knee-jerk reaction that causes you to eat even though you're not hungry. Just knowing you are not hungry most of the time is a helpful piece of information.

You may even have pinpointed the reasons you're thinking of food, reasons that seem to justify eating when you're not hungry. I've heard excuses as varied as "I got so angry because I couldn't get a cab" to "I got caught in a downpour without an umbrella." And someone recently told me they come home at the end of the day and are all hyped up. They tell me food calms them down. Many of these reasons might seem a valid enough reason to make you eat. They are not.

Consider that caffeine all day long stays in your system for ten hours or more. So when evening comes and hypyness ar-rives, you're using even more food/fuel, although what you need are ways to unwind and prepare your mind and body for bed. Adding fuel will energize you. You want to wind down so your sleep will be peaceful.

Certainly, anger might tempt you to use food as a drug to keep the feelings down. If you eat when you're angry, does the anger go away? Or perhaps frustration weakens your resolve. At which point is *your* threshold for discomfort seriously chal-lenged? When you're bored? At exactly which point does a yawn become a yen? When you're tired? When does food become a re-placement for sleep? When you're sad, depressed, lonely? Is food your go-to drug?

Does the emotional pain diminish when you eat? Is the celebration any better because you come home stuffed, bloated, and full of gas, uncomfortable and with lowered self-esteem? Is it worth it?

Consider, if you will, that your past behavior has not worked. A clear vision of what you're trying to accomplish will. Most of all, you need a mind open to *the possibility of change*.

One man I *almost* taught was so afraid to change that he was locked into where he hung his coat, where I sat, and where he sat. He was terrified I was going to pull off his covers and yank away his security blanket of whatever food he was holding onto — whichever food he thought made him *comfortable*. He was so uncomfortable with even the thought of change that he would not tell me how much he weighed, or what he wanted to weigh.

Of course it's possible that some discomfort *might* occur while you're changing. The very act of weighing less than you did before is a change. And there is no change without change. But there are ways to lessen the discomfort of the journey from where you are to where you want to be; to offer options, suggestions, tactics, tips, tried and true assignments that work more and more as they are practiced. After all, you learned to use food to calm yourself down. *You can learn a new method*, a new automatic response.

Do you eat out of habit, not hunger? Identifying habits requires guidance, introspection, and patience, but most of all, honesty. Once you acknowledge, "Yes, I do *that*," you can decide you don't want to do *that* anymore and begin to do something else, instead.

It is unrealistic and self-defeating to expect to go from habitual, compulsive, or addictive eating behavior to being a calm, rational, in-control eating person by reading a book, even this book. You can, however, alter automatic, learned responses by creating new and effective alternative behaviors that will result in permanent change. The new behavioral choices add up to a permanent weight loss, incrementally, not rattattattat. It's worth repeating: Your original patterns *evolved* over a lifetime. Now you can consciously plan the new patterns that will enable you to be the in-control eating person you want to be.

Food does not contain a narcotic. Food only has the power you gave it by doing the same thing with it each time you encountered it. Food has the power you vested in it as part of a ritual distraction with your mind, many times since childhood, when you might have learned how to cope with stressful situations by using food inappropriately. It might have worked then, but it's not working now. Now you need to find a new way that will work for the present.

I'll show you what to do if you are *not* hungry but are tempted. There are many things you can do when food is offered, baked, cooked, prepared, and present just for you. Learn how to handle the compelling urges at the office, in a restaurant, or at home. Learn that an umbrella-topped pushcart, wafting a familiar aroma, doesn't always mean you have to eat a hot dog.

Hunger demands to be fed. An urge passes. Know the difference? The next time you're at home and thinking of food, and you just ate a little while before, set a kitchen timer for twenty minutes and *distract yourself with some activity.* Sometimes I set the timer, get busy with some other project, and when the bell goes off, I not only forget I set the bell, I'm not even sure *why* I set it in the first place.

One woman recalled a walk she took one summer day. She spied a man eating an ice cream cone (a visual stimulus). She used the mental repatterning techniques she'd created to distract herself. She'd practiced and silently repeated the words, "I want to weigh _____ pounds and I Can Do It" while laughing. She reassured herself that everything was going to be okay, and she prompted herself to calm her breathing. "Two minutes later, I'd found a pair of shoes I'd been looking for," she recounted. The moment clearly had passed.

The techniques were there in her memory bank because she had written the specifics of her plan, reviewed it daily to remind herself of the details, envisioned it in her mind, so that when the ice cream cone appeared, her new automatic response to say, "I want to weigh _____ pounds and I Can Do It" kicked in. It is a process everyone can learn. It begins in your mind.

If you do not eat something when you normally would have, you might be particularly motivated to reach your goal weight for an upcoming wedding, class reunion, or birthday celebration. If you use *willpower, self-control, good intentions, and inner resolve*, you'll find the results *temporary*. The next time the same circumstances or food appear, you may be a little less motivated or a little more angry, lonely, tired, or bored, and you'll probably eat the food, only to reinforce your old eating behavior, which is what caused you to gain weight in the first place.

There is no *good intention, self-control, inner resolve* or *willpower* sharp enough to cut through the layers and tentacles of your very practiced and polished ritualized eating habits — habits gone haywire. If you ever had good intention, self-control, will power or inner resolve, you would have used it five, ten, twenty, thirty, or fifty pounds ago.

If, however, you begin to change your overreaction to food by doing something else, you might end up eating the object of your desire, but you'll most likely not put as much on your plate, you'll eat a little less, stop a little sooner, and eat it a little less intensely than if you had not attempted some repatterning techniques.

The first time you do it the new way, it might feel awkward and uncomfortable. It is different from what you've done in the past. But no matter how uncomfortable you feel at the beginning of creating a new habit, nothing is as uncomfortable as having to choose what to wear based on how much of your body it will cover. Nothing is as uncomfortable as selecting what to wear based on what fits on a particular day rather than what is appropriate for a particular occasion.

Maintain a positive, *I can do it* mental attitude, and positive results happen. Avoid negative words about yourself, such as *bad* or *failure* or *I blew it*. They are just words and do not apply to anyone who continues to try. "It ain't over 'till it's over," Yogi Berra said.

For best results, attempt many kinds of change in your life. If drinking water doesn't help by itself, perhaps the water and deep breathing will be helpful. Sometimes water, deep breathing, changing location *and* calling a friend is what you need. *It is the action of taking an action — any action — that gets the result.* It almost doesn't matter which techniques you use to repattern — what is important is that you take a *swift, purposeful,* and *immediate action*. The quicker the action, the quicker the moment of anxiety passes.

It is possible that sometimes you might try every technique available and the moment is still difficult. It happens. But that doesn't mean you should stop trying. It just means your results have not quite accumulated enough to effect a noticeable change. It doesn't mean nothing is happening. It just might be too subtle for you to notice. Keep doing it anyway. It accumulates.

Continue trying, and from each seemingly failed, imperfect human attempt, the structure of the old, destructive habit will be eroded another little bit. And you will be that much closer to success, which is eating only when hungry enough to commit to a meal.

It took many episodes of reinforcing old behavior to create patterns as ingrained as the ones you are trying to change. It takes many steps of new behavior until you're hooked on the new way.

Sometimes one technique works, sometimes another. Every food encounter is different from every other one. Everyone responds to each stimulus differently and responds to repatterning techniques in a different way, too. A combination of several techniques may be just the ticket when one is not enough. Be creative. A man I'm teaching now drinks a lot of coffee and alcohol but doesn't even like sweets or bread. I, on the other hand, do not drink coffee or alcohol except on rare occasion, but I like sweets.

Identify your eating patterns. Even the seemingly insignificant ones, such as *it's only broccoli*, or *I only drink black coffee* add up. Do you mean an orange has the same significance as a piece of candy? Yes.

What ritual thinking is in *your* subconscious? Are leftovers a problem? Does food preparation end up being one for you and one for the pot? Does someone else serve you your food at home, in the office, in a restaurant? Do you finish everything served to you?

One woman I teach had the habit of *eating after eating*. She battled that habit for many months. When I spoke to her last week, however, she reported a two-week period when she did not once eat after dinner. And it was okay. She is fifty-nine years old.

If you buy, prepare, serve, and accept *a little less* food, you'll eat less. Ultimately, *you'll be a little less.*

If you don't bring it into the house, you won't eat it. Out of sight, out of mind.

If it doesn't taste good or look good or satisfy the eye and palate, don't eat it. We all belong to a nation of people who finish everything on their plate. That is not necessary. You *may* leave food over. It's okay. Food is wasted if you put it into a body that doesn't need it. Better to throw it away. If you order less the next time, there will be less to waste.

When you go off your Program because you're human, you didn't blow it, weren't bad, or a failure. Don't beat yourself up.

Get back on your Program at the very next meal. Try to figure out what you could do *next* time the same thing inevitably happens. The quicker you're back on your Program, the more you'll want to stay on your Program. It is becoming comfortable, enjoyable, and preferred behavior.

Think of things you can do if you're thinking about eating but know you're not hungry.

QUESTIONNAIRE

When teaching The Program, participants try to articulate what is happening to them when feeling out of control with certain foods in certain situations.

These are the things I hear most often when participants try to explain what is happening to them when they eat compulsively. Sometimes, one habit will be repeated over and over.

One of my personal habits was continuing to buy a multiple-item package of ice cream, a bagful of cookies, a loaf of bread, or a six-pack of soda. My Addict Brain convinced me *I could handle it.* It was clear I wasn't handling it at all. I'd eat it till it was gone. And the time it took to finish those multiple-item packages was continually growing shorter. That's when I started buying two multiple-item packages of something. I wanted to ensure I never ran out of that item. I was in my addiction when I bought it and ate it, convincing myself I was Skipping and Scattering. I was not.

I call it the Addict Pea Brain; it's that mindless.

Circle the things that pertain to you.

1.   Can you go for a long time without eating, but once you start, you can't stop?

2.   Do you eat when you are angry? Bored? Anxious? Depressed?

3.   Do you feel out of control around certain foods? An abundance of food? Free food?

4.   Are you a secret eater?

5.   Do you always eat take-out food? Do you often have food delivered to your home and office?

6.   Do you buy an extra box of cookies, two bags, or two boxes of anything edible?

7.   Do you drink alcohol when no one else is drinking?

8.   Do you stock up on certain foods because you're afraid to run out of that item?

9.   Do you eat more when you're alone, and hide your overeating from friends and family?

10.   Do you eat a moderate breakfast and lunch only consistently to overeat at dinner?

11.   Are you in control of your eating during mealtime, only to eat non-stop from after dinner to bedtime?

12.   Are you frustrated about your weight, but nothing changes, no matter what you do?

13.   Do you constantly worry that what you ate won't be enough?

14.   Do you eat to the point of physical discomfort?

Acknowledging some or all of the above gets you out of Denial and into the truth. Once you identify the Pitfall Problems, you'll start to come up with the solutions.

THE COST OF ADDICTION

If everything you listed when you set your goal is everything you want, that means you don't have any of those things. That's the **cost of addiction**. Addiction costs you **time, energy, money, and health.**

Time is spent trying on clothing (whether at home or in a store) when you don't like the way you look in them. You're slowing down when you play basketball. Or you use a cart when playing golf. Your additional weight hampers your golf swing. Running errands takes more time. Shopping for extra food takes time. Eating extra food takes time. Every activity is slower.

Energy is spent carrying the extraneous weight around your emotional heart as well as your physical heart.

There's a chair in my office that weighs ten pounds. So imagine: everywhere you're walking, you're carrying two (or three or four or more) chairs on your head, shoulders, stomach, knees, and ankles. You're carrying those chairs in and out of cars, up and down stairs. Every time you get up from a chair, you're lifting those five chairs too. After losing twenty pounds, a Program participant e-mailed saying he was down two chairs.

There is a **monetary cost** to food addiction. You're spending more on food, beverages, alcohol, and bigger clothing than a smaller you might spend. I took far more cabs when I was heavier because I was out of breath if I had to walk even a few blocks. I bought enough junk food to accumulate a noticeable amount of money. If I successfully got past a place I used to purchase junk food, I'd take the amount of money I would have spent and put it in a bowl on a kitchen shelf. What an eye-opener. As I got smaller, the pile of money got bigger. How much does your addiction cost you?

Health is another cost. There's not just stress on knees, ankle joints, your neck and back, but all your organs have to work that much harder to process the extra food. Blood pressure goes up. When your self-esteem is low, it's affecting your mental health.

Last, but not least, your happiness is at stake when you are enslaved to compulsive eating and addiction. When you are in your addiction, you are not present in a conversation or work situation. When was the last time you felt confident wearing fitted clothing? When was the last time you could keep up with your active children and family members? When was the last time you didn't need food to narcotize unwanted feelings of anxiety, stress, and pressure? Food addiction costs you your happiness, whether or not you believe these words.

It's about changing habits, not foods.

It took many attempts before I was automatically able to put my utensils down between bites of food and a week or two to get in the habit of keeping a food log or getting on my scale every morning and evening; Once you form the basic habits, you can do all of the things suggested in this book. Many are quite easy. None are difficult. They are just different.

If you do the new, different way enough times, it will become your comfortable, entrenched way — your default setting. Embrace The Basics.

DON'T DISCUSS YOUR WEIGHT-LOSS PROGRAM WITH ANYONE

"Don't discuss anything about your weight-loss program with anyone," I told Maureen M. at her first session to learn how to conquer her food addiction. "Since everyone's addiction-triggers are different, someone with a thing for bread cannot always understand another person's attraction to coffee. A person overeating to the point of being stuffed at each meal is different than a person in the habit of eating moderately at mealtime, only to eat again right after dinner and until just before bedtime. You don't need everyone's opinion about how to lose weight and what they think you should and shouldn't eat. It will only cause you to second-guess yourself and go off your Program." Maureen nodded in agreement at this advice. "I'll do anything," she said.

At the beginning, almost everyone says, "Yes" to everything I tell them. Then a few weeks later, Maureen told me how when she had contemplated choosing a dessert the second of two days in a row, her husband commented that she'd had dessert the night before.

The Program recommends that part of changing habits is for you — not your spouse — to be able to identify frequency patterns of certain foods you consume one or more times daily. You will become better at changing your habits when you mindfully uncover them rather than relying on someone else being there to help. You also don't want your spouse with his/her nose in your plate. If they could have helped you before, they would have. They didn't. So they can't help you now. Learn how to help yourself.

"He's my husband, and he's been very supportive," she replied sheepishly.

"If he could have helped you before, he would have. He couldn't. He didn't," I said.

"Yeah, but . . ." she responded with the two words all addicts use. "Yeah, but" is where the addict twists around the facts to justify the behavior. The word "but" wipes away all that came before.

"He has a bit of a weight problem himself," I reminded her. "How can you explain it when you don't even understand it yourself?" I asked.

She looked annoyed and frustrated that I was still on the same topic. She wanted to move on. I paraphrased the best-selling inspirational author, Wayne Dyer, by saying, "Do not discuss your aspirations with others: you'll only have to defend or explain them."

What is this compulsion either to tell another person what to do and/or to share every up and down of your own struggle? Why do you think you need approval from a spouse to eat something you enjoy? Many components make up the addiction: the talking; the planning for perfect, or worse, planning to reach for someone else's version of perfect; shopping; preparing, and eating — all are variables with rituals of their own. Trying to achieve someone else's version of what you should do is a no-win situation. How many times had I been coaxed into trying food that was supposed to be amazing but wasn't?

You're dealing with a behavioral addiction. Dieting and deprivation keep habits chronic. Finding new ways of thinking leads to a new way of acting. The weight-weary think they need to recount every up and down, every indiscretion, every bad action and good action. Many of you have been trained since birth to discuss your weight problem. You may describe with every person who wants to listen to the details of every morsel of food, commiserating over the caramelized onions or the chocolate truffles, or describing every piece of clothing and what fits or doesn't fit, and detailing every other behavior related to your struggle with your weight. If you both talk about your eating struggles, you may never find time to reach deeper to discover why you eat when you're not hungry. Discussion is part of the addiction. By talking about it, the entire cycle of addiction is reinforced because you are mentally locking in the patterns.

If you allow your daily food-related behavior to be judged by people who are struggling themselves, you'll continue to struggle. I've been successfully teaching a behavioral approach for thirty-five years. I never discuss my ups and downs but find solutions for myself and pass them along to participants of The Program.

I understand that when people lose weight and are getting closer to the look of the person they want to be, friends, family, and acquaintances all want to know, "How did you do it?" so the bragging gene takes over. The memory of the misery of just a few moments ago becomes murky. Unless friends have read the words and struggled the struggle, they most likely want only to know what you can and cannot eat. You can eat any food at all on The Program. You are changing habits. And that is different for everyone.

Here are some things you can say to others that will soften the anti-discussion edict:

1. I'm trying to understand it myself.

2. It's different and I have to think it all through.

3. It's different for everyone.

4. I'd appreciate this not being a topic of conversation. (This is my favorite non-negotiable rule.)

Practice words and phrases when you don't need them so you'll have them when you do; it's like rehearsing a play. Write your own short and sweet phrases to convey this non-discussion.

This is not cocktail party chit chat. This is a full-blown addiction, and by making fun of it, you trivialize the power your addiction has over you.

Helena W.: I told a roommate I was on a diet, and when she saw me eating a small cup of ice cream one night, she snickered and said, "Aren't you on a diet. What kind of diet are you on?" It was really aggravating, and now I understand what you meant when you told me that if I discuss my weight-loss goals and plans, I will just find myself defending or explaining them. Neither of which I care to do again.

Caryl: On The Program, it's not about eating celery or eating ice cream. It's not about the food choices, but about the habits surrounding that food choice. You can eat ice cream as part of a meal, if you're hungry. If you're trying to narcotize feelings, food don't fix it. In your case, you consciously chose to eat ice cream that evening, but what your roommate saw (in her mind) was that you were out of control with your eating. It does not feel good to be on the defensive when it comes to food, especially when working so hard to change lifelong habits. Next time, let your roommate know that the foods you eat is not a topic of conversation.

Hannah E.: Why should we not talk about The Program with others?

Caryl: It's not a competition. Everyone is different with different experiences, likes and dislikes, as well as depths of habits. When you compare your achievements with someone else's version of success, you lose sight of your goal and what is considered success in your life. You end up trying to achieve someone else's goal. It's a happier experience if you are focused on your own goals.

When I was at the beginning of my weight-loss quest, one evening I was able to throw away a cookie from the bottom of a bag of cookies I'd just eaten. I was so excited knowing that I'd never been able to throw away anything like that before, least of all a cookie! I knew this little baby step was an important one for me, a beginning. I called a friend to brag.

Since she was taught by a deprivational, all-or-nothing society that nothing counts except perfection, rather than being happy about my accomplishment and cheering me on, she said, "You shouldn't have bought the cookies in the first place."

All I could think in response was that if I could have not bought them, I would have done that. At the time, however, I most likely wasn't ready for that step. So I did what I was capable of doing, at the time, under the circumstances. I bought the cookies. I ate most of the cookies, but I threw out one cookie. I was so proud of myself (enough to want to share it with a friend) for having achieved this little first step. It made me realize that nothing horrible happened when I threw out the cookie. It was almost a relief to be rid of them (for that moment). It was then that I decided not to look for anyone to tell me whether I was doing well or not. I needed to focus on my own version of success.

Just a few weeks ago, another participant of The Program told me that her sister insisted on knowing how much weight she'd lost. The sister kept asking and she wouldn't tell her, but finally she acquiesced and told her it was sixteen pounds. The sister looked at her up and down and then said: "Sixteen pounds? It doesn't look like that much."

Friends or acquaintances may be secret or unintentional saboteurs. Some may be jealous of your accomplishments. Others continue to believe the myth that if you really wanted to lose weight, you would. Their standards are too high. Praise yourself for the smallest achievements and accomplishments. Pat yourself on the back for any effort. Only you know how hard you've worked.

One woman wrote that she'd had a No-Meal Meal of half a muffin and half a cup of coffee. "That is my beginning," she bragged. "In the past, I would have had a whole muffin and a larger coffee!" She was clearly proud of herself. Sharing her positive story with me, she lived it one more time — and it lives on here in the book you are reading.

Camelia C.: I know most people don't even notice that I've lost weight.

Caryl: One of the reasons I urge people not to discuss their program with anyone else is that others might not notice your weight loss, but you know you're doing better than you were. That's all that matters. You're trying to reach your goal because you want to look better and feel better. You don't need someone else's bravo. You know how good you look.

Try to incorporate these Program Basic components into your eating life. Think of them as your default setting. Then, when you go off your Program, and you will, you'll know how close or far away you are from where you want to be.

CHAPTER 4

MEAL PARAMETERS

MEAL PARAMETERS

The Meal Parameters are a list of foods from which to choose.

Look at the following items divided into the Top, Middle, and Bottom of a sheet of paper. It's like a menu with cocktails and bread being offered at the start of a meal. Appetizers, Salads, Soups, Proteins, Vegetables, and Potatoes offered as possibilities for an Entrée. And desserts, coffees, and after dinner drinks offered at the end of a meal.

Read (and memorize) the Meal Parameters because the definitions will help you nourish your body in a meaningful way and occasionally have bread or beverage or dessert or alcohol; one of four or none.

The Middle Items, for example, are the most nutrient dense. Whereas the Top and Bottom of The Meal Parameters usually have little or no nutrition.

The definition of each category of food is next. Picture each word as you read it.

TOP OF THE MEAL PARAMETERS LIST

1. Cocktail — If you're having alcohol, then one alcoholic drink as part of a meal (not before the meal.) If you have alcohol before a meal, you're drinking on an empty stomach. "I'd love a glass of water." Wait for food; have a bite or two of food, a sip or two of water, then have a sip of wine. Repeat. Chances are you won't have two drinks.

"And while you're waiting for your drinks
can I get you something from the bar?"

2. Bread — crackers, rolls, muffins, bagels, breadsticks, pita, croissants, matzo, croutons, crust of quiche or pizza, or wraps. May be eaten as part of a meal but No Sandwiches. Note: if you must have a sandwich, remove the top piece and the bottom piece and place both pieces of bread on the side of the plate. This is called *deconstructing a sandwich:* Take a nickel-sized piece of Bread with your fingers; Use a knife and fork to eat the food inside the sandwich. Sip water. Chances are you won't finish two pieces of bread; you might not even finish one piece.

Even if it's a lettuce wrap, any kind of wrap, you want to unwrap it. If you pick up a wrap and put your mouth on the wrap plus the innards of the sandwich, there is no way you could be taking a nickel-sized bite. Deconstruct.

MIDDLE OF THE MEAL PARAMETERS LIST

3. Appetizer — one or two to be served as a main course.

How many times have you had an appetizer and then when the entrée arrived, you knew you weren't hungry. But you ate the food anyway because you had ordered it and paid for it. Same thing if you're thinking of ordering two appetizers and having them delivered separately. You'll eat one and won't be hungry for the next. So side by side if you order two. Take a bite from one and then from the other with water in between. You'll most likely leave food on one or more of the plates.

4. Soup — thick, hearty, substantive. (A cup or bowl, with or without a salad.) If you are at work, you might need a bowl of soup and a salad because you're going to continue working for a while. But if you're going to a movie after work and then go home to go to sleep, a cup of soup might be the right amount.

5. Salad — lettuce, tomato, cucumber, green pepper, coleslaw, sprouts, carrots, etc. (Use any salad components you like; use any dressing you like, but dip, don't drown.) A salad is a handful on a flat plate.

If your salad arrives in a bowl, ask for a flat plate which you'll put before you. Then serve yourself the choicest bits — about a handful. I like to relinquish the rest of the salad to the table.

6. Entrée

Lo-end protein — (lo-end proteins) Poultry (chicken, turkey) fish, veal, some game meats such as rabbit, bison, and deer are usually pretty lean, but check before eating. You want to get as much variety in food, preparation, and seasonings in this category too. These meats are relatively low in cholesterol.

A portion is the size of a deck of cards, not the deck of a boat.

Bonus Protein — The portion of an egg is not enough protein for the day. Each time you have an egg for breakfast or lunch, make sure to have an additional lo-end protein of chicken, veal, or fish at dinner so you've had enough protein for the day. An egg is never enough protein for an entire day.

Hi-End Protein — pork, beef, organ meats such as liver or kidneys, lamb, cold cuts (ham, salami, bologna, corned beef, pastrami), and cheese. *Hi-End Protein contains more fat, cholesterol, and sodium than Lo-End Protein.* (Once every 7 or 10 days it is a good idea to have veal, steak, or hamburger) to get nutrients not found in low-end protein.

7. Vegetables — dark leafy green and orange, including broccoli, carrots, cauliflower, collard greens, asparagus, zucchini, eggplant, kale, string beans, artichoke, spinach, squash, Brussels sprouts. (Choose as part of a meal, like string beans on the side, or as an entire All Vegetable Meal). Hummus can be used in an All-Vegetable meal, whether hot or cold.

8. Starch — beans, corn, rice, pasta, potatoes, and/or yams. (Always have a salad or a vegetable. Never alone.) You can have a vegetable without a starch, but you cannot have a starch without a vegetable.

Brown rice is better than white. Long grain better than short.

Think of starches growing from a plant in the ground. Corn, potato, yam for example fit that criteria. Pasta, though part of every ethnic food, does not come from the ground. It is processed food, like bread. If having any starch, always have it with a green vegetable or a salad.

BOTTOM OF THE MEAL PARAMETERS LIST

9. Dessert — Anything you think of as dessert (cookies, cake, candy), PLUS all fruit, fruit juice, jam, jelly, syrup, honey, PLUS popcorn, potato chips, pretzels, nachos, seeds, nuts, any finger foods. If it's sweet or instant and/or both, it's most likely dessert.

    10. Beverage — coffee, tea, milk, soda (Perrier, Club Soda, Seltzer, and the like) — but no diet soda. There is water and everything else is food.

    11. Wine/Beer — same as #1 above — always with food never alone.

HOW TO USE THE MEAL PARAMETERS GUIDELINES:

1.   If hungry, first choose food from the Middle Items 3-8. Those are the most nutrient-dense foods.

2.   Then choose (or not) one item from either the top two or bottom three items of the Meal Parameters: bread or beverage or dessert or alcohol, one of these four or none. It is so important, I'm saying it again. Bread or beverage or dessert or alcohol, **one of these four or none.**

The only "no" in the entire Program is no diet soda or diet products of any kind. Unless you have a medical reason, use real sugar. Diet products fill you up but have no nutritional value. You don't want to be filled up. You want to nourish your body.

MEAL TERMINOLOGY

Meal. A Meal is nutritious food on a plate, eaten with utensils, of which bread or beverage or dessert or alcohol — one of four or none — may (or may not) be part of a meal that lasts for twenty minutes or more.

The key words are plate and utensils. Just about any food from the middle of The Meal Parameters can be eaten with fingers. What makes it a meal is food on a plate and utensils. It's a break in the middle of each day to rejuvenate yourself. Relax. Unwind. Slow down.

No-Meal Meal. The Program doesn't mention snacks. It covers Meals and No-Meal Meals. I am convinced that the snack food companies were thinking up a cute name, and they wondered what they could call this crap and not let it sound too, um, crappy. They said, "Let's call it a snack."

A No-Meal Meal contains only foods from the top two and bottom three items of the Meal Parameters list. A No-Meal Meal is bread, beverage, dessert, or alcohol consumed alone.

Desserts include: cookies, cake, candy, fruit, fruit juice, jam, jelly, syrup, honey, popcorn, potato chips, pretzels, nuts, seeds, and the like (anything sweet, salty, or both) when eaten alone and not as part of the twenty-minute-food-on-a-plate-eaten-with-utensils consumption of food.

You may be choosing these items because they are quick, instant, usually eaten with fingers, and are easily available. One man told me, "Popcorn is part of the movie-going experience." It is also part of the weight-gaining experience. And popcorn, by itself, is a No-Meal Meal. It's dessert.

A No-Meal Meal is bread, beverage, dessert, or alcohol without any nutrition. Popcorn is dessert. Eaten by itself it is a dessert and a No-Meal Meal.

A No-Meal Meals may look good, smell good, and taste good. But none of those are a reason to eat.

If you're thinking of eating when you're not hungry, think of doing something else. Find other ways to cope with boredom and anxiety. You need to experiment until you find the right combination of actions. Take deep breaths, change locations, drink water, and know the moment will pass. These are easy things you can do anytime, anywhere. Fill up your life, not your belly.

Fourth Meal. A Fourth Meal is a lesser portion of wholesome nutritious food, eaten when additional food is needed because a previous plan didn't work out.

Perhaps you planned on having a dinner of chicken, broccoli, and a salad at 6:00 p.m. But your companion called to say he or she couldn't get home until 7:30 p.m. Having the salad at 6:00 p.m. as a Fourth Meal and the chicken and broccoli at 7:30 p.m. for dinner would most likely work well.

A No-Protein Fourth Meal could be a cup of soup, a cup of cereal, or a salad (a handful on a flat plate) eaten with utensils.

A Protein Fourth Meal could be a half-can portion of tuna, one egg, or two slices of turkey eaten on a flat plate with utensils that lasts twenty minutes or more. If you are reluctant to take those steps, you are most likely not hungry. Before any eating, you want to meet all three criteria.

I remember getting home very early one morning from a weather-delayed plane flight. I hadn't eaten for hours and was hungry. I was also in need of sleep. I went into the kitchen and found a can of tuna. I asked myself, "Am I hungry?" "Yes. Yes," I said.

"Am I hungry enough to get a can of tuna, open the tuna, mix it with mayonnaise, put it on a plate, and eat it with utensils?" "Yes. Yes," I said.

"Am I hungry enough to make it last for twenty minutes or more?" I asked. I thought for a moment and realized, "I'm not that hungry," and went to sleep instead.

Skipping a meal is not on The Program. But the exercise above is for you to get in touch with the feeling of hunger.

If hungry, first choose middle items 3-8.

Then, choose or not, items from either top or bottom of the **Meal Parameters** list, i.e., bread *or* beverage *or* dessert *or* alcohol — one of four or none.

Foods chosen from the middle items, if on a plate and eaten with a knife and fork, are considered a **Meal**.

Foods chosen from the top and bottom items without at least one item from the middle are considered a **No-Meal Meal.** This needs repatterning.

A **Fourth Meal** is only *one* item such as a cup of soup or cereal, a small salad (no protein meals), a hard-boiled egg, ½ can of tuna, or 1 or 2 slices of turkey (protein meals), consumed at 5:00-6:00 p.m., if dinner is to be exceptionally late. Fourth meals cannot contain foods from the top or bottom of the list because a Fourth meal is only one item.

If you swallowed it, you ate it, and it all adds up.

If you look at the Meal Parameters, you will see Alcohol and Bread at the top of the page and Appetizers, Salads, and Soups in the middle. The format follows that of a menu or the order in which food is presented to you at a restaurant.

By learning the definition of each component, you realize that the more nutritious foods are in the middle of the Meal Parameters List.

The less nutrient-dense foods (bread, beverage, dessert, and alcohol) are found at the top and bottom of the menu: the pre-meal alcohol and bread or equivalent, and the after-meal dessert, coffee, drink.

The smaller person you want to be doesn't require a lot of food. You want to make sure most of the food you consume is as nutrient-dense as possible. Then, occasionally, you'll have the bread or beverage or dessert or alcohol — one of four or none.

So if you're hungry, eat. If you're not hungry but thinking of eating, learn to repattern your old actions. Retrain the brain. These are skills you can learn. Henry Ford said "If you can conceive it, and believe it, you can achieve it."

CHANGING HABITS AND PATTERNS

Whether you're thinking differently about what a meal is (or is not), or you're waxing nostalgic about one restaurant over another, you have old cues, habits, patterns, and rituals that are yours and only yours. A combination of new thoughts on how to accomplish your goals, by changing your behavior by thinking, speaking, and moving a little bit differently than what you've been doing.

All those seemingly insignificant attempts add up. Eventually, the new way becomes the comfortable and preferred way.

Just as your old habits solidified, though you didn't like the outcome, so too will your new habits become solidified, but this time with a preferred outcome. In essence, you have been using food to distract you from old feelings and thoughts. Now you want to create new thoughts and actions to distract you from food. Here are two of many helpful repatterning techniques to use when distracted by your old habits:

    a. Delay Technique. Are you still thinking about eating, but you know for sure you're not hungry? Distract yourself using one of my favorites: a fifteen-minute delay technique. Wait fifteen minutes before you put any food into your mouth. And during that fifteen-minute delay, get busy doing something else.

Brush your teeth, call a friend, go for a walk. Any action is better than no action. Sometimes, the fifteen minutes turns into three hours, a clear indication that you were not hungry in the first place. Sometimes, the first fifteen minutes is over and you're still thinking of food. This is seldom. But if it happens and you know you're not hungry, go to sleep early or read your notes for a few minutes. Drink a glass of water. The moment always passes.

    b. Physical Repatterning

When you feel like eating something, but you are not actually hungry, remove yourself from the situation. Leave the site. Leave the room. Leave the planet. Move! When in doubt, get out.

There are other physical things you can do. Circle the ones you think you'll be able to incorporate into your life during a difficult moment. You're creating an arsenal of thought word, and action to counter the old, the mindless, the put-something-into-your-mouth ingrained habit.

Take an Action. Any action. Change location. Throw food away. Go for a walk. Clean the closet. Exercise. Move away from the table. Call a friend. Go to a movie. Brush your teeth. Drink water. Read your Program notes. Walk a dog. Cross the street. Take a deep breath. Do head rolls. Stretch. Change activity. Take a break.

When I'm thinking of food at eleven o'clock at night while working on this book, I know I'm not hungry. I know I need a break. I turn off the computer and turn on the TV. That desire is gone as soon as I leave the site of the discomfort. I didn't need food. I needed a break.

Take a nap. Go to sleep early. Leave the site of your anxiety. Open and read snail mail. I save that for the end of the day. It gives me a sense of accomplishment when I open, glance, and tear up the junk mail.

Check your e-mail. Read your Program notes, including this page. Walk a dog. Cross the street. Water the plants. Play an instrument. Get some fresh air. Try on clothes, and assess success.

Patterns created when you gained weight are what you're looking to change. Initiating any one or more of these Physical Repatterning techniques will help distract you until the moment passes. The moment is a very short period of time. But even better, if used consistently, the new way becomes your comfortable way. The new habits become new rituals. The old habits become less and less compelling.

One participant told me her story of repatterning. She said, "I had a huge win last night. I really wanted to just eat, eat, eat. I even made fancy dinner reservations, planned a movie, too (just because I wanted candy). I stopped for a minute and realized the only voice I had in my head was that of my Addict Pea Brain. So I canceled the reservations, and the movie plans, and went to Barnes and Noble for two hours by myself and read. I'm not going to lie — it wasn't easy — but I did it. I woke up feeling amazing."

I'd rather she think that it was different or challenging (positive thinking) rather than "it wasn't easy" (negative thinking).

Every time you reinforce the new thought or word or action, it strengthens your muscle memory. The next time you face a similar situation, you'll deal with it more quickly and efficiently.

The moment will pass more quickly. Eventually, the new way is your automatic.

In a *New York Times* article by Kate Murphy, she writes, "Whether it's hitting a golf ball, playing the piano or speaking a foreign language, becoming really good at something requires practice. Repetition creates neural pathways in the brain, so the behavior eventually becomes more automatic and outside distractions have less impact. It's called being in the zone."

Others tell me that Physical and Verbal changes seem to help the most. I think Mental Repatterning helps remember the Verbal and Physical things you're trying to accomplish.

List as many Physical Repatterning Techniques as you think might work for you. Be as detailed as possible. If you envision each step, it'll be easier the first time you use it during a meal. One man decided to do pushups during every television commercial. Sometimes just walking into another room is enough to help a moment pass.

1. _____   6. _____
2. _____   7. _____
3. _____   8. _____
4. _____   9. _____
5. _____   10. _____

   c. **Skip and Scatter.** If you choose to have something on a daily basis, such as coffee with every single breakfast, or a sandwich at every single lunch, you will eventually have it twice a day, either at breakfast or between meals throughout the day. But if you consistently skip a day between each dessert (or coffee, or bread, or alcohol), and change the meal in which you have these items (choose sometimes at lunch and sometimes at dinner), you'll get used to that, too. For example, if you have dessert today at lunch, skip a day before having dessert at dinner.

Salads and starches are also part of the equation because many people eat whatever is served to them and most restaurant meals include salad or rice (or a potato, or pasta), which appears to be free.

Good starch is something that comes from the ground: beans, corn, rice, potatoes, and yams. Bread doesn't come from the ground. It is processed. Once it is processed, most of the nutrition is gone. In nutrition's place are additives and preservatives. Pasta is like bread, but it's too ingrained into every culture so it's listed as a Starch, but as with all Starches, it needs to have a vegetable, never eaten alone.

None of these foods are bad or good, but they are usually consumed in a disproportionate portion size and frequency. For instance, eating extra salads might mean not having enough room for a more nutritious balance and mix of foods. And no matter what I order in a Chinese restaurant, it comes with free rice (starch), tea (beverage), and a fortune cookie (dessert). Those are three extra, mindlessly-consumed items. I'm not sure you'd eat any of those items if you had to pay extra for them.

When you diminish the number of times you're having an item, you'll crave it less and less often. Sometimes, you have it, and sometimes, you don't. However, when the frequency of consumption of one item diminishes, but other Fillers, to which you are partial, remain the same in frequency and portion size, you will inevitably regain the weight you have lost. This occurs because as you lose weight, the diminished items will gradually creep back up to match the foods that remained the same in frequency and portion. If that happens, you will regain the lost weight. When all items are Skipped and Scattered and diminished in frequency and portion size, you can keep off the lost weight and enjoy a smaller you.

One man, celebrating twenty-eight years of sobriety tells others, "Sorry, but I'm over my lifetime limit." A woman told me that she tells people she is allergic to food; if she eats too much, she breaks out in fat. Every television show or movie is an opportunity to see how others say no to food; an old movie recently yielded a "maybe later" from one of the lead actors when he was offered a drink. Use your imagination and conjure up a few clever no thank phrases that will bubble up without effort.

There is no change without change. The choice not to do anything is a choice to — not do anything.

Always Keep Trying. Albert Einstein said, "It's not that I'm so smart; it's just that I stay with problems longer." Take his advice and stay the course. If you make a right turn and it doesn't work, try a left turn next time. Each time you make an effort, even if it doesn't seem to be working, some part of the cycle of addiction is weakening. It's like chipping away at a block of marble. Eventually, the shape of the person who was always there emerges. Are you a person who perseveres? You can be.

Bob Mankoff, the recently retired cartoon editor for *The New Yorker* had to make some 2,000 total submissions before he sold his first drawing to the magazine in 1977. Perseverance pays off.

It's a good time to review what you've read until now. See page 314 for Review Number One.

HOW TO CHANGE YOUR CONDITIONED RESPONSES TO CERTAIN FOODS

When trying to lose weight, there are certain foods that each person is more attracted to than other foods. Some find the morning cup of coffee quite addictive. To others, it is bread. Many cannot have dinner in a restaurant without having an alcoholic beverage. With me, it was always something sweet.

TALLY

A good first step is to tally the number of times you consume each category of food in a seven-day period. Then, after the next seven-day period, do it again. Making a list of foods such as bread, salad, starch, dessert, beverage, and alcohol and keeping a count of how many times you eat each category is a good idea. How many breads do you eat in one week? Multiply that by fifty-two. How many cups of coffee? Do you have twenty-one a week? You're trying to achieve a nice balance of food. If one item is consumed two and even three times more than other items, your eating is out of balance. You might have twenty breads and fourteen cups of coffee and zero desserts and alcohol. Few of you have twenty of any other category of food. If you're having any item more than four times a week, you want to Skip and Scatter. This helps you to interrupt the cycle of addiction, i.e., *cycle interruptis*.

ADDICTION MODEL

You're not only trying to lose weight and to feed the smaller person you are becoming, but you are also trying to reverse the progression of the addiction model here.

In a progressive addiction, the portion-size and frequency of usage keep escalating each time you build a tolerance for particular food. This includes alcohol and coffee (if it's not water, it's food). The amount you need increases and the usage becomes more frequent. As you begin to lose weight, the portion-size of food and frequency-of-usage diminish in size, and number of hits.

DIMINISH NUMBER OF TIMES EACH DAY

The most frequently-chosen items are bread, beverage, dessert, and alcohol. Some items may tally anywhere, from zero to fifteen and even twenty, each week, or anywhere from one to four times each day. If, for example, you choose any one item four times a

day, cut it to three, then to two, then to once a day. Cold turkey-
ing does not work. Do things gradually. Cut down the frequency
by perhaps having coffee at one lunch. Afterward, query yourself
by asking whether it was okay. If it was and it mostly likely will
be, then Skip and Scatter. One day try tea. One day hot water (no
lemon or tea), which is very soothing to a lot of us. Shake it up.
You're interrupting the frequency pattern for that particular habit.

ONE OF FOUR OR NONE

Strive to achieve having either *Bread or Beverage or Dessert or
Alcohol,* picking one of four or none per meal. If you are trying
to eat a wide variety of foods, much of this will happen naturally.

MENTAL REPATTERNING

Talking to yourself is helpful as you choose each item less and
less frequently. Think: "Instead of another piece of bread, I'll
have a vegetable," or "Instead of another cup of coffee, this time
I'll have a cup of hot water or tea if it's part of a meal." Remind
yourself, hourly if necessary, "I want to weigh _____ pounds."
Remember some of the action steps you can take to help you get
there. The moments do pass.

A helpful goal: Be pro-active rather than re-active. If you
weren't thinking of an item two minutes before seeing it, you're
responding to a visual stimulus rather than an actual physical
hunger. Inhale. The moment will pass. And exhale.

PORTION SIZE

Get rid of that oversized mug and pour your coffee into an
8-ounce cup. Perhaps you'll feel fine with a few segments of
grapefruit; a few bites of coleslaw. As you lose weight and your
stomach shrinks, you should be satiated sooner and will require
less of everything than you did when you were a bigger person.

DON'T GO NUTS ON NUTS!

The Program does not count calories, but it might be helpful to know that nuts, seeds, popcorn, or potato chips are high in fat and calories. You may have even heard they are healthy and you should eat fourteen nuts each day. It's said that President Obama has seven nuts each evening. But if you're a food addict or compulsive overeater, you might not be able to stop at seven. You may think nuts are healthy, but they yield peanut oil, or popcorn could yield corn oil.

It's good to know that 4 ounces of nuts, seeds, popcorn, or potato chips contains more calories than three dinners with three potatoes, three portions of broccoli, and three portions of chicken.

NUT & SEED SHEET COMMENTARY

The Program does not count calories, but it might be helpful to know that four ounces of nuts, seeds, popcorn, or potato chips is equal to, *or more* than, three meals, each containing a portion of chicken, broccoli, and potato.

Three plates of food, three meals, do not contain as many calories as a handful of nuts.

Three chicken, vegetable, potato meal, with all the chewing, crunching, and enjoyment, *or* a handful of (*Finger Foods*, alert. Alert!) nuts, seeds, popcorn, or potato chips? The choice is yours.

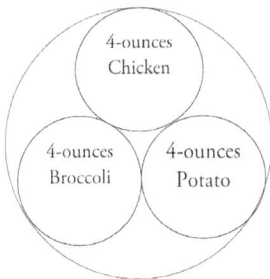

4-ounces Chicken / 4-ounces Broccoli / 4-ounces Potato

Approximately 226 calories.

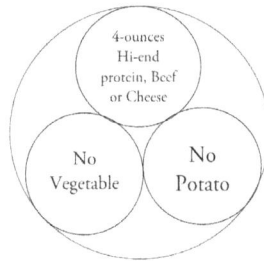

4-ounces Hi-end protein, Beef or Cheese / No Vegetable / No Potato

Approximately 276 calories.

4-ounces Nuts, Seeds, Popcorn, or Potato Chips - - not even a handful

Approximately **600-700**

NUTS & SEEDS	
NUTS	**CALORIES**
(4 ounces)	
Almonds	678
Beechnuts	644
Brazil Nuts	742
Butter Nuts	713
Cashew Nuts	639
Hickory Nuts	767
Macadamia Nuts	784
Peanuts	640
Pecans	779
Pignolias	626
Pistachio Nuts	674
Walnuts	713
SEEDS	
(4 ounces)	
Pumpkin Seeds	627
Sunflower Seeds	635
POPCORN	
(4 ounces)	
Air Popped	640
POTATO CHIPS	
(4 ounces)	
Regular	640

You are trying to reach your weight loss goal, and nuts are too instant and quick, mindless, and finger food. The compulsive in you cannot eat just one or even seven. Your Addict Pea Brain knows: You buy a pound, you eat a pound.

AFTERTHOUGHT

Every day, it seems as if there is an article about nuts being good for you. A doctor on one daytime television show recommends around ten nuts each day. Oh 'twere it possible. More likely, you're not going to stop at ten. You're going to eat it (whatever "it" is for you) until it's gone. You don't know from just a few of anything each day.

You only know, that once you start you cannot stop. You're going to eat it until it's gone. If you buy a pound, you're planning on eating a pound. It may not be today or tomorrow. It might take a week or two or three. But eventually you'll have to buy a new pound. And if that frequency pattern and old portion size holds up, the frequency and portion of these items will increase in frequency and portion size without you giving it two seconds thought. If you think otherwise, you're in your addiction.

REPATTERNING

As item usage diminishes to once a day, the next step might be to Skip and Scatter the frequency of your choices. Writing your intention into your agenda book (or calendar) will be a reminder of what you're trying to accomplish.

If there are many items you choose more than three, four, times each week, pick one at a time and practice choosing things every other day or two, rather than having it one day a week before moving on to the next item. For example, you might have an item Monday, Wednesday, and Friday. A different item might be chosen Tuesday, Thursday, or Saturday, and so on. You're trying to interrupt your old patterns of "usuals" and "favorites," things you have daily or more.

Author Cree LaFavour says ". . .momentum of inevitability beats down the part of the mind that doesn't want to repeat the offense".

No Multiples

Another technique to aim for is No Multiples — no second cup of coffee, no second drink, not another piece of bread after the first, and no second or third helpings, even if it is Thanksgiving. Remember, in a restaurant, you'd never say to the waiter: "Maurice, is there another chicken leg in the kitchen."

Skip-A-Day

As you lose weight and become smaller, your food requirements will be smaller, too. The next level would be to *Skip-A-Day*. If you had one category of food yesterday, skip a day before having it tomorrow. Skipping days will force you to seek more variety and ultimately lessen the hold some items have on you. Choosing any item three or four times a week works out well for most people, but for good health, red meat (beef) should be your choice only once every seven to ten days.

If you are sensitive to refined flour most often found in bread and pasta, choosing it once every third or fourth day might work best. Choosing a baked potato, corn, beans, or a yam every other day in lieu of pasta might be a better choice still. Those foods are chock full of nutrition.

Some days having a dark vegetable instead of *another* salad may be exactly what is needed and will help you achieve the *Skip-A-Day* suggestion. Be aware that you're not having a salad with every lunch and every dinner. That's an old habit. Skipping a day with salads is a skill worth achieving. Even if it comes with the meal.

If you select the same category of food every day, you're eating it 365 days a year, and at the end of the year, you'll have eaten loaves of bread, vats of coffee, pounds of chocolate, gallons of soda, cases of wine, and troughs of salad. By choosing these items every other day, you're only having those items 182½ times a year. That shows up as a noticeable loss of weight and inches. Choosing the same foods all the time cheats you out of valuable nutrition and increases the hold some of those foods had on you. Find a wide selection of food, seasonings, and preparation. Try horseradish sauce and/or wasabi mustard with turkey. Yumm.

Scatter

Shake it all up. If you have coffee at breakfast one morning, select it for lunch or dinner the next time, or not at all. This reduces your reliance on coffee to get you up in the morning. By Skipping and Scattering, you'll get in the mindset of *sometimes I have it, and sometimes I don't.* This helps prove that the opposite of "loving food," is not "hating food," but "indifference" to food. That means you can take it or leave it. Freedom from addiction.

When I drank alcohol regularly and frequented a restaurant near my apartment, the bartender actually knew my usual drink. I was embarrassed to know that someone was watching what I was eating and drinking, that my compulsive, ritual behavior was noticed by someone else. More embarrassing was that the cashier in a local health and beauty aids shop knew my usual choice of candy.

I remember deciding to have no-dessert (candy for me) day, but as I stood at the checkout counter, the cashier reached down to my favorite candy. He put the foil-wrapped bar on the counter, and said: "You forgot your candy." I was so embarrassed that I meekly paid for it along with my other purchases and left the store. Charting these foods might show this type of behavior but it might also show that you're not having enough salads, starches, or dark vegetables, and those items might need to be increased.

Yes, I ate the candy, but the next time — there's always a next time — I had re-patterned enough that I was able to leave the store *without* unplanned food. I kept reminding myself (mental re-patterning): "I'm not hungry; I only eat when I'm hungry, and besides, I want to weigh _____ pounds."

Coping Strategies. When changing behavioral patterns, aim for a wide variety of new ones. Create a written list of things you can say to yourself, things you can say to others, and things you'd

like to change. Review and remind yourself (while envisioning) your goals and stumbles each day. You might, for example,
change your behavior and go right to your bedroom to change
your clothes when entering your own home, rather than going
into the kitchen for food while still wearing your coat.

Brush your teeth after dinner rather than before you go to
sleep. It's always helpful to re-commit to weighing _____
pounds, especially when you're thinking of eating and know you
couldn't possibly be hungry. Tell yourself, "Everything is going to
be okay." All of these efforts and attempts are designed to achieve
cycle interruptus.

Before you go to sleep, picture how you'll look when you reach
your goal. Learn to comfort yourself with something other than
food. Take extra steps by making extra trips around your home,
office, and neighborhood. Now is the time to find new ways to
cope with anxiety or other emotional discomfort. Learn to cope
with life without zoning out, narcotizing, and escaping with the
repetitive actions of a behavioral addiction.

DON'T PANIC CARD

When it is inappropriate or inconvenient to take your logbook
or journey book, to a wedding or cocktail party, a Don't Panic
Card is exactly what you need to combat the temptation while
traveling. A Don't Panic Card contains action steps you can take
or think.

These steps are designed to calm you down. If you prefer, jot
your own ideas on a blank card, or enter them right into your
cellphone.

Photocopy the card and carry it in your pocket or purse; look
at it discreetly when you're searching for your car keys, lipstick,
cellphone, or something in your purse or pocket. Or read it on
your cellphone. Someone will think you're checking your e-mail,

but you'll really be reading I Can Do It. Either use my before, during, and after phrases that worked for me. Or create thoughts and actions that would work for you. Maybe a mix of both is the solution.

DON'T PANIC

1. Don't panic. Change location. Move.

2. Take a deep breath. Exhale slowly. Repeat, if necessary.

3. Calm down. Smile.

4. Think: Everything's going to be okay.

5. Think: I can do it.

6. Step away from the Twinkies. Change location.

7. Remember: You want to weigh _____ pounds.

8. Think: I'm okay.

9. The moment passed.

10.   I'm feeling better than fine. I'm okay.

11.

HOW TO PUSH BACK THE FOOD PUSHER

Is your boyfriend, girlfriend, coworker, family member, or significant other pushing food? Has someone guilted you into eating by telling you, "I've been cooking all day preparing this food"? Do they say, "Taste this, try that. Is that all you're eating"?

Saying *No, thank you* should be enough, but often, a Food Pusher has already put a few tablespoons of food onto your plate even before you are able to look at the food you already have on your own plate. Sometimes an over-zealous table-mate will over- order every course and ask for extra forks and spoons for everyone. In doing this, that person becomes not only your food pusher, but everyone else's food pusher. To my amazement, I once had someone zoom near my mouth with a fork full of food while saying, "Open wide! You gotta taste this." No. You don't gotta taste this.

When someone is trying to control what you eat, he or she may also be trying to control you.

What do you do when this happens?

You may need some new language to refuse food without spurning love or friendship. Saying *No thank you. I'm fine* may not always be enough. Sometimes you have to extend your hand outward while waving off incoming food. This one-two punch of a verbal statement with a physical action might be the perfect recipe to ward off your pusher.

SOME THING YOU CAN SAY:

- No thank you. I'm fine.
- No thanks. I'm good.
- Nothing for me but you go ahead.
- I don't want it. (I don't like it.)
- I'm just not hungry.
- I ate a big lunch.
- I'm okay.
- It's too much food for me; I'm a small person.
- I've had enough.
- Try some of mine. (role reversal)
- I have a business dinner later.
- You go ahead and eat. I'll keep you company.
- I'm just enjoying sitting here with you and relaxing.

SOME THINGS YOU CAN DO:

- Ask questions and wait for answers between bites of food.
- Sip water before resuming eating.

- Distract your Pusher from paying attention to what is on your plate.
- Thank the Pusher for being so kind while you smile and push the food away.
- Stick out your hand and wave away unplanned food. Alert. Alert. Incoming food. Incoming food. Straighten your arm to fend off the uninvited.

If you are taking medication, you'd find a way to say you're not allowed to drink with pills. Or if you need to work when you get home, you'd find a way to defer an alcoholic beverage. And I'll bet if someone put whole boiled octopus eyeballs on your plate, you'd figure out a way to say: "I'm good."

Be creative in your planning. It's all about finding the right words, the right *tone of refusal,* and the right commitment to your more important goal of wanting to weigh _____ pounds. Your mini-goal is to go out with friends after work and not have the need always to say yes to all that is ordered.

This is a good time to find the right words of refusal or the perfect way to say *None for me. I'm good. Thanks, but no.* Give it some thought lest you keep eating to please someone else. Say *I'm fine. I'm not hungry. You go ahead. A big glass of ice water, thanks.* You could say, *I'm taking cold medicine and am not supposed to drink.* Come up with your own tried and true. Every situation is different. Every person is different. Every success feels good.

One woman told me that when she was at a barbecue at her mother's weekend home, she said, "No, thank you" twelve times to her mother.

"How did you happen to know it was twelve times?" I asked.

She said, "Well, in the past when my mother offered me food, I'd say no a few times and then give in. This time, I was so determined to stay on my Program that I had fun finding a different way to say, 'No, thank you.' When I'd used all the arrows in my quiver, I told her I knew where the food was and if I was hungry I'd help myself, so would she please stop pushing food. And she did stop."

"What did you learn?" I asked.

She said, "Next time I'll stop her even sooner. I'm down another pound, and after a weekend like that, I would have most likely gained a few pounds."

FINGER FOODS

If you're really convinced that you're hungry, it's time to eat. This means food on a plate to be eaten with utensils (knife, fork, spoon, chopsticks), not fingers. What a radical thought.

When I was losing weight, a friend called me at work: "Did you have lunch?" Franklin asked.

"No. I just grabbed a hot dog on the corner," I said.

To me, the words *just, grabbed,* and *on the corner"* meant it didn't count because a) it was *only* a hot dog, what I perceived to be a small amount of food, b) I could hold it in my hands, so it was too insignificant to count, and, c) it was eaten on the corner with fresh air and sunshine. How could it be bad?

I thought that eating food sold on a street corner wasn't really a meal. It was . . . well, that's the point. It didn't fit any category. So I ended up having a second lunch with Franklin.

My friend Paula and I were walking down Second Avenue in Manhattan around 5 p.m. as she spied a store that was part of a pizza chain. She said: "Let's have a slice."

Knowing it was a visual stimulus that had pushed her salivating button, I asked: "Are you hungry?"

"Oh yes," she replied. "I'm *starving*."

"Okay" I said. "Then let's have a slice of pizza, which we can eat with a knife and fork, and order a salad, too. It'll be dinner."

"I'm not *that* hungry," she said. What she really wanted was to have a slice of pizza *and* eat dinner, too.

How frequently do you eat finger food and think it doesn't somehow count? I just spoke to someone who thinks that carrot sticks and celery shouldn't count because they are "healthy."

When I talk about putting food on a plate and eating it with a knife and fork, I mean committing to the *structure* of a meal.

If you eat slowly and thoughtfully, cutting, spearing, chewing, sipping, and swallowing, you are present at mealtime. You experience the feelings of enjoyment and satiation. The meal registers. Then, an hour or two later, if you're thinking of eating again because you see or smell something tempting, you know you couldn't possibly be hungry. You just had this terrific breakfast, lunch, or dinner two hours ago. You remember it.

When eating finger foods, the reverse happens. Even a few minutes after consuming a finger food, you think: *I can eat again because I didn't really eat. I only had a bagel chip, some black coffee, one rice cake, a low-fat pretzel, and kale chips. It was nothing. It doesn't really count toward my daily food consumption because it was so small, or so low in calories, or so insignificant. It couldn't possibly count.*

By rushing through the eating experience, by shoving food into your mouth, by not savoring your food, you numbly fill up your body, without satisfying it.

One cracker may contain only 11 calories. That's not the point. The question is: How many crackers are in the box and how many boxes have you knocked off already, and it's only Tuesday in the middle of February, May, September, or whenever?

An apple a day becomes bushels at the end of the year. Do you eat bread so often you could count it in loaves? How much of your food enters your mouth without your seeing it so you think none of it counts?

How often do you mindlessly put your fingers into a box, bag, or basket of something and put the contents into your mouth without thinking about it? Do you wonder every morning why the scale remains where it was the day before, or, more depressingly, goes up?

Are sandwiches, bagels, muffins, and hors d'oeuvres at parties a part of your life? Is a bag of popcorn your appetizer? Are nachos a main course? How many chicken wings make a meal? Hard to count. Hard to know.

Now think: Are you hungry enough to commit to a real meal with food on a plate to be eaten with a knife and fork? Or are you not *that* hungry?

Joseph K.: "I finally understand about food on a plate, eating with utensils. Any bite on the run, even a raw carrot, is totally mindless — I'm not even aware of what I'm doing. And that goes for all sorts of Finger Food — whether it's pretzels, popcorn, or canapés, it just finds its way to my stomach magically."

Karen C.: "Every meal was a special event, even if I was only eating oatmeal. It broke me of my eating-on-the run, eating-on-the-street, and eating-in-the-car habits."

EATING BACKWARDS

Are you afraid that the amount of food you're eating won't be enough? It doesn't really make sense if you think about it. What's the worst thing that could happen if the fuel you've consumed doesn't take you to your desired destination? Will you pass out? Feel a little discomfort? Maybe something in between.

If any of those things happen, you can most likely reach fuel within seconds if you are in your home or office, and perhaps within minutes if you're outside.

The reason I use the term fuel is because that's what it is. If it tastes good, looks good, and smells good, that's a bonus. But food is still fuel.

The problem is that you may be Eating Backwards. You might even be thinking, "I didn't have breakfast and I'll eat less for lunch in order to gorge on tonight's dinner offerings." This mindset is a form of deprivation in order to binge. That's eating backwards. It's like driving from New York to Florida and then filling up your tank. You want to fill up your tank in New York with breakfast; then drive to North Carolina; then fill up your tank again for lunch, and then drive to Florida. This is learning to Eat Forward. Breakfast fuel should take you to lunch. Lunch fuel should take you to dinner. Dinner fuel should take you to bedtime.

Breakfast food/fuel should take you to lunch. For example, if you have breakfast at 7:00 a.m. and lunch at 1:00 p.m., you will need six hours of fuel for your morning activities. For many people, this is a time of day when not a lot of fuel is needed. Hot cereal, cold cereal, or an Egg Meal can take you the distance.

The breakfast fuel carried you around while you awakened, showered, shaved, brushed your teeth, set your hair, and combed your mustache. These six hours of fuel were further used when you dressed, drove, bicycled, or walked to work, went to the market, went shopping, met with others, and walked up and down hallways, up and down stairs, sometimes with a briefcase/backpack.

Lunch food/fuel should take you to dinner. If you had lunch at 1:00 p.m. and dinner is planned for 7:00 p.m., you only need enough fuel to take you to dinner, another six hours. The lunch fuel carries you in and out of meetings, errands, pick-ups, and deliveries. There are phone calls to make, letters to dictate, deals to negotiate, planes to catch, friends to meet, presentations to make, fatigue to shake. It's the end of the day and dinner is imminent.

For some, dinner is where you overeat, not because you are so hungry, but rather you might be rewarding yourself for a good day's work. You might think that more is better. You might be afraid that a hearty bowl of soup won't be enough of a lunch so you make it up at dinner. You can't get hungry while you're eating. If you do get hungry, it can only happen later. Instead of getting hungry for dinner at 7:00 p.m., maybe (just maybe) you'll get hungry a little earlier, perhaps at 6:55 p.m. Maybe not.

Dinner need only take you to bedtime. How much fuel do you need? If dinner is at 7:00 p.m., you should keep in mind, on average, what time you go to sleep. From what I gather from the people I teach, bedtime seems to be on average between 10:00 p.m. and midnight, so I'll use 11:00 p.m. as an example. That means that dinner need only contain enough fuel for four hours. That's four hours of sitting around in your jammies, winding down. Maybe you're balancing your checkbook, or maybe you're sitting around watching television with your family. How much fuel do you need to get from the dining table to the couch to your bed?

After that, you only need enough fuel/energy to keep your heart and lungs moving while you're sleeping. The burning of your stored fat does that fine. At the end of the day, when you're headed to sleep, if you've consumed more fuel throughout the day than you were able to utilize for your activities, all the extra fuel gets converted to fat. It doesn't matter whether the fuel contained fat. You're creating more fat-inventory. And you don't need more fat-inventory. You already have a warehouse of fat. What you want to do is have a sale and get rid of the fat inventory.

EATING FORWARD

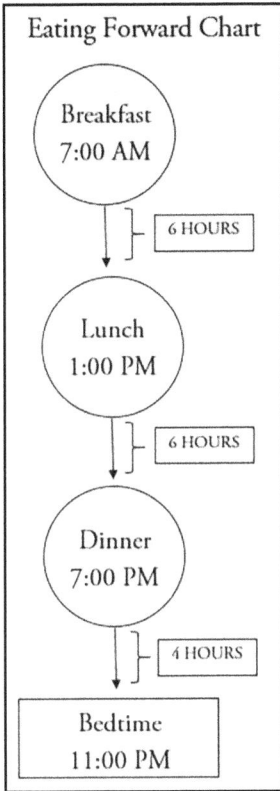

Eating Forward Chart

Breakfast
7:00 AM

6 HOURS

Lunch
1:00 PM

6 HOURS

Dinner
7:00 PM

4 HOURS

Bedtime
11:00 PM

Eating Forward means you want to eat a little slower, a little earlier, and a little more thoughtfully. As you become the smaller person you want to be, you realize that a thick, hearty, substantive soup is more than enough fuel, as is a veggie omelet, a scoop of tuna, or a cool crisp garden salad at your dinner because you're going to sleep in a few hours. If you eat forward, it will always be enough.

Paulo J.: I am a big believer in soup lunches! At breakfast this morning (steak and eggs), I actually felt when I was full. I was reading the paper and had the time to digest and have fullness register with my Addict Pea Brain. At that point, without looking at my plate, I decided, basta (enough); don't need to eat anymore. I ended my meal. It was fine. When I looked down following that, I realized that my plate was more than half-full. I honestly believe this was the first time in my adult life that I gave myself the opportunity to realize and appreciate when I was no longer hungry.

Caryl: And it was fine! Let that thought register. So, next time, you'll put less on your plate because you are a smaller person who requires less food than you used to need. If you have less to begin with, you will automatically eat even slower. You want to eat slowly so you become aware of satiation when it happens. Nice job.

Mary C: What I noticed about myself over the past few months is that if I didn't plan the desserts, I wouldn't have them at all. Then on a holiday or when I am away, I eat desserts five or six times a week. No Skipping and Scattering. It is a constant battle of all-or-nothing.

Caryl: Planned desserts give you a sense of control. In Skipping and Scattering them, you remain conscious. And when you do choose to have that item tomorrow or the next day, try to have it at a different meal than you previously did. As Thomas Palmer said, "If at first you don't succeed, try, try again."

The all-or-nothing mode is extreme. The all part is the out-of-control part. The nothing part may seem as if it is in-control, but it really isn't because it cannot be sustained. Nor would you want to go without any food or food category forever. Planning exactly what you want and where and when you're going to have it will help you maintain calm. Rest easy — you can have the object of your affection tomorrow. And tomorrow you might not even want it.

Many of you only have dessert in a restaurant, and if you do, it is often shared; sometimes a bite or two or three proves to be enough. If it is enough, then that is your portion size — that smaller amount is your amount. It's not small. It's just smaller than the amount you were eating when you were a larger person. When dessert is part of a meal, you don't need or want as much of anything.

When you're eating an item by yourself and it is not because you're hungry, you end up eating the entire amount. Be awake at Point of Purchase. If you can be awake at the checkout counter, you won't be tempted to follow an old food ritual to its natural conclusion of remorse. Purchase the right amount for your meal and you'll eat the right amount at the meal.

PEOPLE EAT FAR TOO LATE IN THE EVENING

A friend called the other day to set up an adult play date: dinner and a movie, or in this instance, dinner after the movie. I like to eat reasonably early.

As you age, you eat earlier than you did when you were younger. Since food is fuel, you need only enough energy to get yourself from where you are to where you want to be. The later you eat, the fewer items you need, so a smaller portion is required. You need not eat more than your body needs for it to have energy to perform your daily activities. Think about the differences in your walking, carrying, cleaning, and working between your morning and evening hours. There is less energy expenditure at night, yet most people increase food intake. Are you one of them?

Iona L: By the time I leave work, shop for food, come home, prepare dinner, and actually sit down to eat, it's often 7:00 p.m. (or later). That's the ideal scenario. But quite often my companion, or my daughter, or a friend calls with a problem. I'm basically receiving e-mails, text messages, and phone calls all night. Everything I do delays dinner. And then I go to sleep at 10:30 p.m.

Caryl: There are a few things that might help.

If possible, when you're preparing food in the evening, make one or two extra portions to freeze in individual portion-sized plastic containers. Then some of the meals you will cook (perhaps on the weekend), but some of the meals will already be prepared so you'll only have to put them in the microwave to warm up.

When I first started eating cereal for breakfast, it seemed hot cereal took so long to prepare that I would end up grabbing the cold cereal all the time. I started preparing hot cereal at night, putting it in a bowl and seasoning it the way I like it. In the morning, I'd add a little water to counter the dehydrating taking place in the refrigerator, zap it in the microwave, and voila! I actually do like hot cereal better than cold. I find it more satisfying on many levels including taste, but that may just be me. It's not better than cold cereal, which I do like, but on a cold rainy morning, I find hot cereal the best.

Eventually, I learned how to make it in the morning without making a big deal of it. All of the processes take time to get incorporated into your other daily rituals. Getting the heat at the correct height and stirring often enough that the cereal doesn't stick to the bottom of the pot took time. But it's become a wonderful peaceful new ritual; almost meditative. I use a certain pot, and a dish that is a different shape than my "good" set of dishes. I know how to season it to my liking. That's a real switch from no breakfast to enjoying breakfast. Take that experience to the dinner meal. Whether hot cereal or hot soup, the later you eat, the less you need.

Every hour you eat closer to your bedtime should reduce the number of items by one.

Since food is fuel/energy, if you eat too late, your sleep might become fitful.

THE FILLERS

A Filler is a food that fills you up but doesn't necessarily nourish your body. Keep track of your Filler consumption. Doing so helps to define the problem clearly. How many desserts do you eat each week? How many cups of coffee do you drink each day, each week? How many salads do you say yes to just because they came with the meal you ordered? The most obvious Fillers are bread (muffins, bagels, rolls), beverage (coffee, tea, soda), dessert (anything sweet), and alcohol. All four are offered when you're ordering dinner in a restaurant.

Most of you have one or two Fillers to which you are attracted. You all know someone who is a bread eater. Another friend has two drinks before each meal. Still another is always buying candy bars and bags of nachos. Those are obvious Fillers. They need to be tracked daily.

Fillers are eaten because they might be served gratis such as bread on the table, choice of a salad or vegetable, which comes with an entrée.

Again, just because something is free does not warrant eating it. Whether you're paying for food, or it came with the meal, or it came with the room, the question is how often are you saying yes to unplanned food? No foods are good or bad. Use the Filler Chart to track items you tend to overeat. Make sure to count all non-water beverages such as coffee, tea, and club soda.

Once you have that count for a week, begin to diminish frequency by Skipping and Scattering. Have dessert one day; then skip a day before choosing another dessert for a different meal. Have coffee at one breakfast; then skip a day before having coffee at another meal. Even better, have tea at another meal and even try hot water for one meal.

Your goal is to interrupt your knee-jerk reaction — your old unthinking, mindless behavior — and consciously replace it with new, planned behavior that is better designed to help you reach your weight-loss goal. Create new food-free methods of dealing with life. This is a process that takes time and consistency. For example, Teresa B. did it this way: "I ate ice cream Monday, and when I thought of having it again the next day, I told myself that I just had this yesterday and did not order it. I Skipped and Scattered, and it was okay."

I discuss sweets throughout the book because they were my Filler food of choice when I weighed fifty pounds more than I do now. I designed The Program for myself so I could continue to eat real chocolate in a more appropriate portion size and at a more appropriate frequency. I customized it for the smaller, chocolate-loving person I wanted to be, which I eventually became and have remained. All my foods are Skipped and Scattered so no one category of food becomes front and center.

Inching forward acknowledges your humanness. Recognize the smallest efforts, the smallest changes. Be pleased with baby steps. Give yourself a thumbs-up. Pat yourself on the back when you're on the right track. Food is not a reward for achieving your goals. A drink is not a reward for getting through your day. Nor is food entertainment. Having your clothing fit better is a reward. Moving the belt notch one hole smaller. Find other ways to end each meal, such as putting down utensils. Then push your plate an inch forward. Push your chair back an inch. Pull your water glass toward you. Think: "I'm fine."

When not hungry, take a deep, satisfying breath. It doesn't have to be entered on your FILLER chart.

THE FILLER CHART

THE FILLER CHART	Seven Day Range	1st Seven Days	2nd Seven Days	3rd Seven Days	4th Seven Days	5th Seven Days	Ect. Seven Days
Date							
Bread	0, 1, 2, 3, or 4						
Salad	3-4						
Hi-end Protein	1						
Starch	3-4						
Dessert	0, 1, 2, 2, or 4						
Bever-age	0, 1, 2, 3, or 4						
Alcohol	0, 1, 2, 3, or 4						
No-meal Meal	0						
BBDA	11						

www.ConquerFood.com to download a Filler Chart.

FILLING OUT THE FILLER CHART

First, become familiar with what a Filler is and what it is not. The most frequently chosen and obvious Fillers are Breads, Beverages, Desserts, and Alcohol (BBDA). But Fillers also include Salads, High-End Proteins, and Starches because they might represent a high percentage of your daily food intake and are usually sides to your meals.

Rice comes free with most Asian cooking. Pasta is usually found in Italian food. And if you order a scrambled egg in New York City, it most likely comes with free hash brown potatoes. Do you ever make hash browns in your own home? No. But there you are (we are) eating them in a diner because they came with the egg and the toast.

Are you eating these items because they came with the meal or because you were going to order them anyway? Rice, pasta, and potatoes are all starches that need to be tracked. They are not good or bad. Just track them. Tracking these various foods will show you either balance or imbalance in your overall food consumption.

If you always say yes to every food that is offered to you, it is reactive behavior. You want to be pro-active. Plan ahead for when you will enjoy these items, and know when you will have them.

The Cold Cereals I recommend (Miniature Shredded Wheat and Grape Nuts) do not contain sugar. If you're hitting the cereal box several times a day, it most likely contains sugar. Toss it and buy the recommended ones. Then add sugar or not, if you like.

The column Range Seven Days indicates the range of the categories of Fillers, each week:

- Bread: 0, 1, 2, 3, 4
- Salad: 3-4
- High-End Protein: 1

- Starch: 3-4
- Dessert: 0, 1, 2, 3, 4
- Beverage: 0, 1, 2, 3, 4
- Alcohol: 0, 1, 2, 3, 4

When filling out the **Filler Chart**, refer back to your **Food Log**. It's good to begin in the same place: the Breakfast of the first day's food. Let's say your food log says you had a breakfast of cereal and coffee. When you enter your breakfast on your Filler Chart, put a tick mark to the right of the word beverage (coffee) under the column heading "1ˢᵗ 7 Days." Cereal is not a Filler. No need to count it on this chart. If you have orange juice, put a tick mark next to dessert.

At the end of the week, add up the number of tick marks and write the sum at the very right of the column. This is the total number of Fillers you consumed during the week. How many breads? How many salads? How many starches, and so on.

Put the totals of each category in the boxes where you put the tick marks. Any category of food where you ate more than four each week means you'll want to Skip and Scatter next week.

When finished with one week's tallying, make a separate total of BBDA (bread, beverage, dessert, and alcohol). Enter that BBDA number on the chart at the bottom next to *BBDA*. If anything is consumed more than four times a week, it is clear you're not skipping and scattering and should be. Eleven BBDA for the week works well for most people. This is half of the twenty-one meals in a week. If your total number of BBDA is greater than eleven, you could apply the following Program suggestions:

- **Skip and Scatter same category foods.** The Program recommends a total of 0, 1, 2, 3, or a maximum of 4 alcoholic beverages each week. Compare this to your total for the alcohol category. Is your total greater than four? Is it eight? This means you can apply the Skip and

Scatter tactic. Shake it all up! If you get a drink with your client one evening, reconsider drinking the usual beer with your meal the next evening. Get into the mindset of "Sometimes I have it, and sometimes I don't."

- **Diminish Portion Size.** If you're noticing that your coffee intake is the culprit of your inflated Filler total, get rid of that oversized mug, and pour your coffee into a regular 8-ounce cup.

- Another option is to **pick one no-coffee day** (this can apply to any of the Fillers: One no-bread/alcohol/dessert day. Plan it out. Write it in your agenda book or electronic calendar.

- **No multiples.** Drink a cup of water rather than reaching for that second cup of coffee, that second bottle of beer, or that second slice of bread. Ask yourself whether you're still hungry. Remind yourself that you want to weigh _____ pounds. The moment will pass.

- **Bread or Beverage or Dessert or Alcohol; ONE of four or none**. This is The Program guideline to follow. Instead of ending your usual meal with a crème brûlée and wine, choose one or the other or none. You'll soon notice how big of a difference this small change makes.

FILLERS AT POINT OF PURCHASE

If the foods you choose are usually purchased in a specific store, walk down different blocks. Shop with an eye toward what you've planned. Remain focused on trying to achieve these new and different techniques. Delay fifteen minutes before buying (or eating) unplanned food. Imagine yourself to be an *indifferent-to-food* person. Keep thinking, "I want to weigh _____ pounds. And I'm no longer hungry anyway." Cross the street. Repeat your goal. Smile. You're winning.

An article in *The New York Times*, "Learning to Dance, One Chunk at a Time" states:

> The seeming effortlessness of a great performance is first learning the choreography and then adding layers of details and color. Finally, the dancers absorb the work so completely, that its elements literally become automatic, leaving the dancer's brain free to focus on the moment-by-moment nuances of the performance. Dancers call it muscle memory.

Learn to choreograph your eating plans. Dance through a cocktail party. Pirouette when food is present. Commit to your muscle memory the hand signal, the "No thank you," a clear vision of a thinner you taking a bow.

Nick J.: On the Filler thing — we ordered pizza the other night with which I would normally have a small soda. I consciously heard that little voice in my head — pizza is cheese and bread, so if you're going to eat bread, forget the soda. I had water with my pizza and it was surprisingly fine.

Caryl: You said you had water with pizza and it was surprisingly fine. Nice. Is this the first time you ate it this way? You've been eating the old way for decades. It takes time and repetition until the new way becomes the usual and truly comfortable way. Good mindfulness.

Pamela M.: My Filler count for this week is Bread-4, Salad-4, Hi-End Protein-0, Starch-1, Dessert-10 (ugh), Beverage-2, Alcohol-7 (not quite an ugh, but not great), and No-Meal Meal-3. Total Fillers-31 and BBDA-23.

Caryl: Addiction is when you keep doing the same thing over and over, and each time you expect a different outcome. Or is that insanity? It's probably the same thing. Anyway, when you continually see the dessert and alcohol numbers way up there compared to other foods, a good rule of thumb is to aim for these items every other day by Skipping and Scattering. Write your intentions in your agenda book so when you wake up in the morning and look at what you're doing and where you're going that day, your food plan is right on the same page. Whether it is a Protein Meal or No-Protein Meal, alcohol, or dessert, even the number of items, write down the details and plan ahead.

When you write your plan of protein and a vegetable, you have a 85-90 percent chance of success as opposed to just thinking about it, which would probably yield around a 20 percent chance of success. Review daily or more often or right before a food encounter, and your success could increase. Writing your plan increases your success.

All three No-Meal Meals are three desserts — quick, instant, portable, low in nutrition. More importantly, you're eating when you're not hungry. You are using food to change your mood. Think of some positive things you can do for those three encounters. If you analyze these now, it will help you the next time. And then when you need those positive thoughts and words, they'll be in your mind waiting to be used, to rise to the occasion because you practiced and thought about them when you didn't need to. Neat the way that all works out, isn't it?

CHOOSE A WIDE VARIETY OF FOOD, SEASONINGS, AND PREPARATION

Eating the same foods each day, drinking your usual cup of coffee, and picking the same pastry creates mindless familiarity with the taste and number of bites, chews, and swallows needed to eat it until it's gone. The entire ritual, from point of purchase to plating, eating, and remorse is pretty unconscious. You might not even realize that the entire process is pretty unconscious.

Eating a wide range of foods with different seasonings, temperature, and preparation will keep you conscious. You might even leave some of the newer items on your plate.

You tend to eat less of a new or unfamiliar food than you do with your usuals and favorites. One man told me he was going to a Grand Central Terminal seafood restaurant near my office to have old-fashioned New England clam chowder. He waxed nostalgic with a look of rapture as he thought about the oyster crackers served with soup — a perfect example of an all too familiar food-combo. He never eats, buys, or seeks out those crackers, except when they are attached to the clam chowder. Having the chowder one night and the crackers on another night with a different food would help change a mindless pattern and feed the smaller person you are becoming. He later recalled, "I realized that once I crumbled the crackers into the already super thick chowder, I lost track of them and never missed not having them."

Jane Brody wrote in *The New York Times*, "Fat is part of a normal diet that adds flavor to food, promotes satiation and carries in essential vitamins."

Yes. Butter on your baked potato is fine on The Program. Oil and vinegar is fine. And vegetable tempura is fine. You want to make sure in between some of those dishes is roasted vegetables, steamed fish, and grilled chicken. Variety of preparation. Satisfaction is texture too. Each cereal is a different shape, crunch, or grit which satisfies as well.

DRINK 8-10 GLASSES OF WATER

Drink 8-10 glasses of water each day in addition to all other beverages. The health benefits are numerous.

Water flushes out toxins and carries nutrients to where they are needed.

Water additionally helps to distract you from difficult moments when in the past you might have been tempted to eat. Drink water the way recommended and see if you notice an improvement in your skin.

I drink water at room temperature throughout the day. When there's a chill in the air, I drink it hot (no lemon or tea). I find it very soothing and think of it as a third hot beverage. A throwback to my mother (Harriet) and grandmother (Annie) who drank hot water to start the day. I realize how soothing and helpful it is. Many participants mention how enjoyable it is for them, too. Others like their water iced. What's your preference?

COUNT THE NUMBER OF ITEMS IN EACH MEAL

As you lose weight, you may reach a time when the scale isn't moving downward as quickly as you had hoped. There is no plateau on The Program. If the scale isn't moving downward, you may be eating too much, too late, or too fast. Or all three.

You are a smaller person and might need to reduce the number of items you eat in each meal. Then count the number of items you consume each day. If it's not water, it's food, so it needs to be counted. Yes, count coffee, salad, a lettuce leaf, a grape — count it all. If you swallowed it, you ate it. It all adds up.

Tally the number of items after completing your log for a week. Divide by seven (days) to yield the average number of items you eat each day. If it is a mélange (or mix) of foods in the same category, think of it as a clump or a handful as being an item. Pasta and vegetables. How many handfuls of pasta? How many handfuls of vegetables? Is it a two, three, or four item meal? Are you counting chicken and broccoli as two items? Or is it really chicken, chicken, broccoli, broccoli?

Once you have determined the number of items you eat each day to maintain your current weight, an easy thing to do is to reduce your food consumption by one item each day. At the end of the week, that adds up to two or three extra meals you didn't eat. Had you eaten those meals, you would, in essence, have been trying to burn off eight or nine day's worth of food, in seven days. It can't be done on a consistent basis. And it is food you most likely would have eaten mindlessly.

Here is an example of a Food Log:

Food Log/ Filler Chart- Participant Example**

Day/Date	2/3	2/4	2/5	2/6	2/7	2/8	2/9		
AM Weight	181	180	181	182	180	179	179		
BREAKFAST	Egg 1	--	Hot cereal 1	Oatmeal 1	Cold cereal 1	Cold cereal 1	egg 1	6	20
LUNCH	Chicken, broccoli	Soup 1	Chicken, wings, salad 2	Roast beef, salad 2	Bread x 2, meatloaf, coleslaw 4	Mixed vegetables 2	Chicken 1	14	
DINNER	Mixed vegetables, rice 3	Cod, steamed vegetables, noodles 3	Salad, fish, rice 3	Mixed vegetables, beer, eggroll 3	Soup, bread pudding, beef 3	Chili, beef jerkey, dessert, beer 4	Broccoli, chicken 2	22	
PM Weight	182	182	181	182	180	180	180		
# Total Items	6	4	6	7	8	7	4	45	
THE FILLERS								TOTAL FILLERS	
Bread (0,1,2,3,4)					xx			Bread	2
Salad (3-4)			x	x				Salad	2
Hi-End Protein (1)				x			x	Hi-End Protein	2
Starch (3-4)	x	x	xx	x			x	Starch	6
Dessert (0,1,2,3,4)				x	x	x		Dessert	3
Beverage								Beverage	0
Alcohol (0,1,2,3,4)				x	x	x		Alcohol	3
No-Meal Meal (1)								No-Meal meal	0
								BBDA	8

**The content of this Food Log/Filler Chart Combo is an example of how the same Program participant categorized food items and calculated Number of Items and Fillers.

LOOKING AT THIS LOG:

- If you add up the number of items in breakfast you'd have 6 items.
- If you add up the number of items in lunch you'd have 14 items.
- If you add up the number of items in dinner you'd have 22 items.

- This participant is eating more at dinner (22 items) than breakfast and lunch combined (20 items).

A good rule of thumb is to sometimes choose a one-item dinner and some two-item dinners. For breakfast one with an occasional two items, one to three items for lunch, and one to three items for dinner. One-item meals need to be sprinkled throughout each day, especially sometimes for dinner or lunch. If a bowl of cereal is enough for breakfast, that amount of food will be enough in the evening, too. But don't have one item for breakfast and lunch only to have a side of beef for dinner. That would be a version of deprivation in order to binge, an old habit that never worked. Consistency will get you to your goal.

Coffee, tea, and soda are items that usually need Skipping and Scattering. If you eat slowly enough, while sipping water between bites of food, you'll automatically begin to leave food on your plate (and in your glass), and you won't need as much food as you needed before.

One participant wrote, "I have been in Portland Oregon since Wednesday. Returning home today. I have eaten out for the last six meals. I have said, 'No thank you' to bread six times, coffee or coffee refills three times, nuts once. I have pushed side dishes of rice, cheesy potatoes, goat cheese, and fruit garnish aside. Mindful of my item count, I have asked that everything normally lathered on the simplest items (veggie burger with goat cheese, peppers, and mango) be brought on the side including salad dressing and sauces so I could "dip not drown." I am amazed at my diminished appetite and the number of calories I would have consumed if I wasn't on the Program. And I know we don't count calories, but you know what I mean."

HONEST PORTION SIZE

At restaurants and take-out places, most portion sizes are some-one else's version of how much you should eat based on what the restaurant wants to charge.

In order to reach your weight-loss goal, and keep the weight off, you need to understand that you only need to eat a portion size that is designed for the smaller person you want to be.

Know your portion size in your home and office so when dining out, you can identify *your* portion size of food across a crowded plate, across a crowded restaurant, or on a tri-level buffet table. Your portion size of each item is four ounces, the size of a deck of cards, not the deck of a boat.

Four ounces is a handful of vegetables, a clump of salad, or a medium-sized potato. Three four-ounce portions is three-quar-ters of a pound of food. When you are counting the number of items, do you count pizza as one item? Even an unadorned slice is bread and cheese, two items. Another item like sausage or veggies would make it a three-item meal. Are you eating it with a knife and fork? You should be.

QUANTUM LEAPS

Committed efforts and attempts to change begin with baby steps that, upon repetition, become Quantum Leaps. Acknowledging the successful outcome of a new action — something you're doing now that you've never been able to do before, is a Quantum Leap.

It's important for you to write about such leaps in your jour-nal; write about all you've accomplished whether it is a "direct" Quantum Leap; something you've learned on The Program like asking if you're hungry before eating, and it's okay.

Or it could be "ancillary," fitting into clothes I couldn't wear a few weeks ago, enjoying compliments, or I'm at a smaller belt notch.

If you leave over one bite of something and you've never left it over before, write it down. Under a challenging circumstance, did you do a little better than you might have in the past? Write it down. When you review a little each day, you'll eventually bump into your Quantum Leaps Page. You'll be reading that you had soup for dinner and that it was okay. You'll then think, *It was okay then. It'll be okay now. I can do it again. And besides, I'm smaller than I was and I don't need as much food anymore.*

Or your Quantum Leaps list will remind you of something that may have dropped along the way that you can incorporate into your daily rituals once again. One woman wrote, "No popcorn in the movie and nobody died." And another said, "I can tie my shoelaces without causing internal bleeding." Many have told me of their pride that they no longer need to carry a seatbelt extension when they are on a plane. And it was awesome. That's a Quantum Leap!

NEEDS WORK

For every strategy you successfully achieve, there's always one that might need work. You might even be resisting working on that particular component. Writing it down in your journal is simply reminding you of something you'd eventually like to accomplish. Every day, pick two or three things from your Needs Work page and work on them. Review daily. When the time is right, you'll internalize some of these actions into your repertoire. Finish working on one thing. Pick another. Keep working on them until they fall off your to-do list and end up on your Quantum Leaps list

Watch for habits that might want to creep back. Like a juggler whose goal is to keep everything in the air, it's the same with The Program's concepts. Some days you might need more variety. Other days you might need to work on getting enough water. Maybe your nickel-sized bites have turned into quarters. Whatever you've accomplished, there's always something to polish. More to do. Eventually, the new way becomes automatic, comfortable, and preferred. The new way becomes your default setting.

I CAN DO IT! — DAILY AFFIRMATION

The *I Can Do It!* daily affirmation will help you believe you can reach your weight-loss goal. Yes, it may seem unsophisticated. It may seem a little optimistic. It may even seem embarrassingly easy. But you need positive brainwashing to drown out the negative thinking you've been practicing. Say the following aloud with a big beginning and a big finish! Nobody is watching. You want to reach your goal. Read with emphasis and exuberance. Let me hear you say:

- I *can* do it!
- I *can* weigh _____ pounds. I *can* do it.
- I *choose* to weigh _____ pounds 365 days a year; not just when it's convenient.
- I *choose* to feel better and look better physically and mentally, about my appearance and about myself.
- I *choose* to be free of the excess weight and all the excuses that hampered my success in the past.
- I *choose* to succeed.
- I *can* succeed.
- I *will* succeed.
- I *will* weigh _____ pounds and *will* do everything possible to achieve this goal — *my* goal.

- I *choose* to feel better about myself because I'm worth it! (Read this sentence slowly, three times, because you may have forgotten you are worth it. Have you put your spouse, family, friends, and coworkers ahead of yourself? Move yourself to the front of the line. Everyone will benefit.)
- I *can* conceive of this success.
- I believe I *can* succeed.

(Now a big finish. Let me hear it. Convince me. Convince you.)

- I *choose* to weigh _____ pounds.
- I *will* weigh _____ pounds.
- I *can* do it!

Rewrite the I Can Do It affirmations into your workbook. Review them daily. They're a reminder of what you eventually want to accomplish.

CREATE A HOME BASE

A Home Base is a safe harbor. It consists of *people* (friends, family, coworkers) who do not push food on you or guilt you into eating more than you need or want. They accept whatever you choose and don't try to seduce (or guilt) you into having more food or a drink when you don't want any. Sometimes you have to remind someone who is pushing food not to do that.

A Home Base could also be a *place,* such as a restaurant, where you can order what *you* need, not necessarily what is offered. In an Italian restaurant, for example, I like the sauce used when preparing eggplant parmesan, but I don't like cheese. Years ago, I asked a waiter whether he could put mushrooms on the eggplant instead of the cheese, but to use the same sauce. So delicious. Since then, I've never been refused. Friends enjoy it, too. There's nothing wrong with eggplant parmesan. But I wanted an All-Vegetable Meal at that time, and I didn't want a Hi-End Protein of cheese at that meal either.

A Home Base is helpful to have. Make a list of a few people and places that constitute a safe harbor where it's easy to achieve your Program goals.

Gina B: A very strange thing happened last night. I went out with some friends, and I messed up my Program. I had pizza with wine — forgot the BBDA rule of one of four or none and had both bread and alcohol. And when I got home, I didn't care about my Program anymore because I had already messed it up, so I had a frozen yogurt.

Caryl: That pattern is an old and popular one. I screwed up so I'll make it worse.

If I can't do it perfectly, I won't do it at all. There is no perfect. Perfection is an illusion. You'll never get to be perfect. But did you do better at any meal or day or food encounter than you might have? Yes? Then that's great. And as Maya Angelou said, "When you know better, you'll do better."

Caryl: When you are on your Program, you are basically concentrating on what I call your Home Base. That is your home, office, certain friends, certain restaurants, and certain situations that happen again and again. You get comfortable eating with certain people and in certain situations. Then when you go off your Program, it is not because you messed up, but because you encountered an eating situation with already established patterns, portion sizes, and frequencies that were different from your Home Base. So you do what you always do — eat too much, eat to socialize, eat to relieve discomfort, and eat without planning. This situation ends in remorse.

Did you repattern? Did you breathe, change location, brush your teeth, check your e-mail, retrieve text messages, change clothes, read program notes? No? Then that needs work. Had you done (or tried to do) all or some of those things, you still might have eaten, but you would've eaten less and stopped sooner because of your efforts.

It doesn't help one bit to beat yourself up and have frozen yogurt. And you're most likely in denial. You're keeping extra, instant food in your freezer rather than purchasing dessert for one meal at a time. You did what you've always done. You went to the freezer and something instant was there so you ate it. If it hadn't been there, you would have gone to sleep with a glass of water.

Think about what you could do next time the same thing happens; then you'll do even better than you did this time. It takes time to absorb all the assignments and their place in your eating life. Keep reading and reviewing. The Program will eventually make sense, and its processes will become comfortable and automatic.

It's a good time to review what you've read until now. See page 318 for Review Number Two.

CHAPTER 5

Repatterning: Making a Habit of Breaking a Habit

DUTIFUL CHILD

You learned almost everything you know.

When you were born, you were an innocent child. Eventually, you learned how to eat and breathe and swallow at the same time without drooling or choking. Baby food was added to liquids. Then solid foods were added. You learned how to take care of that change, too. You knew how to cry when you were hungry. You figured that out. You learned every other habit.

Many habits you now have were most likely passed along by your parents, or some other role model, such as a sibling, teacher, coach, or perhaps an aunt or grandparent. It might be a habit such as looking both ways before crossing the street, or paying your bills the day they arrive. It doesn't matter how long it took to learn as long as you eventually learned. Mastering a cellphone, iPod, or computer took a period of adjustment until the steps became comfortable and automatic. When you begin to learn new habits, they are not immediately comfortable. Learning to feel feelings without trying to stuff them down with food takes practice, too.

All that repetition in doing each step with each ritualized habit creates a certain rhythm and routine to which you have become accustomed. Many of you can turn on your computer, go into another room, and know at what point it is in the signing on process just by hearing the clicks and clacks. A cellphone has its own musical hums and buzzes. It is the same way with eating habits.

There's a certain physical rhythm: a number of bites, chews, sips, and swallows until you are no longer hungry. How long does each meal need to last until you no longer feel hungry? For each person it is different. Studies have been done that show a person has the same amount of volume at almost each meal, though calories vary. Since you learned what you are now doing and you don't like the outcome, realize that you can learn a new way, get into a different rhythm of eating, chewing, sipping and swallowing like a thinner person does, and you will like the outcome. You can achieve this because you follow the rules. You're trainable. You are a Dutiful Child.

Being a Dutiful Child, you keep figuring out how to make the eating process even more efficient by trying to get more food and drink into your mouth in a shorter period of time. Can heartburn (acid reflux, gas, or stomach discomfort) be far behind? Wanting to please everyone, you gave others what they wanted. Mother wanted you to finish everything on your plate, so you learned to finish everything on your plate. Father wanted you to eat quickly so you could get a few hours of baseball in before dark. You learned to eat quickly.

Those two habits, finishing everything on your plate and eating quickly, have been repeated since childhood and reinforced throughout your life because you are a Dutiful Child. Just as you have practiced other habits that are not destructive to your weight-loss goals (such as making your bed in the morning and locking your doors before you leave your home), you've practiced some habits that are destructive to reaching your weight-loss goal. It might be buying unplanned food, eating on the run, eating when you're not hungry, bringing foods into your home for a larger group of people than just you and your cat and imagining you can handle it. You cannot.

Other components and patterns that should be of particular interest to the overweight person are: frequency of eating, portion size of food, and the time needed to buy, prepare, and eat the food. Let's look at each of these patterns in more detail.

EATING FREQUENCY

During an addiction's development, the frequency of your eating behavior increases. An occasional alcoholic drink at a parents' anniversary or holiday party when you were younger is now a glass of wine every time you're in a restaurant. Having a drink on occasion turned into drinking once a month, then once a week, then daily, then twice daily, then every single time you are with others. Sometimes you order a bottle. Even though your companion only wants one glass, you finish the rest of the bottle yourself.

Are you now buying wine and drinking alone in front of the television? This is an example of a progressive disease. You build a tolerance and the time between each glass of wine (bag of chips, six-pack of soda), gets shorter and shorter.

For some, it is the ritual of drinking coffee at every breakfast, eating bread with every lunch, or having dessert at every dinner to end a meal. These behaviors are very progressive. The frequency becomes more frequent. It happens so quickly that you might not realize it's happening until your clothes become snug or even tight.

PORTION SIZE

Portions also grow. A splash of alcohol doubles. Coffee cups escalate from regular, to large, to grande, to giganticus! Ordering a small cup of coffee is no longer an option. A walk to a grocery store reveals the amazing size of fruits and vegetables. Colorful advertisements of fast-food restaurants show oversized sandwiches using oversized bread. It's the new norm. The documentary *Supersize Me* brought home the point beautifully. Everything, including the body, is growing. At one fast-food restaurant, you order your sandwich by asking for a six-inch or a twelve-inch sub. Food by the inch!

Victoria M.: Determined to have a one-item lunch, I stopped at the deli that usually has shrimp salad. Alas, none to be had. But I did think the turkeyloaf looked tasty. I pondered whether I should get one piece or two . . . after all, it's all turkeyloaf so it's one item, right? But I really knew it was two servings, so that's two items. The longer I stood there, the smaller the servings looked, so I convinced myself two was the right portion.

On my walk to the office, I took some breaths, got in touch with how loose my pants and coat are. When I got up to my desk, I offered one piece to the Help Desk supervisor who happily took me up on my offer.

I had purposely picked up lunch on my way in because I'm getting to the office late. My one serving of meatloaf sang to me from its perch on my desk. So I put it in a file cabinet to help me drown out the song of the Lorelei until lunch. I had breakfast early today so lunch by 12:00 would be reasonable. This was 11:30.

I returned some calls, installed a patch, and did testing to see if it worked (nope), and all the while felt the call of the meatloaf. I drank a glass of water.

I made it until noon, put it on a plate with utensils and spent twenty minutes eating it. It was tasty. It was enough. And, you know the end of the story. Nobody died. And I'm really happy with myself.

Caryl: It's actually a Victoria Victory as you did all the work, all the arguing with your addict brain, made all the choices, gave away one part of the food, and persevered to the finish line, arms raised in Victory as you won the battle using your new, thinner Program voice.

Every step of the way you could have gone either way. At the end of every race is the start of another. Each step you chose a new way, a different way, and ultimately a better way, and it was all okay. Better than okay because nobody died. You get to put that in your Quantum Leaps List. You get to re-live your wonderful success every time you read that page. If you did it once, you can do it again. Next time it gets easier and easier. Less sturm and drang, for now you know the outcome was perfectly satisfying, perfectly enough.

Every step you took was being interrupted by your addiction and you fought it and you won. Doesn't that feel great? Doesn't that feel empowering? Of course, next time you won't spin your head with one slice or two, big size or small, this container or that. You'll know the one slice, smaller size container is plenty, is enough. The secretary won't have that second piece because there won't be a second piece. Next time, you'll have the deli person weigh it so you know exactly how much you're buying and more importantly, how it looks. Then you can identify your portion on a crowded plate, on a crowded buffet table, in a cafeteria hot table.

Yaaaaay!! Now do it again with some hot water. Perfect.

TIME

Food addiction takes up time. Time is dedicated to buying, preparing, and eating.

First you need to get the *drug*, which could be food for some of you. Then prepare the drug. Ingest (insert, chew, swallow) the drug. You need to clean up afterward. All of this takes time. You feel remorse. The behavior is repeated and repeated and repeated until it is automatic and mindless, though it might be familiar and comfortable. You continue doing it, just to feel normal. All the steps take time to execute. As frequency increases, you're ingesting food more times per day. An ever-increasing amount of time is spent shopping for and consuming food. Remember: If it's not water, it is food.

Not all habits are horrible. When it is an innocent habit like brushing your teeth or paying your bills the day they arrive, the behavior might even have positive benefits. But when you are the Dutiful Child, following your overeating rituals and habits, the results might not be to your liking.

Once you practice dealing with frequency, portion size, and time — and learn that it is okay to say, "No," and it is okay to leave food on your plate when you are no longer hungry — you will master these new habits and rituals. You'll keep improving each new constructive habit because you are a Dutiful Child.

Wilma M.: I went to dinner with a coworker, and the meal was very satisfying. Afterward, my coworker asked whether I wanted dessert. I was no longer hungry, but I did want dessert. We went to a place a few blocks from the restaurant. By the time we got there, I wasn't hungry for dessert anymore, but I ordered anyway. She did, too. I watched my friend have a few bites of her dessert and then push the plate away. I couldn't. I knew I was satisfied after a few bites, but I ate it all anyway. Why do I continue to eat when I'm not hungry?

Caryl: You may have learned to finish everything on your plate, or not to waste food. It almost doesn't matter how you began this now automatic habit. The question isn't, "Why do I continue to eat when I'm not hungry?" But rather, "What could I do next time?"

How about going for a walk with your coworker? Or come right out and tell someone, I'm not hungry, but I wanted to spend time with you.

I just read an article in *The New York Times* about the comedian Sara Silverman being interviewed in a busy restaurant who declined food because she was meeting a friend later for lunch.

Think about your options now so you'll have them at the ready should you need help in the future. Writing things down makes them more accessible and prevents a good idea from disappearing, never to be seen again. "Every moment — every blink — is composed of a series of discrete moving parts, and every one of those parts offers an opportunity for intervention, for reform, and for correction," says Malcolm Gladwell, author of *Blink*. I like that: "for intervention, for reform, and for correction." That fits right in with The Program's edict, "If not hungry, do something else instead. Plan. Execute. Evaluate. And adjust."

As Maxwell Gladwell makes clear, every blink, every moment, every act builds on the previous, and at each blink we have a choice — make a left turn instead of a right one, and the day will be different.

In the blink of eye, you can choose to change. In other words, each blink is one more opportunity to change your habits. And each change or choice you make for the better, no matter how small, I call it "inching forward." For you, that change occurs through repetition. That moment of discomfort (disappointment, anxiety, stress, guilt about sitting and not ordering) and your resulting decision not to act to relieve your discomfort by eating. It's a time to calm yourself without food.

The question is really about why you're eating to please someone else. You can keep a friend company and order water. You could say (when asked), "I'm not hungry, but I'll keep you company." You might say, "I changed my mind."

Make a list of twenty-seven ways to say "No thank you." If you create the list when you don't need it, and practice and rehearse these phrases, they'll just bubble up the next time you need them. What will you say next time so you reinforce your Program, which will enable you to weigh _____ pounds? By eating unplanned food without working on repatterning techniques, you merely keep that old behavior chronic.

THE ACCUMULATORS

Two people e-mailed saying they were within a few pounds of their goal weights for a few weeks, but they couldn't seem to nail it. Both seemed confused. Do you know the difference between a smidgeon, a drop, a smattering, a tad, a bit, a mite, a bite, a scrap, a part, and a particle of food? Do you see why you cannot seem to reach your goal? You're most likely accumulating foods you deem too small to keep track of. You forget them, but they accumulate whether you acknowledge them or not.

I call people with this issue The Accumulators: people who eat a big slice of some food, one sliver at a time, over time, again and again. The Accumulators eat bites and pieces of food before, during, and after each meal, while nibbling after dinner until bedtime. Chefs are some of the most frequent Accumulators.

Is your portion size a realistic amount of food? Or is your portion size a fantasy of fabulous food images from magazine and newspaper advertising? If you don't realize what and how much food you're eating to contribute to your weight gain, you are most likely in denial about why you weigh what you weigh. People with lots of mindless habits do many things that fly under the radar screen. It's when you start to see all the little things that add up, that you'll be out of denial, one item at a time.

You might not only be underestimating what you are eating, but also overestimating the amount of food you actually need. You may continue thinking daily physical activity will keep the pounds at bay only to be disappointed one more time. But thankfully, food and weight are not the only things that accumulate. All efforts and attempts to change your old eating habits to new eating habits, also accumulate.

Questions to ask yourself while you're preparing to eat seemingly harmless, healthy, low-calorie foods such as celery and carrot sticks are: How often am I doing this? Two times a week is 104 times a year. How often am I having drinks and finger foods with friends? Once a week? That's another 52 times. How often do you have three or more items for dinner? Twice a week? That's another 104 times you're eating more than you might (probably) need. These overeating episodes add up. They accumulate. You may be thinking about how much is in each meal, but you need to think about the bigger picture. How frequently do you act out your habits and rituals? These rituals and habits accumulate. They become solidified.

Camelia C.: I just received your book and liked the first few pages I've read. I'm very discouraged about my weight loss. I'm one of those high number people (started at 512 pounds). I have lost 129 pounds over the past two years, but it is so slow as to make me want to ask for weight-loss surgery of some type just to have it happen in a more reasonable time frame. I know surgery is not the answer.

Caryl: You know surgery is not an answer, but you may not realize why. My feeling is that most people who lose weight cannot realize they are much smaller, and they continue feeding the bigger person they were rather than the smaller person they've become. Even with the surgery, the lost weight is sometimes regained. Yes, people figure out how to overeat even with a reduced stomach.

Camelia C.: In the past ten months, I've gained back twenty-three of the 129 pounds I've lost, and I am scared. So I have no idea what's going on, why I'm having so much trouble again, or why I'm gaining instead of losing. Obviously, I know it's how I'm eating (portions, food choices, etc.), but I am at a loss as to why these issues weren't present two years ago when I began and was successful. They didn't seem to be interfering then. Why now? Maybe there's no reason other than that I'm an addict and my addiction is rearing its ugly head, but somehow I don't think this is the case. I refuse to give up, but I am exceedingly discouraged.

Caryl: Try not to be scared, but realize you are continuing to feed the bigger person you were. You have those old habits practiced and perfected. You have an established frequency and portion size of all foods for all circumstances. The thing to do is to change your habits, perceptions, and automatic behavior so you yield the result you want.

Be confident — one day, one moment, one second at a time. The Program asks you to ask yourself whether you are hungry, and if not, to try to figure out what is really happening in your life. A seemingly insignificant, non-hungry eating episode could turn into a moment. Maybe it's not a session with your therapist or something a friend said that triggers an eating episode, but perhaps you are tired; then it starts to rain, and then you receive stressful news, and bingo — the perfect accumulation of little things build up and you're looking to distract yourself from the discomfort of the little things by eating when you're not hungry.

Have you cleaned out your home and office of all kinds of foods that don't require preparation? Have you worked on finding the right thoughts, words, and actions for each food encounter? Have you practiced those strategies? They only become comfortable after doing them again and again until the new way becomes the comfortable way and the old way becomes less compelling. Have you noticed more frequent "snacking" or eating little bits of food that you consider too little to count? Remember, every little bit of food counts. If you ate it, log it.

Eddy K.: No matter how hard I try the Program methods I use, I cannot seem to get rid of the last five pounds to my goal weight. I plan my meals so specifically that I don't even eat the same meal as the rest of my family. I am the chef in the house, so I cook everyone's meal, including mine. I always spend at least twenty minutes eating, and I stop when I feel I am no longer hungry. So why can't I lose those last five, pesky pounds?

Caryl: Are you an Accumulator? Think back to when you are cooking everyone's meals. Do you taste the food as you make it? Do you eat little pieces of this and that while you're cooking? Everything counts. Even the smallest morsels of food will add up after so many episodes. Eating while cooking is mindless behavior. You might think that it's too little to count, but before you know it, you've eaten one, maybe two, extra food items. Those items add up quickly and can hinder your weight-loss progress. Mid-meal it's helpful to ask whether you're still hungry. Probably not.

Think that you are smaller. Sometimes you plan a two-item meal and you might think it is so much less than you used to eat when you were fifty pounds heavier and become mindless again and finish everything on your plate. What you want to think is, "At what point am I no longer hungry?"

THE PHANTOM FIFTH

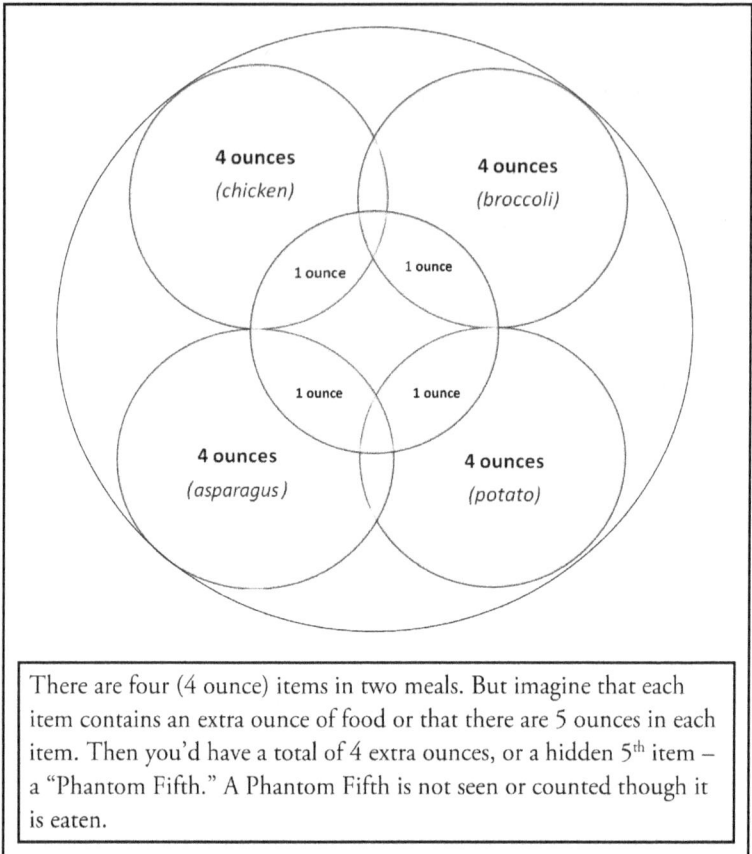

4 ounces
(chicken)

4 ounces
(broccoli)

1 ounce

1 ounce

1 ounce

1 ounce

4 ounces
(asparagus)

4 ounces
(potato)

There are four (4 ounce) items in two meals. But imagine that each item contains an extra ounce of food or that there are 5 ounces in each item. Then you'd have a total of 4 extra ounces, or a hidden 5th item – a "Phantom Fifth." A Phantom Fifth is not seen or counted though it is eaten.

When looking at the **Phantom Fifth** illustration, think of the two circles at the top, containing chicken and broccoli, as being Lunch. Think of the bottom two items, asparagus and potato, as an All-Vegetable Dinner.

The Phantom Fifth illustration shows four, 4-ounce items that comprise two meals, Lunch and Dinner. I'd like you to imagine that each item contains an extra ounce of food or that rather than four, 4-ounce items, there are four, 5-ounce items. This would give you a total of four extra ounces, or a hidden four-ounce fifth item — a Phantom Fifth.

Oftentimes, you may think your portion sizes are remaining consistent at four ounces. However, portion sizes have a habit of creeping back up from whence they came. As a result, a Phantom Fifth is often not noticed, logged, or counted, though it is eaten.

You didn't even notice that *extra item*. It may not seem like enough to log. But it can rapidly accumulate — an extra bite of the fish at dinner, two bites of dessert when you weren't hungry, more than you needed of a too large salad, and a taste of bread you tried at the insistence of your friends — it does add to your daily, weekly, and monthly tallying. It was all so small it couldn't possibly count. You may even be thinking, *I got away with it.* You didn't get away with anything. Eventually, all those extra (though unseen) items will show up on the scale. But why did it take so long to show on the scale? The Frequency increased. The Portion size increased. And the scale stopped going in the right direction. It might have been a while until it was noticeable.

There are many other Program things you *are* doing. Perhaps you're now keeping a log, asking whether you're hungry before eating, taking nickel-sized bites most of the time, and realizing that one item meals are often fine. All those and many other efforts accumulate. Those efforts show up on the scale as weight-loss.

Then you start making exceptions to the rules when you attend your company's annual meeting, eat more than you want or need at a baby shower, or help plan your daughter's summer wedding. You consume a bite, a slice, a sliver, a sip, and a swallow more than you're able to burn. All those unnoticed bites become noticeable on the scale as weight gain.

The things you are doing got together with all the things you are not doing and you have a wash. Those efforts (going in two different directions), meet in the middle and your weight re-mains the same. You think you've hit a plateau. But there are no plateaus on The Program. You're either eating too much, too late, or too fast. Or all three.

What is happening is that all your Phantom Fifths are accumulating. The frequency of your habits is increasing. You may convince yourself that if it's "only tea, or only coffee, or only a salad, it's healthy." There's an ancient weight-control business out there that either directly, or through omission, seems to encourage people to have unlimited salads and unlimited vegetables. If you have unlimited anything, you'll have an unlimited body.

Your goal is to serve yourself the same portion of food whether it is a salad or a steak, hot or cold, spicy or not, so you'll get in the habit of a certain amount of nickel-sized bites of food, a certain amount of sips of water, a certain amount of chit chat or reading your notes or a newspaper, until you are no longer hungry. Just today a participant recounted how she put much less on her plate for lunch and took such a long time to eat it, she realized, before she'd finished everything on her plate, that she was no longer hungry and left food. She hadn't done that in decades.

When you know what an honest portion looks like, you can identify your portion wherever you are. And now you'll be able to identify a Phantom Fifth hiding under a lettuce leaf.

Thank You, But No.
27 Ways to Say No Thank You Without Spurning Love, Friendship, or Partnership
Verbal Repatterning Techniques

1. I am sticking with water.
2. I need more water first.
3. I had a late lunch.
4. I don't want to drink on an empty stomach.
5. One is never enough, so none for me!
6. This is exactly what I wanted. I'm fine.

7. Eating too much makes me tired.
8. That's so lovely but I couldn't have another bite.
9. One drink is perfect for me tonight.
10. I'm the designated driver.
11. I've had the perfect amount of food.
12. I'm very satisfied.
13. I'm just not hungry.
14. I have a physical tomorrow.
15. Trying to get into a Speedo by the end of summer — so I just can't.
16. I have been eating out too much lately.
17. Maybe later.
18. My company's financial planner magazine wants me as the swimsuit centerfold.
19. I'm good. I'm fine. Thanks, no.
20. I'm going to a pool party next week.
21. I'm enjoying just sitting here and visiting.
22. I have some work to do tonight.
23. Looks good, but I'm saving my appetite for dinner.
24. Too much sugar makes me crash.
25. Maybe later.
26. My doctor says I need to drink more water.
27. I'm not hungry, yet.

And even more suggestions from others:

28. I am already drunk.
29. I am worried about being arrested for DUI.
30. I hit my quota for day.
31. I am kinda dehydrated — sticking with water.
32. Don't like drinking on an empty stomach.
33. Had cocktail for breakfast.
34. Saving up for weekly quota on Saturday.
35. Hit my quota for the week.

36.   I don't have time.

37.   I am already buzzed.

38.   You are intoxicating enough without my drinking.

39.   Have big meeting in the morning.

40.   I have some work to do tonight.

How can you say no when you're not hungry?

List some of your own ways to say no to drinks or food. This is all Verbal Repatterning. Be creative, be funny, and be ready! Strengthen your Program Voice.

A Smaller You Needs Less Frequent, Smaller, Food Portions

As you lose weight, it will be apparent you do not need as much food as you did before. People pounce on the number of items. "I am eating such a small amount now, I couldn't possibly eat less," they argue. And yes, you *can* eat less. You need less food than the amount of food you were eating to have sustained the bigger you. But you're smaller, and you need less than you did yesterday, less than you ate last week, and less than you ate last month — until you reach your goal. Then you don't need less or more, but to strive toward enough.

Remain mindful at Point of Planning and Point of Purchase. Know that if you buy food (in any amount), you'll most likely eat whatever you bought. Reduce portions of everything you now buy. You'll get comfortable with it. I'd rather you purchase a cookie than a box of cookies. Then when it's gone, it's gone. By the time you Skip and Scatter, and purchase dessert again, it might even be more than a day. This helps interrupt the entrenched frequency pattern.

Find other ways to comfort yourself; other ways to de-stress, unwind, and relax without using the inappropriate act of putting food in your mouth when you're not hungry enough to commit to a meal. If you do decide to eat, that meal contains nickel-sized bites, fork down between bites of food, sipping water between bites of food, making sure mouth is empty before inserting more food, and making it last for twenty minutes or more.

Is your portion size a realistic amount of food? Or is your portion size learned from food images from over the top food shows and magazine articles? I'm not sure who the audience is for those shows and articles, but you don't want to be ordering food by the pound anymore. There is no need to fill up your plate or even to finish everything placed on your plate.

What should you say if someone comments, "You're not having an appetizer?" You might experiment with some of these responses:

1. If I eat an appetizer, I won't be hungry
    by the time my entrée arrives.
2. It's too much food; I'm fine.
3. I'm not that hungry. This is plenty.
4. I had a big lunch. (Not that you should eat a big lunch,
    which really means: I ate more than I am able to burn.)

Or as you get smaller, closer to your goal, you might say:

5. I'm a little person — look at the size
    of this portion; want some?
6. I don't need so much; want some?
7. This portion is so big it could feed
    a family of four; want some?

In saying these things, you are not only telling the other person, but you also are telling yourself you are fine with the amount you've chosen to eat. You are creating and hearing The Program voice.

If you say, "I'm fine" enough times, one day you'll realize you really are fine.

Sara H.: You asked me if our field trip together to the food market in Grand Central Terminal helped. You better believe it helped. I keep hearing you say, "Not your portion." I'm even cutting up my beets that I'm having for lunch into little pieces and feeding the smaller person I am. I keep learning something new.

At our last meeting I learned about the fifteen-minute delay technique, and that needs more work. Your "Not my portion" reminder and the visuals associated with it were very enlightening. I was eating too much salad-type foods. Interestingly, though, I didn't have large portions of dessert. Now I'm making all portions equal size like I did at lunch the other day with the crème caramel, soup, and vegetables.

Caryl: Good awareness. And I hear pride in your words. Be proud. You're fine tuning all of this. Not only are you at your goal, but you're keeping it off day after day, after week, after food encounters, after business trips, after a holiday in Mexico.

Review your portion size often to make sure it's not slowly increasing. When you can identify your portion among the excess served to you, and you are leaving over everything that doesn't look like your portion, you are at the top of your game. Even after you've reached your goal, it is important to review it daily, even for five minutes, or by reading just a few pages of your logbook. A little effort can make a big difference. Any effort is better than no effort. A choice to not do anything is still a choice.

Cindy G: I served myself a plate of lunch yesterday, and then ate only about half of it until I was full. It was rewarding to see practically another meal left on my plate. In the past, I would have thought I would be hungry after eating only the amount I had served myself. I wasn't. Wow.

Caryl: This is a nice, positive story of awareness. You're proud of your accomplishment. You are awake and aware. Try eating until you are *no longer hungry, not full*. When you continually leave food on a plate after eating for twenty minutes, the next time order a little less, buy a little less, prepare a little less, serve a little less, and eat a little less because you are a little less. Nice awareness.

PUSHING THE ENVELOPE

As a child, your parents wanted you to go to bed at seven o'clock. You may have pushed the envelope by begging for another few minutes, one more TV show, or one more story. It all seemed harmless. But behaviors are often progressive. A woman I teach, Goldie, has difficulty saying, "No" to an alcoholic drink. It has such a hold on her. Her food could just as easily have been coffee, bread, or dessert. I suggested she try to go a week without a drink, just to see whether she could do it. She should easily be able to if alcohol doesn't have a hold on her. If she's indifferent to alcohol rather than being someone who's *gotta have it,* then sometimes she'll be able to say "Yes," and more importantly, sometimes she will be able to say, "No." Either way, we agreed she would go a week without choosing alcohol.

The next day, she e-mailed me, "I'm going to dinner with a friend I haven't seen in a while. Can I start the week tomorrow?"

"No," I answered. "Begin today." There'll always be another dinner with another friend.

Goldie was Pushing the Envelope. That's what addicts do; they have one more sip of a drink, one more drink, one more bite of bread, one more cup of coffee, one more inhalation of a cigarette, one more pack.

Now you want to eat or drink just because you're bored or tired. Maybe you're eating because you're thinking: *One bite can't make a difference. I'm up anyway. It's so small. I'll start tomorrow. I'll begin after the wedding, after vacation, after the party next week, after next month, after income tax time, after all that* — *then I'll start my new weight-loss program.* That's part of resistance to change.

You may discover you are not yet comfortable being with others unless you're eating or drinking the way you used to. So, you wait one more meal or day or function to begin your weight-loss program. You continually test yourself by Pushing the Envelope about how much food is enough, how often is enough, how much you can eat and still lose weight.

So why are you Pushing the Envelope?

There are certain Program concepts that you left when you read them the first time. There were so many other things you could do without discomfort. That might be one factor. Another factor might be that things are slipping; perhaps the nickel-sized bite is now a quarter. Or the number of items have increased, especially at dinner. Are you back to having an alcoholic drink every time you meet to eat with a friend?

It's time to create a new way of thinking: Instead of thinking what is the most you can eat and drink and still lose or maintain weight, why not think, *What is the smallest amount of food I can eat and not feel deprived and not pass out in the street and still lose weight?* Between those two extremes is a nice middle ground.

Often, if you're eating slowly enough, you'll realize that the new amount is fine, and it is certainly enough to feed the smaller person you are becoming, the smaller person you are.

It is at the precise moment of discomfort that you want to create a new action that, when practiced, becomes your new automatic and comfortable response when emotional discomfort or food is present. Since habits are acquired behavior patterns (in other words, you learned your habits; you weren't born with them), you can create a new habit to eat only when you're hungry — another habit to change your errant thinking.

If you push the new habit with creative, well-thought-out so-lutions, the moments of temptation will pass and *cycle interruptus* occurs. The moments of temptation (and they abound) are when you are responding to the *memory of a previous food encounter you are trying to replicate.* That's what the Addict Pea Brain does to seduce you, to tempt you. The Program Brain knows that the moment does pass, and the new way eventually becomes com-fortable. The new way eventually becomes the preferred way.

If you continue Pushing the Envelope by eating when you're not hungry, you're creating a structure that locks in and becomes the default setting.

Push the Envelope in the other direction by reading your notes one more time, having a one-item dinner one more eve-ning, taking nickel-sized bites one more meal, having hot or cold cereal for breakfast one more day, delaying eating unless you're hungry for one more week, and writing new achievements on your Quantum Leaps list.

Even though healthy, cold cereal is almost too instant. I eat it but still find oatmeal more satisfying than any of the others. I cook hot cereal with water so it's saving milk every time I have cereal. Even when traveling, I take a bite of shredded wheat and a sip of water.

Marsha M. doesn't eat much throughout the workday (candy/coffee/diet soda) and then binges when she eats out or at dinner-time — big portions, steak, pasta, too many cocktails with her girlfriends, and mindless nibbling on whatever the server puts on the table. She regrets it in the morning, but then she starts the same, destructive cycle again. Here is the conversation I had with her to help her resolve her binge-eating.

Marsha M.: What do I do when I go out with my coworkers every night and end up drinking too many drinks and eating too much food?

Caryl: Now that you know the eating patterns you keep reinforcing (that's what keeps the cycle chronic), it is helpful if you think about some of the changes you would like to make. Rather than trying to do everything at the very next meal, pick one little thing you can do each evening. It takes time to create habits, so don't expect it all to be 100 percent comfortable overnight. It's a process. Patterns take time to form.

For me, water is an essential part of every outing. And so is speaking up. You might say, "Nothing for me, but I'll keep you company." You might say, "I'll have water, thank you. I can't drink on an empty stomach," or "I have to drive home," or "I have to be up early," or any number of phrases that would work. Make a list now and rehearse so when it's showtime, you'll have re-patterning techniques when you need them.

Going out after work with friends is part of life. Once you are in the restaurant, it's too late to think about what you're going to do. If you only had $10 in your wallet, you'd think beforehand which items you would buy. Give your food (and drink) intake the same thoughtfulness. If you are taking medication, you'd find a way to say you're not allowed to drink with the pills.

Or if you need to work when you get home, you'd find a way to defer an alcoholic drink. Be creative in your planning. It's all about finding the right words, the right tone of refusal, and the right commitment to your goal of wanting to weigh _____ pounds. Pushing the Envelope doesn't work.

Focus on one small goal at a time when going out with friends. The first night you might keep it to one drink by having four sips of water for every sip of wine. The next time, you could do that and also look for an appetizer (yes, even standing at a bar you can still get served) because you tell your companions, "I can't drink on an empty stomach anymore." Then have a bite of food and water before having a sip of wine. Repeat.

Of course, if you are drinking to get wasted (drunk, to zone out, to escape), there is nothing I can tell you that will make a difference. But if you want to weigh _____ pounds, there will always be the next outing or girls' night (or guys' night) out to make changes. Make small changes now in areas where you find yourself Pushing the Envelope. I remember ordering soup and a salad one night when everyone else was ordering an appetizer, a main course, and mindlessly eating the bread on the table. And it was okay. It was thoroughly enjoyable. And no one else cared what I did or didn't eat.

Wanda J.: I need lots of ideas about repatterning techniques. I know I need to think, speak, and act differently, but when I'm near food, I'm like a deer caught in headlights stunned by my compulsion.

Caryl: Use a fifteen-minute delay technique: Instead of reaching out your hand to put something into your mouth, move and get some water. Do something else. Recommit to your goal of weighing _____ pounds. Think about what you can do to kill fifteen minutes. Wait fifteen minutes while repatterning by doing something else; call a friend, check e-mail, go for a walk, read the newspaper. I'll bet if you look around your surroundings, something needs tidying up. At the end of the fifteen minutes, ask yourself, "Am I hungry?" If so, then commit to a Meal by Program standards: Use knife and fork, take nickel-sized bites, sip water in between bites of food, choose the number of items, choose a Filler or not, and make it last at least twenty minutes.

Instead of eating brie with your fingers, cut it into pieces and toss it in with a salad. Get sliced turkey and cut it into pieces as well. Put a toothpick into each little square if you absolutely cannot find a fork.

If you constantly eat, which you do, you'll never get hungry. You're not eating for nourishment. You are eating to fill up your belly. It appears as if you're stuffing things down with the continuous conveyor belt of food, distracting yourself from stress (and accompanying feelings and emotions) by eating all the time. You're not present. You're either getting food, or eating it, or thinking about getting more. That's addiction.

Name three things you can work on this week. Some examples might be to Skip and Scatter, apply the fifteen-minute delay technique, or eat the correct portions of nutrient-dense foods. If you at least try to interrupt the cycle of addiction, you'll end up eating less often and less volume. It will all work out. Even one bite less each meal is more than a thousand bites at the end of the year. That's a big pile of food.

We Don't Count Calories But You Need To Know

100 Calories a day
x 365 Days a year
36,500 Calories per year
÷ 3,500 Calories (equals a pound)
= 10.4 Pounds per year

100 Calories more than you need each day, i.e., a can of tuna, a piece of bread, or an apple, fifteen nuts, or 4 ounces of soda, consumed every day, 365 days a year equals 36,500 calories, divided by 3,500 calories which is one pound equals 10.4 pounds by year's end. 200 calories equals 20½ pounds by the end of the year. It's all consumed one bite or one swallow at a time. One item more than you need every single day. Was that portion of fish more than 4 ounces? It was good. But not a reason to overeat. Take it home and freeze for another lovely meal. If you think you'll eat upon arriving home, leave it in the restaurant.

Dana K.: I feel totally at odds right now. Saturday morning, I reached my goal weight. I went out to dinner that night and did really well. But then I went to my parents' house in Connecticut on Sunday and ate way too much and for the wrong reasons — I was tired, bored, and my mother was telling me that I've lost more than enough weight and that she didn't want me to lose any more. She usually nags at me and tells me I am overweight and shouldn't be eating. This was something new. Feeling like a wholly changed and untouchable person, I proceeded to eat a ton of junk — cookies, chocolate, and ice cream. That was Saturday night.

Then I woke up Sunday morning feeling really horrible about what I had eaten the night before. So I ate a normal breakfast of cold cereal. But by lunchtime, I went into the cabinets and ate more junk.

I feel really disappointed with myself right now and can barely face myself in the mirror. I feel like I have completely gone off The Program. I know I need to get right back on, but I feel so ashamed of myself and like such a failure. I know this is the addict in me talking. Right now, I just want to starve myself and go to the gym. I haven't gotten on the scale since Saturday, and I know I need to. I feel so helpless right now, but I need to pull myself together, get through the workday, and get back on The Program. I haven't had breakfast yet, but I'm not hungry.

Caryl: Sometimes when you reach that irresistible goal, you think you deserve or can afford to eat whatever you want and all of life will be fine. But you realize that nothing has really changed. All that happens is that you are thinner. Your issues with your mother, or life, or anything do not change. You have the same problems. The disappointment reminds you that eating doesn't change anything — it just exacerbates your feelings of helplessness. It takes time to become the person you want to be using pro-active repatterning techniques.

It is your life. Thank your mother for her opinion rather than debating it or feeling bad about it. She's got her own issues with food. No shame. No failure. This is the addiction. And although you've figured out how to work through the Home Base, you have not changed the habits at your mother's. In your mother's home, you are still the little girl, and she is the omnipotent know-it-all. Perhaps you need to meet your mother on a more neutral ground. Tell her your weight is not a topic of conversation.

Revisiting your encounter at your mother's, I was curious to know whether there was alcohol involved. Alcohol causes lack of resolve and you might end up eating (and drinking) more than you planned. Even with all your weight loss, you still have the same mother. She says what she says and you react the way you do. Someone has to change or the outcome will always remain the same. If you change even a little bit, then she will change a little bit, and that is hopefully how it goes. The question remains. What will you do next time? You gotta have a plan.

It's helpful to relive the moment in your memory. At exactly what point did your mother make you not want to weigh your goal weight anymore? What did she say? And think about all the things you could do and say next time so the new smaller you will get more and more comfortable sticking to your plan. It always feels better in the end.

YOU CAN HAVE YOUR CAKE AND EAT IT, TOO

Each week (month, year) brings a conveyor belt of food encounters: one more sports packed weekend, a family tradition, an unexpected winter get-away — all designed to whet the weakest appetite and erode the strongest weight-loss resolve. Or maybe the winter months become one more excuse to halt your weight-loss efforts until the spring thaws. Beautiful buffets, Super Bowl feasts, and Valentine's Day dinners are waiting for you to do exactly what you did last year with disastrous results.

You can learn to eat real food in the real world and still reach and maintain your goal weight. It doesn't have to be an all-or-nothing extreme. Here's a plan of behavioral strategies to get you through the next year of eating engagements. After years of observations, the strategies are easy-to-achieve behavioral tips and tactics. All the tips will prepare every Knicks, Nets, or _____ fan to anticipate and plan for a host of eating challenges.

To help the weight-weary cope with the constant onslaught of food, I've boiled down eating strategies to what to do *before*, *during*, and *after* each event.

BEFORE AN EATING ENCOUNTER

- Eat breakfast and lunch. Starving all day as an excuse to overeat at a function will only convince you to eat more than you are able to burn before bedtime.
- Recommit to weighing _____ pounds.
- Make sure your neon sign of wanting to weigh _____ pounds is glowing above your head.
- Before leaving for the festivities, plan the food you're going to consume. Avoid the mediocre items you'd never select if you were paying for each one individually. Do you really need to eat one more salad just because someone tossed it? Thank you very much, but none for me.
- It's okay to say "No, thank you," if you're no longer hungry. Your host/hostess *wants you to* have a good time; feeling stuffed, bloated, or uncomfortable in your clothes does not enhance the event's enjoyment.
- Wear a belt rather than elastic-waisted pants or skirt.

DURING AN EATING ENCOUNTER

- Upon arriving, get a glass of water to drink while you mingle. It will give you something to hold during socially anxious moments or periods of boredom. If you like, put water in a wine glass. No one will know. No one will care.

- Drinking alcohol lowers inhibitions, especially when consumed on an empty stomach. Save the drink for when you finally sit down to eat. Once you've begun to eat, then between sips of water, take a sip of alcohol. The smaller you are, the less tolerant you'll be to the drug alcohol. Personally, I found that once the food arrived, I was more interested in it than in the alcohol.

- Keep moving by helping your host(ess). Talk to everyone in the room before looking at the food. Walk. Talk. Cha Cha Cha.

- Make sure your favorite foods are included in your daily (weekly) meal plan so you can have your cake and eat it, too. A glass of wine on Tuesday night, a decaf cappuccino on Thursday, and delicious dessert at Sunday brunch might be the perfect recipe for your weight-loss success.

- Slow down. It's a meal, not a marathon.

- Choose your food as if you were ordering á la carte in a restaurant, even if it is offered buffet style.

- One couple said that if the food is the most interesting thing at a get together, they leave.

AFTER AN EATING ENCOUNTER

- If in your own home, send leftovers out the door with friends. If you keep leftovers, freeze individual portions. If you're too tired to do that before bedtime, throw them away, lest you go back in the morning and think, "One more shrimp puff, two more bites of leftover cheese."

- Relish the fact that you can attend a function where food is served, have a nice time, enjoy your meal, and come home with your clothes still fitting and your self-esteem intact.

The part of the meal that you find most challenging is a perfect time to create new coping strategies. Everyone's moment can be different. The start and the finish cause me to be super-vigilant. You can get up. Go to the bathroom. Help the hostess. Call your office. It doesn't matter what you do. Do something. During an anxious moment, that new automatic response replaces an old automatic response. After following some (or all) of the strategies, you will be confident and more in control of your inappropriate use of food.

Instead of being overwhelmed, remember there will always be another meal, another occasion. Keep in mind how much more fun these encounters will be with a more in-control you wearing a smaller-size outfit. When you plan in advance, you can have your cake and eat it, too. But the new, smaller you will most likely want less of it.

Serena B.: I have cut down my portions a lot and it has shown on the scale. I am down four more pounds since Tuesday. I listened to what you said and have tried different foods each day, except that stupid banana and, of course, the dreaded soda that I can't seem to resist having every day. I know, I know. Two No-Meal meals every day. But I am taking baby steps to try to change.

Caryl: Nothing wrong with a banana, but you'd had a banana every single day between meals and did the same with your soda habit — two No-Meal Meals every single day. And no Skipping or Scattering.

Eat when you're hungry — Bread or beverage or dessert or alcohol, one of four or none, might or might not be a part of that meal. Banana and soda are dessert and beverage. Two No-Meal Meals daily. Why not have a banana one day and soda on another? Diminish portion size. Maybe if part of a meal, it's a half or third of a banana. Pour the soda into a glass; a portion is 8 ounces, and you'll be sipping water between bites of food and sips of soda. Those are skills you can achieve.

Serena B.: Tomorrow night, my husband and I are going out for dinner with his partner and his wife and then to a birthday party. I am planning to drink a lot of water, and this is going to be the first time out with a couple since I started The Program, so I am planning ahead. This weekend, I have a lot going on and am a bit concerned how to approach everything, but I am planning it in my head and will do the best I can.

Caryl: Brava! You see how all those little efforts paid off big time. Nice job. You're almost in a new decade (of weight when you go from the 150s to the 140s). I think that planning in writing is ultimately more effective than planning in your head. Acknowledge that your goal is to get into a conversation with a variety of people before looking at the food.

Caryl: With both the dinner and the party, it is enormously helpful to take a few quiet moments after you've dressed, but before you leave for the food encounter, to read your goal sheet, your "I can do it" sheet, and think how committed you've been and how it has paid off. Recommit to your Program. Even if you're feeling a little bit uncomfortable, so what? The moment will pass. If you leave the table, it will pass that much more quickly.

Can't move you? Move it. When it is late, I am tired, and lack of resolve has kicked in, I like to make a wall out of the salt and pepper shakers, my water glass, flowers, a candle and anything else on the table to separate me from anything that might call my name when it wasn't on my plan. No one knows it is a coping strategy. It reduces my discomfort by giving me something to do until the moment passes.

Michael: What do you do if you've eaten a wholesome meal, but you are starving long before it's time to eat the next one?

Caryl: Have you had enough protein for the day? You're most likely not starving or even hungry but bored or tired. Drink water. Keep a toothbrush and toothpaste at the office. Take a nap. Try doing something else for a few minutes. Perhaps you just need a rest. Take a break. After the time is up, if you're hungry, have a Fourth Meal. Water is always a good option too. Even better if you have to get it before you can drink it. An action step as well as doing something to refresh yourself.

Keep a stash of Fourth Meals (a tuna pouch, a plastic bag of cold cereal, a hardboiled egg, a container of soup you can warm in the microwave) in your home and office. You might travel with a disposable plastic container of cold cereal, tuna, or turkey. Purchase some pretty paper plates and plastic utensils to have on hand. Take food out of the containers and place on plate.

Gayle F.: I am a little frustrated with myself today. Even if I think I'm having a good day, I add up the number of items per day, and I'm still at seven or eight. The scale either stays the same or seems to go up every few days.

Caryl: It might be helpful to count as you go along, plotting and planning for it to be five or six items. As these habits become established, it is possible that the portions are diminishing, though the number of items is not yet where you want them. I'll bet it is still fewer than what you used to consume. Personally, it's easier for me to aim for one- or two-item lunches and dinners so by the time I have a three-item meal, it feels like I'm overeating. The number of items falls in the four five or six items daily range, but all I have to think about are the one or two items I have at each meal. It is always doable.

Gayle F.: I am having one-item meals, but to have two and not three items at least for one meal a day is very hard.

Caryl: Think that it is different or challenging rather than hard. It is different from what you're used to eating. It is also what made you gain weight. You don't need as much food. If you practice two-item meals for a week, it won't be hard. It won't be different. It'll be comfortable. If one or two items are okay for breakfast, you'll find they are physically enough for lunch and dinner. It is making them emotionally enough that takes time.

You're smaller. You may want those extra items, though you no longer need them. If you're trying to feed an emotional hunger, you could back up a truck full of food and it wouldn't be enough food. "One's too many; a hundred's never enough," said a character in the 1940s movie *Lost Weekend*. He was talking about alcohol, but the same could be said about food addiction.

Brie S.: I don't want my weight to fluctuate anymore. I want to lose the weight and keep it off forever.

Caryl: The only way your twenty-eight-year-old addiction can be gone and stay gone is to practice and perform the new habits until they become the default settings. The new habits are, relatively speaking, quite new. You've only done them a few days or weeks. Keep working on them. It is when you surrender to an old seductive food ritual when with another person and think, "I can get away with something," or "It's so small it can't count" that you know you're in your addiction. (Errant thinking).

When you project into the future or beat yourself up for past behavior, you're not present. When you're focused on present strategies that help you change habits now, the weight will stay off. It is more than thirty years since I lost the weight. I still live The Program. There are a lot of old food memories out there. But I don't act on them.

TOO MANY EXCEPTIONS, NOT ENOUGH RULES

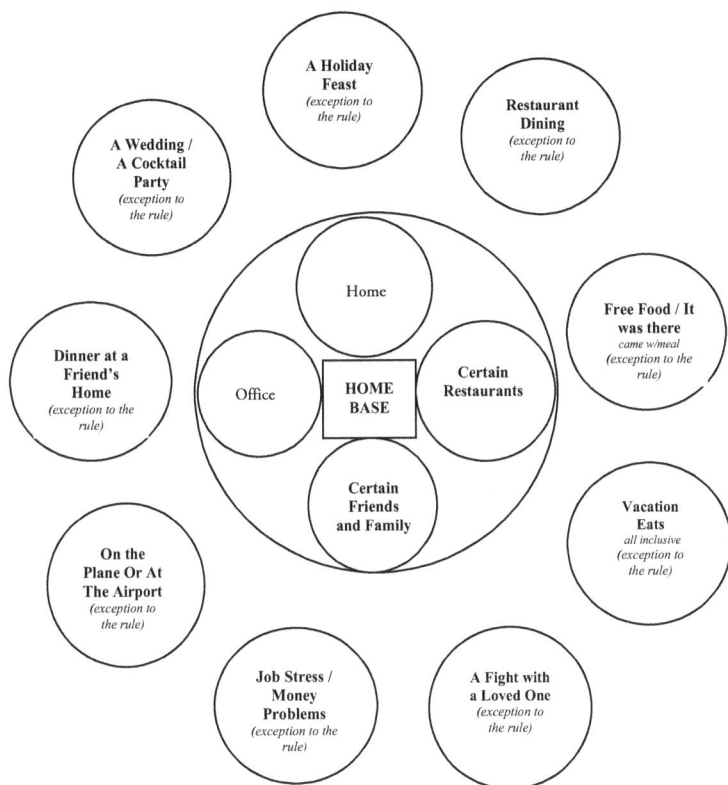

Your Home Base is where you feel comfortable, in certain places, with certain people and with certain foods. Every time you make an eating encounter an *exception to the rule,* you erode your Home Base. Your Goal is to enlarge your Home Base, to eat only when hungry, anywhere in the world, with any number of people. In this way you'll have more rules and fewer exceptions.

You want to do what The Program suggests and do it consistently (it's all in the details) — even when you don't need it — so that all the new thoughts, words, and actions will appear effortlessly when you do need them. By repeating the process, each step becomes familiar and comfortable enough so you can do it again. You're finding new ways to conduct yourself around food no matter where you are, and with whom you are. Whether you are in your own city or another country, whether you are with friends or total strangers, you will have The Program to help guide and nourish you.

The more you expand your Home Base, the more the new way becomes the comfortable and preferred way no matter what situation in which you find yourself in. All the successfully traversed big events should be part of your Home Base, too.

One college student said to me: "I wanted to have the college experience and overeat and drink at a tailgate party." It took her an entire week to get back to the weight she was before the tailgate party. Each exception to the rule reinforces the old way one more time, keeping it chronic.

You want to enlarge your Home Base so that no matter where you are, Plan A is in your cellphone along with twenty-seven ways to say "No, Thank You."

Look at each circle and decide if it is an Exception to the Rule for you, or if it is not a problem for you. If it is an Exception to the Rule, think about how many times you follow that old pattern in a week? Month? Year? Guestimate. After you've thought about each circle, add them up.

One person identified five situations where he tends to overeat. One situation was an exception six times a year. Every couple of months. Three situations where he overate 36 times a year and one was 24 times a year for a total of 66 times a year where he was off his Program, surrendering to unplanned food, food he didn't need, food he wasn't thinking about until he was surrounded by it at some holiday, business, or family function. This is where an arsenal of thought, word, and action will come in handy. What could you do or say or think to create new behavior for the smaller person you want to be and will be taking to the next food-laden get together?

How many times a year do you eat something because it was free at a restaurant, trade show, or check- out counter? Was your vacation an exception to the rule? A holiday feast? At the airport?

Each exception has rituals of its own. When at the airport you have that muscle memory of packages of peanuts coming down the aisle. I would always ask the flight attendant for a second package. I never asked myself if I was hungry. I never read the package information. I never ate peanuts at any other time. It's the old rituals that calm us down.

No matter what kind of trade show, most booths tempt with chocolate, popcorn, and other lovely things to eat.

See how many exceptions to the rules you find. How many problems do you identify with? How many solutions will you be using?

It's a good time to review what you've read until now. See page 321 for Review Number Three.

CHAPTER 6

Away From
Home Base

FIVE FOOD FUMBLES THAT DEFEAT YOUR BEST WEIGHT-LOSS INTENTIONS

Are any of the following an Exception to the Rule?

Waiting for friends to arrive at a restaurant, I see the diners at every table doing things I did for years before I lost fifty pounds: mindlessly eating much of the contents of a basket of bread (slathered with butter or dipped into herbed olive oil), sipping a glass of wine as if it were water, and nibbling on olives that were put on the table — a food you'd most likely never order.

Although many eating opportunities — parties, holidays, smorgasbords, and salad bars —are a challenge, eating a sit-down dinner in a restaurant may be a throwback to your first out-of-home eating experience, a special occasion where you were encouraged to order anything on the menu, or at least to taste a wide variety of food offerings. Moreover, you may have eaten the free food such as bread, salad, starch that came with the meal. You still may think, "It's free; eat it!" Free food is not a good reason to eat. Consider the five most common restaurant food-traps and how to traverse the terrain:

1. **Everyone else is eating everything. I don't want to be left out.** At a popular restaurant or with friends who have the recipe of the week, it's hard to refuse the braised truffle salad, kiwi fruit-tart, or other recently popularized food. But eating all the offered food won't make you smaller than you are. You don't have to say, "Yes" to everything. You don't have to eat it all, just because it's put on your plate.

Find things to say to those with whom you are eating; it's a gathering to visit with others. Food is just a part of the festivities.

2. **I see it. I want it. I order it. I eat it.** People with weight problems tend to order impulsively based on the menu or circumstance. The connection between action at mealtime and the consequence at weigh-in time is usually obscured by forgetfulness. To succeed, you have to anticipate, plan ahead, call ahead, and be mindfully present at each food encounter. Every restaurant now has a website showing its menu. What a nice addition for all of us to use. Plan ahead in writing.

Enjoy conversation and the ambiance and concentrate on your goal: Remember: It's just food. A few minutes ago, it was produce. And in a few days, it will be fat.

3. **It looks good. It smells good.** Yes. It does look and smell good. But the idea is to eat only when you're hungry. And if at the time you are eating, the food tastes, looks, or smells good, it's a bonus. Taste, look, and smell are not sufficient reasons to eat. Eat to nourish your body, not to entertain yourself or distract yourself from feeling sad or glad.

Whenever eating, wear a belt buckled on snug. Remain conscious around food. Be present in your own life.

4. **It's my favorite. It's the specialty of the house. It's the best "whatever" I ever tasted.** Favorite foods will always be around to call your name. Your desire for them heightens

when someone else is pushing you to say, "Yes" in order to please him or her. By doing this, you're putting your desire to weigh _____ pounds on the back burner. You can always have the object of your affection when you've planned it, not when you happen upon it. You weren't thinking of it a minute ago, were you? It is a visual or sensory stimulation.

Turn your head. Change location. Move you. Move it. Try to stick to your plan.

Find other things on which to focus. I used to tell my friends what I wanted and then I'd go to the lady's room. By the time I returned it was a done deal. I didn't have to be tempted by a waiter embellishing the descriptions of the entrées or describing a "special" on the menu. I didn't get tempted by what others at the table were ordering. Eventually I could order it myself and didn't have to excuse myself from the table. It's a process.

5. **It was a price-fixed meal. I paid for it. It came with the meal.** It's so hard for most overeaters to forsake food that has already been purchased. But steer clear of the bargains. Order á la carte instead of a *prix fixe* meal. In this way, you'll get closer to the amount of food you need, instead of succumbing to what someone else wants you to have based on what they want to charge.

Serve yourself French style (food on an individual plate for each person), rather than Family style (food on a serving platter from which you serve yourself). Even some individual portions of food are enormous. My assistant brought me leftovers from her meal the night before. I had it for dinner one night and there was still another portion that we threw away. She'd had the first portion in the restaurant. She paid for one meal but received three.

Transfer take-out food from the container onto a flat plate one spoonful at a time. You'll gain a whole new perspective about how much is enough while reaching your goal. Select the choicest pieces. Get the items you planned on having, rather than being tempted to put (and eat) second and third helpings on your plate just because they are there.

Think of restaurants and any food-laden big event as an extension of your kitchen except someone else is shopping, mincing, chopping, sautéing, cooking, and cleaning up afterward. You wouldn't serve yourself a drink, a basket of bread, an appetizer, main course, dessert, and coffee if you were home alone, would you? Of course not, because you want to weigh _____ pounds. And it's too much trouble. So are you eating so much more in a restaurant just because someone else is cooking? That's not a reason to eat either.

When dining out, these are just a few of the numerous triggers that have a practiced reaction. Which Food Fumbles do you need to repattern?

Dianne R. found herself unable to eat regular meals because she worked in the Emergency Room of a local hospital, which was constantly busy with patients. She kept candy bars and other such instant foods in her pocket and tried to steal a minute away when she could eat. When she came home, she often found herself bingeing on whatever instant food she found in her cabinets.

Dianne R.: What if I were mindfully to eat a candy bar?

Caryl: If you're hungry and eat a candy bar, your brain will not register satiation. Sugar doesn't satisfy a craving for sugar. It creates a craving for *more* sugar. You'll still be hungry and want more food or perhaps more candy. You're reinforcing an old habit that will yield an old weight. Reinforcing a habit keeps it habitual.

How about keeping a tuna pouch, a hard-boiled egg, or some sliced turkey in the office. You can cut the turkey into cubes so you can spear it with a fork. Mix the tuna with mayo before you get to the office. Even cold cereal that you can eat a bite at a time is better than a candy bar.

Gia V.: I am up to my ears in boxes and amidst apartment chaos in the midst of a move. Aside from that, all is well. I have been doing the Program as best as I can, though I could be doing a lot better. I am staying on track with the food pretty well and maintaining weight loss with only a few pounds to go. I think I will be more focused after this move and I have my kitchen back.

Caryl: It sounds as if you are doing better than had you not been doing your Program. You are mindful and conscious, and in the past, you might have eaten differently or more often. You're down another two pounds from when you'd gained it and lost it before. No matter what, chaos is not a reason to eat. You can take a break every now and then without having to use the excuse that you're stopping work because you want to eat. It's enough to say you need a break.

Lucia M.: I went to a friend's house for dinner and held to my plan notwithstanding that the host is like an insecure Jewish mother: "How do you like my soup; isn't it good? What do you mean you want only two chops from the rack of lamb?" I practiced working on counting items yesterday and kept to my plan. It was fewer items and it was fine.

Caryl: Your narrative is so funny. I can almost picture him standing near you with a platter of something like dinner for four in the serving spoon poised above your left shoulder. Better even than the fabulous Quantum Leaps you've described is that you were aware and mindful and conscious, and it was all okay.

THE POINT OF PURCHASE

Is this an Exception to the Rule?

Are you one of those people who eats every bit of food you bring into your home? Do you finish every last drop of food on your plate? If you buy a pound of food, do you feel compelled to eat it because you paid for it? If you wait until you're about to eat, or you're thinking about what to do mid-meal, it is often too late to take constructive action. It needs to be done prior to the time you begin your slide into the speedy trajectory of your habit. Where do you begin to change? Change begins at the Point of Purchase.

Whether it is at the cash register in a small grocery store near your home (where there is a wall of candy and breath mints below the counter by the cash register), or a salad bar the size of a dance floor in a banquet hall, or in a chi-chi-poo-poo restaurant, you want to plan ahead and think ahead. You only have to ask yourself at the Point of Purchase whether you were thinking of any of the food you're about to purchase before you left your home. Was the food you now cannot seem to live without on your shopping list? Was it on your planning list? Any list? No? Then pull out your bag of coping strategies.

Years ago I'd fill up my grocery cart and then end up eating more than I needed so it wouldn't spoil. A no-win game.

Now when I shop, I think of which meal I'll eat at home and how many portions of vegetables or salads and protein I'll need and for which days. This way of shopping insures variety too.

Make a shopping list. Working with a shopping list reinforces mindful (rather than mindless) purchases. One thing I remind myself is that I won't remember later any of the should-I-shouldn't-I battles I have between the Addict Pea Brain voice and The Program voice. You just have to get past the Point of Purchase and then everything is going to be okay. What can you do to help the moment pass?

The following recaptures a personal battle between the Addict Pea Brain and The Program Brain from my past: I'm tired this afternoon — emotionally fatigued. After deciding to have dessert with dinner, I find a candy I like in a grocery store and I decide to buy it. Only problem is I'm playing lockstep with the cement floor, the question being: Should I buy one bar or two? Bingo — I'm in my addiction cycle. Should I? Shouldn't I? I want it — Yes. No. Yes. No. Yes. No. Yes! Should I? Shouldn't I? My mind makes pro and con lists. Weight-control mantras are repeated: I want to weigh _____ pounds. I only eat when I'm hungry. I'm not hungry now. I recall the remorse. I breathe deeply. I exhale all the pent-up tension. I remind myself none of this is a reason to eat. I tell myself: move, change location, turn around, walk. I unclench my fists. My breathing slows. My jaw unclenches. I'm calmer now. I pick one object of my affection. The moment has passed.

Later that night, I decide to have a hearty soup for dinner followed by my dessert. It is cut into pieces on a plate, with each piece slowly speared with a fork, like I had practiced, savored, stretched, and enjoyed with water sipped on the side. Dinner ends. Lovely.

Then later, around 12:30 a.m., I'm tired and should've gone to bed earlier. I browse for food, open cabinets in the kitchen. Nothing. Nothing. Nothing. I open the refrigerator and freezer looking for instant food. Nothing. Nothing. Nothing is there either. I double-check them; then I check e-mail, then turn off the computer. I drink some water. I check the television — it's reruns. I'll write. The moment passes.

If you buy one of anything, it'll be enough. If the second dessert were here, I would have eaten it. It was at the Point of Purchase that I won the day. Of course, if you don't succeed the first time at the point of purchase, clean out your cupboards and throw food away. Don't want to do that? Then buy less next time.

Teresa B. would always stop by her local candy store for a sweet. She also enjoyed giving treats to her children and grandchildren.

Teresa: I know I need to approach my sweets addiction differently, but how? Could you please clarify and give me some more specific direction? I'd really appreciate it.

Caryl: Get to the point where you're only eating when you're hungry enough to put food on a plate and make the meal last for twenty minutes or more. Then, after you've made sure your nutritional needs are met, you choose (or not) from the top or bottom (bread, beverage, dessert, alcohol, one of four or none) from the Meal Parameters list. The more you plan it, the easier it is to succeed.

Being mindful and aware at Point of Purchase is critical. Begin by purchasing one soda to have with a specific meal. Then when you plan another soda, you may purchase another. If you're purchasing instant foods in boxfuls, bagsful, and six-packs, you'll nibble away until they're gone. That's the cycle of addiction. Gonna eat it 'til it's gone. It's like a fifty-dollar bill. I can carry one around for months. But once I break it, the two twenties and a ten, become all tens, then fives, then singles, and then they're gone.

Work on repatterning your behavior at the place where you're buying food to bring home. Plan what you're going to do at the Point of Purchase. And follow through with new thoughts, words, and actions.

Water is a most beneficial tool. It flushes out toxins, brings nutrients to where they need to be, moisturizes the skin, and you can drink it during moments of stress. A few sips of water will help a moment pass when you didn't really feel hungry. If you tried the water and were still hungry, then a Fourth Meal might be helpful.

Jeff D.: Not only is bread the most longed-for part of my intake, but it turns out that sandwiches are by far the least messy lunch to have at my desk. There's very little opportunity for me to have lunch elsewhere. Is there any solution?

Caryl: When I was working in the evenings, freelancing as a typist while starting my business, a container of soup was the easiest and most varietal food I could bring to work. I could eat it hot or cold and as slowly or quickly as I wanted. It was tasty and satisfying. I'd have a bite or two and close the container. Then I'd sip some water until I was ready for my next bite. In between, I typed.

Years ago, when I began my quest to lose weight and keep it off, there was me and Campbell's Chicken Noodle Soup. Today, numerous places offer as many as a dozen fresh soups daily. Most homes and offices have a microwave to warm your food purchases. The comedian Ray Romano said about soup on the *Late Show with David Letterman*: Hot. Cold. A meal. Perfect.

If you have two slices of bread in a sandwich daily for a year (five days a week, fifty-two weeks a year) you'll have it 260 times, or 520 slices if you're eating a sandwich each day. That's approximately twenty-five loaves of bread. But if you Skip and Scatter every other day, and have one piece instead of two, you'll only have it 130 times a year, so you'll end up with a noticeable weight loss. Have a half-piece of bread instead of a whole piece — consistently — and you'll lose even more. You're smaller. You don't need as much food.

It takes six to eight weeks for your physical weight loss to catch up with your brain. You might still see yourself as the bigger person you were and try to feed that person. You are smaller, so you don't need as much food.

It is at Point of Purchase that you at least want to try the small soup container. There's a real fear that "It won't be enough," no matter what "it" is. So trying a different size portion might be scary. That's a perfect time for some mental repatterning. Think,

"If the cup of soup isn't enough, I'll have a Fourth Meal." If you're eating those nickel-sized bites, putting the spoon down between bites of soup, and sipping water between bites of food, the new size will be enough.

Talking yourself through a moment of indecision, you might tell yourself, "Everything's going to be okay; the moment will pass; I don't need as much food as I used to think I needed."

You can get used to everything, as evidenced by your habit of eating pasta and potatoes because that's what your wife cooks.

You could also have the turkey from a sandwich (deconstructing a sandwich by always putting bread on the side). Take one nickel-sized bite of bread, use a knife and fork for the turkey (tuna/chicken/shrimp), and sip water between bites. Chances are you won't finish two pieces of bread. Most likely, you won't finish one piece. When variety becomes a habit, it's unlikely you'll want to eat the same foods and beverages for two meals, or two days in a row.

Make Up Your Mind Before a Reservation

Is this an Exception to the Rule?

When in a restaurant, you may think the key decision is to order a salad instead of a steak, steamed vegetables instead of a shimmering soufflé, or a simple side dish instead of a sinful dessert. But is it? When you're already seated in a restaurant, it may be too late to decide what to eat. Habits and memories abound.

With a waiter looking to increase his tip and the maitre d' offering a complimentary cocktail, free bread, and an extra cup of coffee, it is hard to say, "No, thank you." And what about the sights, smells, and sounds of the foods being described? It's all designed to whet the weakest appetite and erode the strongest weight-loss resolve.

So how do you hop over hurdles? Traverse the temptations? Obliterate the obstacles? You make up your mind *before* you sit down, whether at home or in a restaurant. You need to decide what to do *in advance* of the avalanche. It's then a matter of purchasing and preparing, or ordering, the food you planned on eating rather than merely surrendering to the seduction of what is there. It's being pro-active rather than reactive.

However, if you arrive at your eating destination without a specific plan and you choose what to eat at the last minute, then you didn't really decide. A businessperson would never walk into a meeting without knowing what he or she was trying to accomplish. An attorney would never walk into a courtroom without knowing what he or she was going to say. You're a person with a mission to reach your weight-loss goal, so you need to have a plan. A goal without a plan is just a daydream.

If you anticipate the offerings in the sane quietude of your home or office, you'll be able to decide what you need. Then you can find what you're looking for. Almost every restaurant now has its menu posted online, which is enormously helpful. If it doesn't, the restaurant staff will usually be happy to fax a menu to you, or even discuss the menu with you over the phone. It helps if you plan ahead so you don't slow down the festivities at the dinner table. It also helps to eliminate meal-time stress, or at least reduce it.

If you don't know ahead of time where you're going to eat because of the situation or circumstances, you can't always plan ahead or get what you've planned. This may be true, but you can still plan the number of items you're going to eat at that meal. You can still plan, in advance, if you'll have (or not) bread, or beverage, or dessert, or alcohol. Those are things you can do.

You can think about whether it is a Protein or No-Protein Meal. Even if it is far from what you wanted, you can still take nickel-sized bites.

If you spend a lot of time in airports or in other people's homes, there are two types of meals: a Protein Meal (chicken or fish meal) and a No-Protein Meal (soup, all-vegetable). Once you've established which category you need, protein or no-protein, it's easy enough to find that item almost anywhere you eat. Even if an official All-Vegetable Meal isn't available, most restaurants are happy to accommodate special requests. They always have a vegetable in the kitchen and usually a baked potato or other starch. You'll find things to eat. Again, know the *category of food*, and *the number of items* in advance of putting your hand on a restaurant door.

Beforehand, write down which courses you're going to order. The choice isn't always between the lettuce and the lentil soup. Sometimes the questions are: Are you hungry? Where are you going to use this food/fuel after the meal? How much of what is served will help you reach your weight-loss goal? If you write your plan, rather than only thinking of doing something, you have a better chance of success. Just scribble on a piece of paper whether your Protein or No-Protein Meal is going to be a one-item, two-item, or three-item meal.

Assess Success

Do a reality check mid-meal. See how well your plan is going. Did you find the foods for which you were looking? Did you manage to refuse gracefully any unplanned foods? *Not doing anything is a choice not to do anything.* Sometimes leaving the table mid-meal — finding a bathroom, a view, a public phone — breaks the thrall of food and the habit of shoveling. Upon returning to the table, you may only be hungry enough for one or two more bites of food. If you'd stayed in your seat, you may have eaten many more bites than that. One, two, three, move.

"Habit is habit," said Mark Twain, "and not to be flung out the window by any man, but to be coaxed downstairs a step at a time."

Mary W.: On Sunday, I had two killer finals in the morning and planned to meet a friend for a movie around 1 p.m. My plan was to eat lunch first and then skip popcorn. Unfortunately, I got back from classes very late and had no time to eat lunch. By the time I got to the movie, the popcorn whispered sweet poppings in my ear. When I arrived at the movie theatre, I was famished and dived into the popcorn.

Caryl: There's a saying that is always true: No matter how long you think something is going to take, it takes longer. Next time, try a Fourth Meal such as a hard-boiled egg, turkey, or bring a tuna pouch to have at the ready along with plastic utensils. If you need it, you'll be prepared, but only if you think to plan ahead.

Would you leave your home without an umbrella if you knew it was going to rain? Of course not. Would you dial a phone number unless you knew what you wanted of the person at the other end? Be prepared by integrating your eating into your life. Enter meal plans into your agenda book. Plot your weight-control goal on the front burner of your life rather than on a back burner like an embarrassing relative.

Fred S. often has to go to lunches or dinners with potential clients. He has a nervous disposition, and socializing with friends, coworkers, and other people in his industry calms him down. He likes to eat at nice restaurants, which often serve large portions. After dinner, he and his companions usually go to a bar for drinks.

Fred S.: I like the company, but I'm not sure how to offer someone a drink and not drink with them.

Caryl: Yes, The Program covers many particulars about eating out: weddings, bar mitzvahs, cocktail parties, holidays, weekends away, and drinks with friends and potential clients. This is a good time to find the right *tone of refusal.* The perfect phrase to say could be, "None for me, but I'll keep you company." Give it some thought lest you keep eating to please someone else. Other phrases might be, "I'm fine," "I'm not hungry," "You go ahead," "A big glass of ice water, thanks," and "I'm the designated driver." Come up with a few of your own tried and true phrases.

Uma M.: Tonight, I have one of those celebration challenges. We are celebrating my parents' fiftieth wedding anniversary at the River Café. It is a three-course, *prix fixe* meal, and I would like some tips on how to handle myself.

Caryl: A three-course *prix fixe* meal can yield six to eight items. At a recent dinner I attended near Broadway, free refills of the main course were periodically offered, which included various chicken, pasta/rice/potato, and vegetable or salad selections. All this was in addition to the appetizer, dessert, and coffee, as well as a big basket of bread on the table.

My point: Plan in advance. Select two or three things and write them down. A three-course *prix fixe* meal contains many more than three items. The main course usually comes with a salad and a starch. Are you going to eat both items? One? Are you going to have bread *or* beverage *or* dessert *or* alcohol? One of four or none? Do you want to weigh your old weight when you're finished with dinner or be closer to your goal weight? Mid-meal, ask yourself, "Am I still hungry?"

What time is the meal? You might want to eat a Fourth Meal before you leave for the restaurant so you won't be overly hungry when everyone is going through the bread, alcohol, and appetizers. Recommit to your goal before you leave for the party. The choice isn't prime rib or Chilean sea bass. The choice is: Do you want to weigh your present overweight weight? Or do you want to weigh your goal weight of _____ pounds? This is a perfect time to utilize some of those new action steps you've been practicing. Remember: It's not like you're doing anything to burn off your dinner. You'll be sitting all evening.

Annie L.: I travel almost every week for work, and eating out becomes one of the only non-work-related activities that gets me out of the hotel. I've gained fifty-five pounds in the past fifteen years.

Caryl: I totally relate. When we were children, a visit to a restaurant was most likely a rare event: someone's wedding, your grandparents' fiftieth anniversary, to celebrate a milestone in someone's life. Now you (and I) eat in restaurants as a regular part of our lives. Do you still think of a restaurant mainly as a place to celebrate with food? Probably.

Think of a restaurant as an extension of your own home. If you were serving yourself at home, would you put a basket of bread on the table and have two alcoholic drinks, an appetizer, a three-item main course, plus dessert, and coffee? Of course you would not. When thinking of getting food, especially in a restaurant, try to replicate the number of items or amounts you have at home — which is enough.

Learn to deal with the momentary emotional discomfort in a different, food-free way.

Learn to be around food — it's everywhere — by planning ahead. If one or two items is enough in your Home Base, extend those concepts to a restaurant, your friend's home, or a business meeting. No matter where you are in the world, you're eating the same amount of food as you do when you're in your own home. Consistency leads to success.

Gisela C. is constantly on the run and tends to eat a lot of fast food. She finds that pizza is a quick and easy meal. She often has to entertain her clients at night and frequently finds herself drinking at a bar.

Gisela C.: If I have to go out for drinks with clients, what should I do?

Caryl: Try drinking water until mealtime. If you drink alcohol at the bar, you would basically be having a No-Meal Meal on an empty stomach. Alcohol causes lack of resolve. You'll end up eating unplanned food. Order bottled water. Or sit at a table and order something to eat. Get a glass of water to sip between bites and swallows. Order something that needs to be eaten with utensils so you'll have something to cushion the alcohol's effects. Intersperse with plenty of water and conversation.

Most business meetings are an excuse to talk business and having alcohol clouds the mind. Keep working on this one. Every person I teach comes up with a different workable solution. What works for you?

If necessary, I offer to be the designated driver. And frankly, no one seems to care whether or not I drink. There are a million reasons not to drink while others are drinking. Find a few phrases that will work for you.

Lena M.: If you go to a Chinese [buffet] restaurant with a bunch of people, is it still critical to limit the number of items rather than just quantity? Does the same question go for a cocktail party when you won't have a chance to eat dinner later?

Caryl: Yes. You want to weigh _____ pounds, and the smaller you doesn't need a lot of food, no matter where you are. No matter the circumstances

You are a smaller person and need fewer items of food at each meal. Each exception to the rule (like the times you eat too quickly without utensils) becomes another and another and another exception. Part of the goal is to try to do your Program no matter where you are or who you are with.

Prepare phrases to say to people with whom you're eating. You can say, "I just had a big lunch and this is plenty." Or, "I'm fine, but you go ahead." I tell people who inquire that what I ordered was exactly what I wanted. And it is because I always look online to see the menu of a restaurant I'll be going to.

Rehearse a couple of "No thank yous." There is no change without change. All effort accumulates. Remember, even one bite of food left on your plate each meal is more than a thousand bites at the end of the year. All those bites add up to a lot of items.

Ian S.: My family gets together once a week to eat a meal together and catch up. My mother cooks a feast for us. I don't think I'm addicted to food and am pretty careful with how I eat, but the food selection is very starch, sugar, and carbohydrate heavy. My family serves a lot of potatoes, pasta salads, along with many side dishes in every meal. I can see that my family members eat very poorly, and I could easily fall into that as well. How can you modify the behavior of an entire family when everybody is using the same foods so abundantly?

Caryl: You cannot change others. Everyone has to do it for him- or herself. You can, however, think about what you will do *under the circumstances*. The choice of what you eat is always yours. Even if there is chicken, broccoli, and a potato served in a meal, that doesn't mean you have to choose to eat all three of the items. It means that sometimes you might say, "Yes" to two of the items — say, the broccoli and the chicken. Sometimes the chicken is enough food. Depends on where you need this food/fuel to take you. You might want the broccoli and potato at one meal for an All-Vegetable meal. With regard to your family, it's hard enough to change yourself. The best you can do is to take care of yourself. If you bring food for yourself, bring it for another five or more people too. Walk in with your dish already prepared so you don't have to borrow already stressed oven time. Maybe roasted veggies you might only have to microwave. Bringing a salad is usually appreciated.

Jarrad G.: I weighed 238.5 pounds this morning (round down to 238) — down two from Thursday and down nine pounds since we started ten days ago. The weekend was tough —birthday party plus a two-plus hour formal dinner at a Greek restaurant. And yet I know I did better than I would have. I knew there would be an abundance of red wine being served, so as soon as we were seated, I told the waiter, "I would love lots of icy cold water, and keep it coming!" and refused to have my glass filled with red wine even though my five dining companions all got their glasses filled (very challenging — never did that before). I was fine; actually, better than fine — great!

Caryl: Never refused several glasses of wine before? And you lived to tell the tale. You found other techniques to deal with discomfort. With so many people around you, you found ways to cope with the anxiety of feeding the smaller person you are. Keep polishing those fragile steps. As your resolve to reach your goal (and stay at your goal weight) gets stronger and stronger, you'll be more resolved with your assignments. You'll find it helpful to use positive words, phrases, and tones when facing these food encounters. Think that the weekend was different or challenging rather than tough.

Jarrad G.: I did sample each of the appetizers, small portions over thirty minutes. Even though my Addict Pea Brain was dumb enough to order lamb chops for a main course, I took two bites, realized I was no longer hungry, passed the plate to my wife, and asked the waitress to wrap it up to go.

Caryl: You were sated with the appetizers, but you ordered lamb chops. Excellent rebound realizing you were no longer hungry. This new smaller you doesn't require as much food. This new you fills up on the ambiance and chit-chat. Nice job. Next time, you most likely won't order the main course.

BIG EVENT EATING STRATEGY SHEET

Is this an Exception to the Rule?

- Eat breakfast and lunch the day of the event. Starving all day as an excuse to overeat doesn't work. Plan ahead instead.
- In a relaxed, quiet atmosphere, envision what food and drink you'll be encountering and plan, in advance, in writing, what you want to do. How many items are appropriate? What are they to be? Are you planning on bread or beverage or dessert or alcohol? Remember, one of four or none. What behavioral techniques do you plan to use to help lessen food-related anxiety?
- Wear a belt with a buckle, whenever eating and whenever necessary. Clothing with a waistband is better than something with elastic or some other stretchy material.
- While in attendance, keep moving. Help the hostess, play with children. Talk to everyone in the room before looking at the food. Don't linger near the buffet table.
- Get a glass of water to carry around and drink. Throughout the party and whenever needed, relax, deep breath, and stretch to reduce socially-anxious moments. If wall-to-wall food is imminent, consider arriving a little late.
- If it is a buffet meal, first walk around the table *without a plate*. Identify the foods on the table; i.e., that's a protein. That's a green vegetable. I don't know what the brown thing is. Then, pick up a plate and make your own selections — is it a one-item, a two-item, or a three-item meal? Remember, it's not the last supper; it's just another meal.
- Decide, *before* arriving, whether you'll choose bread *or* beverage *or* dessert *or* alcohol rather than deciding you'll

have all four. (Is the bread really unique, the coffee unusual, the extra drink adding to your enjoyment?)

- Find a place to eat where you can enjoy your meal in a relaxed manner while using a knife and fork. If this is not possible, stand and eat slowly while sipping water. One man told me there were no utensils, but he put his fingers down between bites of food. Was that okay? It was, but look for a fork.

- It is okay to tell your hosts you don't want a second helping of everything. They only want you to have a good time. You won't be having a good time if you eat too much and your clothes become tight. Overeating is not a reward. Fill up on the ambiance.

- Eat slowly and thoughtfully. Make each meal last a relaxing twenty minutes or more. Intersperse plenty of good conversation between bites.

- Less and less alcohol is needed as your total body weight diminishes. If alcohol is your choice instead of bread, beverage, or dessert, toast the holiday. But try to drink two sips of water for each sip of alcohol. Make sure to have a few bites of food before one sip of alcohol. No one else will know and no one else will care.

- Remember there will always be another meal, another holiday, another party. Keep in mind how much more fun they will be with a slimmer waistline.

- Do the best you can. There are a lot of choices to make. The first time, your plan may not turn out exactly as you pictured it to be. By reading your strategies and planning in advance what you want to accomplish, chances are you'll eat a little less, move a little more, put your fork down sooner, and feel a little better than had you not had a plan.

- Most of all, have a nice time. Being stuffed, bloated, or uncomfortable in your clothes does not enhance the enjoyment of the event. More is not better; it's only more.
- Enter into your smartphone as many strategies as you think will help — press one button and read *Everything's going to be okay; You won't remember any of it anyway,* and *I can do it.*
- If all else fails, flee the city with a friend.

MAKING UP YOUR MIND IS NOT ENOUGH

There are almost as many reasons why you eat as there are food products on the shelves. A grocery store chain in New York City contains upwards of 25,000 different items in the smallest branch of stores and more than 50,000 or more items in a suburban supermarket. The items on the shelves are all saying, "Buy me! Eat me! Enjoy me!" That message is here, there, everywhere. In a New York City Fifth Avenue department store, there is a display of candy for sale next to each cash register. No matter how bored or anxious you are while shopping, it's still not a reason to eat.

I hear it all the time — sentiments voiced by people who come to my office to lose weight, or send me e-mails, or leave messages on my answering machine. They tell me, "If I really wanted to lose weight, I probably would." Or "If I'd make up my mind not to eat such and such, I should be able to do it." Or they guess, "I really don't want to lose weight or I would have already done so." A young chef told me on the phone the other day, "I learned what to eat and how to cook correctly when I was in culinary school, but I can't seem to do it for myself."

A man I met for lunch commented (between eating a rather large sour pickle in two bites and consuming a grilled cheese sandwich in four bites), "I know what to do. I just don't do it."

Nothing could be further from the truth. *To know and not to do is not to know at all.*

It's not as simple as making up your mind; it's a rather complex tapestry woven of thoughts and actions, repeated food encounter after food encounter, until overeating has become so mindless you're not even aware of all the components that have gone into the mix.

Most of you are hardworking, accomplished individuals who have achieved success with school, business, and family. Yet reaching your weight-loss goal is the one thing you are unable to achieve.

There are many reasons why you eat more than you are able to burn. Finishing everything set before you will result in eating more than you need fuel-wise. All those reasons make it nearly impossible simply to make up your mind to stop eating and then accomplish it. Since those reasons and your habits keep you following a path of one step after another after another until you reach the heaviest you've ever been, you need to create a new set of steps to follow until you reach your ideal weight.

You can change your habits by filling up your life with new thoughts, hobbies, and projects to fill up the time you used to fill up with food. When you create a new life containing new thoughts, words, and actions, the weight loss is an inevitable fringe benefit.

Caryl: I'd say that 75 percent of the alcohol I drank when I moved to New York was because everyone else was drinking. I watched what others did and copied them so I would look like I knew what I was doing. I didn't.

As Aristotle said, "Excellence is not an act but a habit."

BEWARE OF THE FOOD PUSHER

Is this an Exception to the Rule?

If someone is trying to control what you eat, he or she may be trying to control you.

Be prepared so when asked what you want, you'll have an answer. Checking a menu online before heading out to eat is always a good idea.

If the Food Pusher is being particularly pushy, ask the person why your eating is so important to him or her.

Keep saying, "No thank you," but also turn the tables and say, "Would you like some of mine?"

And the ever popular "That's so kind, but no." You'd think saying, "No" would be enough. Sometimes you have to say it more than once.

No time of your own

Is this an Exception to the Rule?

Parents tell me how they are almost attacked by their children as soon as they walk into their homes. The kids are so excited and want to share their day with their parents. Then there is dinner to prepare, mail to be sorted, homework to be reviewed, e-mail to be checked, cleaning up after dinner. Whew! Not one moment of transition from *the working day* to the second job at home: *the working night.*

"It seems that the only time my children leave me alone is when I'm eating," one parent recounts. "It's not that I don't love them; I do. It's just that I've been going since 5:30 in the morning. and there is no time for myself. I'm just exhausted." Another reflects, "When I'm eating, I sort of zone out."

Once you pinpoint some of the reasons you're eating, you won't be able to ignore the myriad of other reasons you're eating when you're not hungry. Those underlying reasons drive you to use food as a drug because of tremendous fatigue, unexpressed anger, frustration, anxiety, stress, and a newly identified method of self-silencing, among other things.

One of your goals is to replace your automatic responses to the stimuli (lonely, tired, it was there, it smelled good) with newly created responses. Ask yourself, "Why am I thinking of eating when I know I am not hungry?" And remind yourself, "I do want to weigh ____ pounds."

Learn to comfort yourself without food. If you feel stuffed, bloated, and not so good about yourself, then food is not a comfort. Food is not a friend. Find food-free things that will work for you. Put it in writing. Envision each thought, word, or action you intend to use. Create coping strategies. Imagine success. Making up your mind is not enough.

Brie S.: I have lost weight before and swore to myself that when I reached my goal, I would stay there, but the weight eventually crept back on.

Caryl: Making up your mind is not enough. Weight creeps back if the old behaviors creep back. If you do The Program, it works. If you stop doing it, it stops working.

Your goal is to polish all the new behaviors and new Program habits until they are familiar, automatic, and the default setting. Yours. If they start to slip, you'll notice right away and get those habits back into the flow.

You want to work to keep the old way dormant while bringing the new way to the forefront. "Power," says author Stephen R. Covey, "also includes the capacity to overcome deeply embedded habits and to cultivate higher, more effective ones."

Many people who lose weight by doing specific things eventually reach their goals. Then they erroneously think, "I don't have to do those specific things anymore." Yes, you do, my little buttercup. And then you must do them again.

Heidi M.: I have read your book and have been doing very well so far. But last night I had my first bite of chocolate as a dessert and totally lost control. I couldn't stop eating chocolate for the rest of the night. Does this mean I should not eat chocolate ever again?

Caryl: You should eat chocolate again. But there are other things to ask: Were you eating the chocolate as part of a meal that was eaten with a knife and fork (utensils) and lasted for twenty minutes or more? Yes? Then you're fine. If not, you may have been eating a No-Meal Meal and the sugar was not cushioned with the consumption of other food. That's not fine.

Did you bring extra dessert into your home thinking you could handle it? That's not fine. Other variables to ask yourself are: What happened when you went from *I'm okay, I'm okay,* to *I'm not okay?* Were you tired or bored or angry from something that happened earlier in the day?

Heidi M.: Now I know. When my cellphone rings, it's either my boss telling me I'm not where he wants me to be, which is on-call twenty-four hours a day, or it's my companion of fifteen years wanting to know why I'm not coming home right after work. I'm so busy taking care of them, I have no time to take care of myself. So I eat, I drink, I chew gum.

Caryl: Did you read your notes, review sections of the book, drink water, and move? Did you do anything to repattern? Or did you surrender to the thrall of food only to reinforce *that* behavior once again. And notice the remorse afterward. That's part of the cycle of addiction, too.

You want to weigh _____ pounds because you are worth it. You are worth taking care of in a meaningful way. You're taking care of your boss (twenty-four hours on call — whew!) and your companion, and you're in the back of the line. Taking care of yourself first takes getting used to but pays off. When you feel better and look better, everyone will benefit.

Take a deep breath. You're not a machine. It takes time to learn to do all the assignments, and it is a process until it all gels together. It's the journey. Embrace each new concept until it is your own. What will you do next time? Think about it because there will be a next time. And a time after that. Something triggered the situation. Move you or it. Throw things away. Recommit to your goal. Get back on your program.

Katie F. was a sixty-five-year old who'd had a tough time dealing with her recent divorce and found herself feeling very lonely at nights.

Katie F.: Why do I continue to eat while I sit there thinking, "I'm not hungry; why am I eating?" I'm even embarrassed to tell anyone about it. Sometimes it makes me afraid to be alone in my house.

Caryl: You may be angry that you're no longer married. Perhaps angry at your husband for not helping work it out, angry at yourself for not keeping it together, angry at being vulnerable and lonely. A million reasons, and yet, none of them is a valid reason to eat. The out-of-control-with-food person is sitting there thinking, "I'm not hungry; why am I eating?" and yet continues to eat. You may need to go through a mourning period: the end of your old way of life, the beginning of a new way of living.

Part of your cycle is being embarrassed to tell anyone about it — keeping it a secret. Part of your cycle is eating and staying occupied. In this way, you don't have to face the fact that you are alone and afraid in your house. You eat to relieve the discomfort of not eating. All of those behaviors keep you locked into where you are.

Think about other things you could do that might work better for you. Perhaps moving, finding a volunteer job, learning a language, going to the movies, or doing a jigsaw puzzle will occupy your mind to help a difficult moment pass. Just seeking out another person to tell your troubles to will be enormously helpful. Find one person who will listen to what you have in your heart. What other ways can friends help you? Call them.

EXCEPTION TO THE RULE

Why do cocktail parties and celebrations seem more difficult to navigate food-wise than your everyday food life?

You may think you have one big eating disorder that encompasses all your eating encounters, including business, travel, vacation, and special occasions. In reality, each one of those situations has rituals of its own.

It may be that because for three or four months you've remained on your Program at your current weight, you erroneously imagine you'll do the same things when you are on vacation or a business trip. It's a nice thought. But not necessarily true. Vacations have their own food and eating traditions.

Home Base is the place you spend most of your time — your home, office, with friends and coworkers — where you may have eaten in the past when you weren't hungry, but no longer do. The movie theater is becoming part of your Home Base when you buy water because you only eat when committing to a meal. Of course, if you want the popcorn as a side with the chicken *cordon bleu*, then do so. But eating in the movie theater does not meet that Home Base criteria. Eating in the movie theater is an Exception to the Rule.

One man told me that, "*Popcorn in the movies is part of the experience.*" It's also part of his weight-gaining experience. You've conquered the most frequently executed habits by changing these habits with new thoughts, words, and actions. Now, you may handle each one of the previous food encounters a little better than you previously handled them.

A food encounter when traveling may seem similar to your Home Base. It is not. The Home Base has many actions and reactions practiced for days or weeks or months, usually on a daily basis. Traveling long distances is not usually a daily act. As a newly smaller person, you're in for a lot of firsts: the first ride to the airport, first time through tightened security, first time wearing a tightened seat belt, first time through a buffet table the size of a basketball court. The Addict Pea Brain thinks, "I don't do this all the time. I'll just have such and such. It looks so good, and it can't hurt since it's not *all* the time." You think you're eating it because it looks great or it smells great. You think you cannot resist. It isn't any of those things. You think it's okay to eat more than you're able to burn, to eat more than you need or want or planned just this once because this is a rare and isolated experience. It's not, and you're in denial.

When you travel, you follow a previously practiced path of actions and reactions that you have practiced and perfected from the time you took your first trip. And each trip thereafter, you added to your traveling rituals. The frequent traveler has ritualized his routine. When you are at the airport or in the hotel room, you're doing things differently from the Home Base you created. For example, when at the airport, I'd buy magazines I'd never buy in the City. I'd buy desserts when I knew I wasn't hungry. I'd look for the small bag of nuts coming down the airplane aisle. I was in a mindless travel mode.

At the airport, you might mindlessly order a fast-food meal — the same one you've been ordering for years. Would you be eating that when at home? At your hotel, you might be used to ordering room service at any time of day just because you can. Do you do that at your Home Base? I don't think so.

You're making exceptions to all your rules. There may be too many exceptions and no rule. You're reinforcing an infrequently used, but nevertheless, ritualized version of what you do on vacation such as: how you eat at a food court, what you do at someone's sweet sixteen or sixtieth surprise birthday party, or what you do at a friend's thirtieth wedding anniversary or because one of your best friends got her doctorate degree after ten years. You use celebrating as an excuse to make exceptions to the rules. Take a deep satisfying breath and exhale slowly.

I used to purchase a certain candy in New York. When I went on vacation I saw the same candy, which was only of interest because it was fifty cents less than in the City. I had no established habits of buying that candy while on vacation in that store but had many rituals created around buying candy near my apartment. Same candy. Two different experiences.

When you fall into the old patterns, different from your plan, you think you failed. You didn't fail. You bumped into a ritualized snarl of food-related habits and you did what you always did. You ate. The (flawed) perception is that you're making a conscious choice. The opposite is true. You most likely weren't thinking about eating a lot of unplanned food moments before you saw it, smelled it, or heard it described delectably in dulcet tones by a food purveyor: *Have this. Taste that. This is fabulous.* You say, "Yes" as if you'll never pass this way again.

Though it seems natural for you to think you're in control and making a decision to eat food you had not planned on eating, you're not. An in-control-around-food person is indifferent to food; indifferent to the smells and sights, the snap, crackle, and pop of it all. An indifferent-to-food person isn't interested in food unless he or she is hungry. An indifferent-to-food person only uses food as fuel. He or she can appreciate all the time and effort that has gone into the preparation of the food, thoroughly enjoys the taste and savors each bite, but knows that's not a reason to eat and will respond, "Looks good, but no thanks; I'm not hungry." It helps to integrate all your eating into a comprehensive whole, not "This is what I do at home and this is what I do on vacation."

I take a vacation trip every few years to visit friends and family in Las Vegas, and North Carolina. It is familiar and comfortable and somewhat ritualized. However, the six to eight times I've taken the trip in the past twenty years has led to the development of habits that are nothing like the daily and twice-daily (or more) rituals concocted over the same twenty years while at home.

When you revisit an infrequently visited scenario, you haven't had a chance to evaluate the old habits of travel, vacation, and fifty-year anniversaries. There has been no time to create a new scenario, to reinforce a more constructive pattern of thoughts; as a result, no matter where you are, you keep reinforcing The Exception to the Rules instead of The Program principles.

Plan ahead in writing all the things you're trying to accomplish. That would be the Basics of The Program. There's the keeping of the log, asking whether you're hungry or not, fork down between bites of food and sips of beverage, having soup or all-vegetable lunches and dinner once each day, weighing twice daily and other things you've read so far in this book. Make the time to think and plan ahead. Then there'll be more Rules and fewer Exceptions to the Rules.

Murray T.: My son and nephew are visiting for a month. I'll be fine. They'll eat anything.

Caryl: Since the scale is going in the wrong direction, perhaps you should be a little more thoughtful about food and the family visit. Visits from your family are powerful stimuli. It's easier to eat slowly when alone, and if you are practicing it consistently, you'll have the skills.

Your Home Base can additionally be thrown off by new visitors who bring their own habits with them. Those old habits are familiar and even comfortable. If you're not mindful, it's easy to drift back to the old way. Those old habits are more entrenched than the new habits. Exceptions don't just happen when you're out of your element, but also when another element enters your everyday life — enters your Home Base.

Find some satisfying soup and All-Vegetable Meals you can all enjoy. Watch your portion size. You can't compete with two teenage boys' eating habits. Rather than try to think of what everyone else is going to eat, it is easier for you to figure out where you can get your All-Vegetable Meal, a Soup Meal, cereal for breakfast, and the number of items you need.

Seneca B.: Tonight I am going for Happy Hour with friends. I am planning on eating something before I meet them; otherwise, I will end up eating junk later. I am going to have some wine. I am sure all the girls will end up ordering wings, nachos, and other bar food. My plan is to order either soup or an All-Vegetable Meal to eat while they munch on the things they order.

Caryl: You plan to have a Fourth Meal before you meet your friends. It will be very clear you're not hungry when you enter Happy Hour Heaven. Even if you decide to eat at the restaurant, order an appetizer portion, more as a courtesy. You don't have to do much but cut with knife and fork, sip water, have a few bites, and end the meal. The wine should be part of the meal. Sip water and wine. If you drink alcohol on an empty stomach, it causes lack of resolve and you'll end up eating things you had not planned. When in doubt, or even contemplating something you hadn't planned, get up from the table and find the bathroom, find a phone, find a view, or go outside to stretch and get some air. Move. When you calm yourself down, return to the table.

Georgina L.: The only positive story for yesterday was lunch. Nice and quiet, three items, no junk food. But dinner with the kids brought me to the pizza parlor where I ate a standard junk meal with ice cream to top it all off.

Caryl: You had pizza and ice cream, which is bread *and* cheese *and* dessert, another three-item meal. Three items are too much for you if you are not going to burn them off between dinner and bedtime. Today, aim for two-item meals and see what happens. If you eat slowly enough, even a one-item meal is enough. That's where repatterning techniques come in. If one item is not enough, have a Fourth Meal. Remember to choose either bread (crust of the pizza) *or* dessert (the ice cream) or alcohol or beverage; one of four or none.

Georgina L.: I guess I do sort of zone out. I eat junk food when the kids are hungry. It's easier than trying to find time for myself later. To be honest, I did the same thing the following day. I gave myself a peaceful lunch but then got sucked into Halloween junk candy and indulged in five pieces. I got back on track with dinner. Then I got swept into the ice cream.

Caryl: You're still in denial when you use terms such as *got sucked into Halloween junk, indulged in pieces,* and *swept into the ice cream,* as if it is some magical force. You are the force. Then you go on to think *you can handle it.* That's denial. You did not handle it. If you knew how to handle it, you would have handled it two, four, sixteen pounds ago.

There are no fat fairies who wrestle you to the ground and pour hot fudge in your mouth. Part of conquering your addiction to food is to get out of denial. You make it sound as if someone or something came along, hurricane-like, and swept you away from your plan.

There are only two questions to ask: Did you do better this time than you might have had you not been reading your notes?

What could you do next time? Only next time, you'll be a little thinner and a little more thoughtful. You'll buy a little less and not eat when you are lonely, stressed, bored, worried, happy, or excited. Look for thoughts you can tell yourself and words you can tell others that will work for Halloween as well as other ice cream-laden festivities.

You appear to be jumping from junk food to pizza to Halloween candy. It's all the same category: instant, quick, finger food. These are the things that need repatterning. You have to find new ways to cope with anxiety and boredom without always looking for some instant way to relieve your anxiety. Is there a green vegetable in your future? Some lean protein? Nutrition?

In your case, compulsivity is what needs to be repatterned. Did you ask, "Am I hungry? Am I hungry enough to put food on a plate? To make it last for twenty minutes?" Not that hungry? Do something else. And that is the crux of it. You want to address each assignment with relish (and maybe some mustard).

If you have too many Exceptions to the Rule, you'll have no Rules, just Exceptions. If you drop a stich here, here, and there, eventually the whole sweater unravels.

Paulo J.: Positive story is, at the airport early Saturday morning, while (sort of) rushing to the plane, I stopped for breakfast. Only thing available was egg and cheese on a roll. Got out the knife and fork, removed the four sections of roll, ate the egg omelet with knife and fork, drank lots of water, talked to my traveling companion (about your Program), and scraped a little cheese off the roll for taste. It probably took ten, maybe more, minutes eating this one egg omelet. Felt satisfied, no longer hungry, and still made the plane.

Caryl: Remember this moment so the next time it happens, and there are even more delays and more temptations, you will recall that it was all okay. If it is okay in the present, then it will certainly be okay in the future because in the future, you will be a smaller person and you won't need the same quantity of food to feel satisfied that you used to think you needed. You are internalizing The Program, and I'm sure it is showing in your clothing, choices, weight, and self-esteem.

In the past, you might have convinced yourself it was okay to overeat, to reward yourself for some real or imagined achievement, an Exception to the Rule. But this time, you were thoughtful and did so much better than what you used to do. You worked your Program and stuck to your plan of eating with utensils, deconstructing a sandwich, and even felt proud of what you did. If you put that story on your Quantum Leaps list, you'll come across it when reviewing. You'll see this story and think you did it once and it was okay, so you can do it again.

You didn't make any exceptions to your rules even though you had all the opportunities. You could have ordered a worse type of fast food. You could have given into feeling rushed and devoured the entire sandwich without using utensils. You could have spent one minute doing all of that and felt justified because you were rushing to catch your plane. But you didn't, and that is why you are continuing onward and downward!

Rebecca J.: My clothes are fitting better. There are such immediate big benefits from the smallest of efforts. I am slowing down and eating less. I am sipping water between bites of food; things I never did before. And it all is okay. I haven't had heartburn since I started slowing down.

I am cutting down on portions a little bit and drinking plenty of water. But what I wanted to tell you is how my Thanksgiving Day meal plan turned out. In the past, I've eaten a little (okay, a lot) of everything — even dishes I can have year-round and things I didn't even like. I always felt lousy afterward. This year, I decided not to make my Thanksgiving Day meal an Exception to my Program Rules. I wanted to try it and see how it went. I planned the items I would eat before I approached the dinner table: turkey, stuffing, and whole cranberries.

Many of the items like salad, string beans, Brussels sprouts, and sweet potatoes I can have year-round. I conversed with family and friends, put my utensils down in between bites, drank a lot of water, and to my surprise, I was satisfied. Even better, I didn't feel guilty or lethargic after. Everyone else was tired and weighed down from all the food they ate, but I was up and active. I even offered to do all the dishes and help clean-up. Now I know I can do this again and feel great doing it.

Caryl: Those are the same three items I choose. It's very satisfying. This is definitely a Quantum Leap! Write it down on your Quantum Leaps list so you remember you did it once and you can do it again. You should be proud that you didn't make an exception to a major holiday that is centered around overeating. I am sure you put a great amount of effort into staying on your Program, but do it often enough, meal after meal, and it will become the preferred way.

Ariana: Yesterday, my weight was down so my positive story is that I was on the way downward again. Today, I gained weight. Seems that the Super Bowl party last night did not follow The Program. I will also work on sending you some stuff about being caffeine-free and how I love it this week.

Caryl: As for working on sending me some things about being caffeine-free and loving it: Excellent. As for going off your Program, realize that you walked into an eating encounter (the Super Bowl party) that had an established food fest ritual with an established frequency and portion size of its own. You stumbled. The question is: Did you do better than you might have in the past? Did you stop sooner? Or eat a little less than you might have? You most likely did. You're doing fine. This is all about learning what you can do to continue moving your weight in the right direction. What are some of the stimuli that make you stumble?

Call ahead and ask the host(ess) what is being served. Bring something to complement the host(ess) plan. Make sure it is ready to eat without any added preparation for which the host has not planned.

Supply your own serving platter, tongs, or large spoons if needed. I once had oatmeal while getting dressed to go to a friend's wedding. From everything I was told, it didn't sound as if anything but finger foods and alcohol would be served until 9:00 p.m. when there was a sit-down dinner. I think I was the only one not foraging at the reception's food-laden buffet tables.

I also made arrangements with the man tending bar to keep my water glass filled, and I'd keep going back from time to time to sip.

CHAPTER 7

REMEMBER, IT'S JUST FOOD

EXPLODING SOME WEIGHT-LOSS MYTHS

Do you ever see weight-loss products or services promising a result too good to be true? They probably are. Advertising is seductive. One weight control method pushes meat over other choices, convincing millions of desperate people that it is a healthy choice. Marketers misdirect your attention.

One weight-loss method I just saw on television is about food extraction. The narrator said, "You will feel full all day."

You are told by media that the way to control weight is by adding berries to pancakes or fruit and nuts to chocolate and vanilla pudding. If you follow that advice and add the suggested amounts of berries, almonds, flaxseed oil, green tea, an ounce of chocolate, a glass of wine, and a partridge in a pear tree, each evening to an already food-ladened intake, you will gain weight. It's not that the item in question is unhealthy or high in calories (though nuts are mind-bogglingly high in calories and fat); it's the frequency of consumption that tilts the scales in the wrong directions.

It is further suggested you dip apple slices into melted cara-mel, chocolate, or peanut butter, or sprinkle cocoa powder on microwave popcorn and cereal! Some suggest buying small cups of low-fat pudding instead of cookies or drinking four glasses of milk in twenty-four hours as a weight-loss tool. The problem with all of these suggestions is that the amount of food you're eating with each of those items is increased without reducing the basic foods you're being told to eat. Oatmeal every day for thirty days might lower cholesterol by seven points if you don't do anything else. But if the oatmeal is in addition to toast and coffee, a bagel and cream cheese, or bacon and eggs, then you might lower your cholesterol (though it is doubtful), but you'll also gain weight.

I read one product that advertised low calorie desserts. If you're not hungry to begin with, a low calorie dessert most likely won't deliver what you think it will, so you end up eating two, if not more. Some in the public eye say to include more vegetables, use skim milk instead of cream, or eat a certain cereal that guar-antees a six-pound weight loss in two weeks. You're promised that one food will keep you feeling fuller longer. Many food products are low-fat, making it difficult for you to absorb nutrients found in vegetables. Reduced fat in some foods reduces your body's ability to move waste materials through the intestines. Another company draws consumers in by putting fruit in the bottom of yogurt. This just increases sugar content to make it sweeter and less healthy than having (on occasion) those items separately with real fruit.

What about the theory that six little meals a day are better than three? Research shows that the *more times a day you eat, the more calories you consume.*

What about soft drinks? A twelve-ounce can of soda has nine teaspoons of sugar and no nutrients, pretty much the same for sugar-sweetened breakfast cereal. What about diet soda? Besides diet soda being chock-full of chemicals, you don't just want to fill up your body. You want to nourish it. Soda, diet or otherwise, does not nourish your body.

Many overweight people think a gastric bypass will be the end of their problems. It is not. A woman from Belgium told me that after years of health problems that made it almost impossible for her to lose weight, she had a gastric bypass. She called to tell me that until she learned to change her habits, even with the gastric bypass, she gained back some of the weight. Surgery alone isn't going to keep off your weight unless you change your habits. A compulsive overeater needs to change ritualized behavioral patterns, not find yet one more bite of food (low calorie or not, healthy or not) to stuff into an already stuffed body.

Myth-making also occurs in food packaging. Food packaging plays with size, graphics, and price, making you think it is so small. Small? Compared to what? A building? "Everything from menu design and graphics to wording of item descriptions can affect what guests order and how much you spend," says Gregg Rapp, a Palm Springs, California-based menu engineer.

Lighting, color, sound, price, and the menu all can influence and alter your decision-making process in a restaurant. Even the look and location of your seat in a restaurant adds to what you consider ordering. It is much better to decide what category of food(s) you want, number of items you'd eat if you were home, and whether one of the food items is a Filler or not.

Restaurateurs are in it to make a profit from your overeating tendencies. They have to cover their insurance, employee wages, utilities, and rent fees. So the more food you order, the more their plan is working.

Just this morning, a man asked me whether it wasn't better to have six small meals each day as he does. He was tall and thin, a salesman in a cabinetry shop. I told him that might work for someone without this problem. A person using food inappropriately is not clear about boundaries. The six small meals he or she would plan would turn into eight or ten, and eventually, it would be called "grazing." The frequency would increase and so would the portion. The small would grow to medium and then big. To be very clear: six small meals a day thinking is a part of your addiction thinking. The question isn't: What is the most I can eat and still lose weight? The question is: What is the smallest amount I can eat, still feel satisfied, and still lose weight?

Leilani J.: I was at one time 100 pounds overweight. I lost fifty by going to a weight-loss program, but when the weight started to creep back on, I got really scared, and that is when I decided to try something more serious. I tried low calorie, fewer carbohydrates, and only salad regimens. The weight still increased.

Caryl: Some weight-loss programs have created a nation of compulsive overeaters by encouraging people to eat when they are not hungry and to eat unlimited amounts of food, especially salads, vegetables, and diet sodas. I heard a guest nutritionist on a television show tell people that you should eat plenty of vegetables because they will fill you up. Vegetables are food. They count. They add up.

You don't want to *fill up*. You want to stop eating when you are no longer hungry. Your goal is to differentiate between when you are hungry and when you are using food as a distraction.

Other programs urge people to eat large quantities of low-calorie foods. Of course, if you're eating large quantities of anything, the question is: How often are you doing this? Large amounts of food fill up your stomach. Then when you go to eat something not exactly low in calories, you still expect to eat until you are full. You won't know when to stop eating because your usual stop signal is feeling full and squeezing out of your pants.

The smaller person you are becoming will feel loose in his/her clothes. That's the goal.

Liza M.: Did you see that the *Wall Street Journal* said older women showed far better cognitive and memory activity if they have one drink a day?

Caryl: They're looking at the average person. It is not a one-size-fits-all edict. And for someone with a weight problem or an addiction to alcohol, consider all the food you eat that you wouldn't have eaten had you not had a drink. Your physical body will feel stuffed and bloated and tired when it has to process all that extra fuel, not to mention the psychological remorse you'll feel afterward. Even though the Program doesn't count calories, you at least have to be aware of some of these things.

Murray T.: I read that three teaspoons of flaxseed oil every day is good for your health.

Caryl: Part of resistance to change is the insistence that you can eat it all. If you're thinking that a tablespoon of flaxseed oil each day is no big deal, that's denial. All food adds up — every scrap from the table, every lettuce leaf, every teaspoon of flaxseed oil, every blueberry, every kernel of popcorn, every almond. And if you are adding this seemingly inconsequential amount of food without subtracting something you are already eating, then the extra calories accumulate, get converted to fat and stored, and your scale goes up. The point is that you don't have to consume a lot for the act of consumption to result in gaining weight. You're eating more than you're able to burn *each day*. The unused fuel gets converted to fat.

Esther C.: A lot of diets encourage drinking unlimited volumes of calorie-free diet drinks or low-calorie beverages like coffee and tea. Why does The Program discourage this? Can't I have tea (caffeine-free, herbal, regular) in unlimited quantities, like water?

Caryl: Anything other than water fills you up, but does not nourish your body. Tea or coffee needs to go through your whole body to reach the end. Your body will think, "All that work and not a vitamin or mineral? Not one shred of nutrition?" If you consume too many foods with little or no nutrition, your new smaller stomach won't have room for the nutrition you do need in addition to the 8-10 glasses of water each day. You're also getting in the habit of putting something in your mouth even though you're not hungry. Tea is fine as part of a meal, on occasion, when it is Skipped and Scattered — sometimes you have it, sometimes you don't. Coffee and tea do contain calories even if you drink them without cream or sugar.

Whether it is too much beverage it might also be too much salad or starch or more protein than you need. Skipping and Scattering all food, you diminish consumption by 50%. You might say, "It's only two calories!" And I say, "It all counts." Eventually, you have to purchase another pound of coffee or another box of tea.

Larry J. is 5' 9" and 180 pounds, in good shape, but trying to lose the extra weight around the middle. He recently switched to a low carbohydrate diet and swims intensively three or four times a week for ninety minutes or so. He is trying to figure out how to balance his food intake with exercise.

Larry J.: About a day and a half after a swim, I will crave carbohydrates — the worst kind of pastries and sweets — so bad that it feels very animalistic. What can I do/eat/avoid that will not make me crave bad carbohydrates so much? I thought eating protein instead of carbohydrates was supposed to keep me feeling full and satiated.

Caryl: After a workout, your body most likely needs nutrition in the form of a protein. It is needed more frequently than every day and a half. It's unlikely that a craving happens a day and a half after working out. If need be, bring food to the gym. Try a hard-boiled egg or some thin-sliced turkey (or tuna), immediately before your workout — a Fourth Meal. See what happens. You might need to have protein at breakfast (an egg) and protein at lunch (chicken/fish/veal) on the days you work out. So, at dinner on those days, plan to have your All-Vegetable or Soup Meal. Maybe your day-and-half-later cravings are to reward yourself for the workout. Food is not a reward for getting through a day.

WHAT'S ALL THE BUZZ ABOUT? (CAFFEINE/COFFEE)

Out of the eight or so food categories mentioned in the Meal Parameters of the Program (protein, vegetable, salad, starch, bread, alcohol, dessert, and beverage), coffee is the most frequently consumed beverage of the people I teach. Other than caffeine, coffee contains hundreds of other substances, including tannic acid, the stuff used to tan leather. *Better Life Journal* strongly recommends it as "a cleaner for kitchen floors, white wall tires, and stainless steel."

Caffeine is a diuretic that relaxes the muscles of the digestive tract and the kidneys —meaning that it makes you urinate. And because caffeine is a diuretic, it has a dehydrating effect on the body. Coffee would most likely not be approved today if it were presented to the Food and Drug Administration for consideration. There is a wide variety of side effects from caffeine: irregular heartbeat, dizziness, indigestion, high blood pressure, and hypoglycemia. A small amount (one eight-ounce cup) can trigger alertness by blocking receptors in the brain that signal the body's natural need to sleep. Caffeine can remain in the system up to ten hours. That jumpy mouth hunger in the evening could be a reaction to caffeine consumed hours before.

Heavy caffeine users may become psychologically dependent (believing the drug is an essential part of their lives) and develop a tolerance (requiring more caffeine over time to get the same effects). "Withdrawal symptoms include headache, drowsiness, irritability, and difficulty concentrating. Many people discover that they are dependent on caffeine when they go for a day or two without coffee and get a splitting headache," reports Source Media Resources, Inc. "For example, I recently gave up drinking coffee," says Renee Phillips, *The Artrepreneur* coach, motivational speaker, and author. "That one step led to creating new habits and a much better, healthier lifestyle, such as eating a more nourishing breakfast to replace the *zing* effect I used to get from the coffee. Since becoming caffeine-free I relax more, meditate more easily, have more patience, and I feel a tremendous sense of self-confidence for having accomplished this single goal."

Cynthia Kilian of Pulsefood says, "Things like anxiety, insomnia, some kinds of panic disorder, stomach problems, some kinds of cardiovascular problems — those all may be made worse (with caffeine)."

One Program participant told me that when he gave up coffee, not only did his acid reflux almost completely diminish, but he quit taking over-the-counter drugs for it. He also lost two pounds within the first few weeks.

What I will tell you is that you want to bring all foods (and that includes coffee and alcohol) to the right frequency and correct portion for the smaller person you want to be.

If you bring all the nutritious food down in size and frequency, and leave caffeine and alcohol at their original portions and frequencies, you'll be levitating. Is that hyped-up feeling your new normal?

Gina C. had recently gone back to school to continue her education, on top of her full work schedule, when she came to me as a Program Participant. She was chronically dependent on coffee for that extra "kick" in the morning and to beat the mid-afternoon energy slump.

Gina C.: I'm having a hard time getting my mind around the fact that coffee needs to be part of a meal. I'm having the same problem with the cheese and alcohol. I really need and enjoy coffee in the morning. I also routinely drink it around 3:30 p.m. when my coworkers and I hit the coffee shop by work to re-energize.

Caryl: It's not that you can't have coffee or cheese or alcohol. It's that you only want to eat when you're hungry enough to commit to a meal of which these foods are (or are not) a part. Food needs to nourish your body. The coffee and alcohol do not have nutrition in the way of vitamins, minerals, or fiber contained in other foods. Cheese is very high in fat and cholesterol. When your meal consists of only those three items, it may fill you up (though that's not a reason to eat), but it has little or no nutrient-redeeming value. Coffee or alcohol as part of a meal is fine as one-third of your meal or less, but not as two-thirds of your meal. It's about finding balance.

It seems you are dependent on coffee. Make sure you are not cutting out nutritious food-items just to replace them with excessive amounts of coffee. The best suggestion I have for you is to pour a little less each day. Going cold turkey here will not work because of years of using coffee to keep you awake.

You can use Skip and Scatter techniques here. You can start by cutting down coffee to once a day; then progress to drinking coffee every other day. Keep track of your number of cups of coffee and make it your goal to decrease your intake a little bit each week.

If you are anxious when making these choices, you want to do some pro-active inhalation and exhalation. Calm down. You're responding to a long-practiced habit. You have a wonderful opportunity to create something new: feeling calm when making these choices. That takes time. *Ask yourself: Are you drinking coffee to relieve the discomfort of not drinking coffee?*

Gina C.: I still had coffee, but the good news is I had one scrambled egg and I was fine. What do you think? A big part of me still does not want to deal with the coffee.

Caryl: It is great that you are drinking coffee as part of a meal. Continue this behavior and soon you will associate coffee with a meal rather than mindlessly consuming it throughout the day.

Coffee contains a drug, caffeine. You get addicted to the frequency, the portion, and the drug itself. As you get smaller, you'll want to buy, order, prepare, serve, and eat a little less of everything, including your beverage of choice, coffee. Pour less. Get it out of the oversized mug and into a normal 8-ounce sized cup.

Skip and Scatter the days you choose it. One day try hot water in lieu of coffee or tea. Sometimes have nothing. Shake it all up. Get variety. Just reading those possibilities, you're thinking: I can do that. I can get a normal-sized 8-ounce cup. That little bit of effort will yield wonderful results.

Leah H. got in the habit of drinking coffee in the mornings. When I spoke to her, she was finding it difficult to stop. Although not overweight, she was concerned that she was not as thin as her friends. She said she was little by little gaining more control over the five to seven cups of coffee. She occasionally replaced them with tea with milk and honey and hoped to get to plain hot water.

Leah H.: I wanted to tell you how happy I am with my progress with coffee. I feel much calmer and it's easier for me to fall asleep now that I'm not drinking coffee throughout the day.

Caryl: You are gaining more control of your coffee by weaning yourself from the six daily cups. What you're doing now gives you pride and increased self-esteem. Not to mention how much calmer you'll be with less caffeine. Nice job.

A few tips: Pour all beverages into eight-ounce cups. Pour a little less. Leave a teaspoon (or more) at the bottom of your cup. Have beverages at a different meal than the previous day. Skip days between cups of coffee if possible. Sip coffee along with sips of water.

Nick J.: The portion size thing is interesting. Saturday morning, I went to Starbucks and ordered a small decaf. I asked the woman behind the counter how many ounces in the small cup, and she said twelve. When I got home, I poured half the coffee into a coffee cup from my cupboard and it almost filled up another ceramic mug. And when I had it with breakfast, I realized it was enough for me. I threw out the remainder and, you guessed it, I was fine. Never did that before. Check that — would have never even *thought* about doing that before.

Caryl: So wonderful. These realizations are terrific. Is this the same person who didn't want to set goals? You seem to be enjoying setting the goals and achieving them. With the smaller coffee that turned out to be enough and fine, you now realize how many extra mouthfuls of everything you've been eating just because it was there or that was the portion that was served. Now you're finding your portion among the excess. Terrific!

ARE YOUR FRIENDS CONTRIBUTING TO YOUR WEIGHT GAIN?

The book *The Biology of Appetite* cites a study from Georgia State University that found that eating in a group of six or more boosts your food intake by a whopping 76 percent. I think it is because you get sucked into the speed, conversation, and frenetic eating habits of your tablemates. It's a subconscious reaction to wanting to belong, wanting to be part of the group. Overeating when others are overeating helps quell the anxiety of not fitting in because now you're one of the crowd. If you're eating with just one other person, meal size increases by 28 percent.

When I thought about that information, I realized the study was correct. When I'm at home and working, I'll open a can of tuna, put a little mayonnaise in it, and that'll be lunch. But when a friend comes over, I'm making a platter! My friend most likely doesn't want the platter either because when she's home she's opening that can of tuna, adding a little mayonnaise, and having her own lunch.

Multiply any one action with the number of times you re-inforce it over the course of the year and the scale goes up. If you're Skipping and Scattering, the scale will reflect your efforts and go down.

It's a good time to review what you've read until now. See page 324 for Review Number Four.

CHAPTER 8

QUANTUM LEAPS

WHAT'S A QUANTUM LEAP?

Quantum Leaps are successful outcomes of food encounters — when you are able, comfortably, to do some behaviors you never thought of doing in the past. And it's okay. When you become victorious with conquering an entrenched behavior that it took repeated efforts and attempts to change, chip away, and neutralize, that needs to be acknowledged. That is a Quantum Leap. Habits are changing, and that's good and needs to be acknowledged, too.

Continued mindfulness and reinforcing new ways of coping with the ups and downs of every day life, solidify the new habits until they become involuntary, familiar, automatic, and comfortable. You're doing something now that you've never been able to do before, and you begin to make it a solid, concrete habit.

A Quantum Leap can be anything from traveling with a scale "to eight hotels in four time zones on a trip up the Amazon" to wearing clothes that you haven't been able to fit into for the last ten years. Think about things of a physical and mental nature with regard to the foods you have chosen, the way you feel about yourself, your new weight, and your new awareness. No matter how small the effort, it accumulates. After each Quantum Leap, write that it was okay, or awesome, fantastic, terrific. Then when you re-read your Quantum Leaps list, you'll read "I left over food, and it was okay." Rather than, "I left over food; poor me." And if it was okay once, then you can do it again.

There are two kinds of Quantum Leaps: Direct and Ancillary:

1.   **A Direct Quantum Leap** is something you're doing that you learned directly from The Program. For example: eating with utensils, finding and enjoying All-Vegetable and Soup Meals, keeping a log of all consumed foods, or learning that one- and two-item meals are very satisfying.

2.   **An Ancillary Quantum Leap** is something that has happened as a result of doing your Program. Some examples are: clothes are hanging rather than being tight. Rings on your fingers are spinning rather than stuck. You're enjoying and believing the compliments you're receiving. You're getting better sleep.

One participant said, "I can bend over without internal injury." Another woman told me, "My wrap-around robe actually wraps around me!" And still another Program participant said he was dancing on the scale, so excited was he to see each morning's weight. When you stop being happy, and avoid the scale, you're in your addiction.

Acknowledging Ancillary Quantum Leaps allows you to make a connection between your getting comfortable with Program concepts by doing them and the positive results you're achieving.

Some Quantum Leaps cross over. You can write them on either list, or on both.

QUANTUM LEAPS I HAVE JUMPED

Are you a person who's in the habit of beating yourself up for the slightest indiscretion, the implication being, "In order to lose weight, I have to be perfect." Of course, all you can ever hope for is to do the very best you can under the circumstances. And if you're able to accomplish that, you cannot beat yourself up. The new way to think is, "Whatever I did, I ate less of it, stopped sooner, and didn't have remorse for overeating as I once did."

All those instances when you thought you blew it were merely you bumping into stimuli you had not anticipated. You reverted to your previous practiced, familiar, almost involuntary behavior. By continuing the old way, you reinforce that old behavior once again, locking it in even more tightly — keeping it chronic. This is a chronic, progressive disease.

The solution to removing those old habits is to custom-design new habits that are created specifically to chip away and neutralize your practiced, automatic behaviors until they are different and result in a different outcome. You don't have to succeed 100 percent of the time. Your efforts and attempts to change are what become Quantum Leaps. By acknowledging the successful outcome of an assignment — something you're doing now that you've never been able to do before — you begin to create a solid, concrete habit. The first time you're laying down the foundation. Every repetition makes the foundation more locked in and solid.

Quantum Leaps do not happen overnight. It takes a lot of consistent and committed efforts to change your habits. You should be proud of your accomplishments. You want to remember them. You want to write them down. Capture your Quantum Leaps in writing. Give yourself a chance to recognize the enormity of the effort. For example, if you've never left anything on your plate, and you're now leaving something on your plate, it deserves to be acknowledged. One of my favorite comments was from a woman who stated, "No popcorn during the movie, and nobody died."

"Quantum Leaps I Have Jumped" is an assignment to acknowledge how far you've come on your Program. Write down the things you've become aware of having changed; read them again and again when you review your notes. You'll realize how far you've come with your progress in changing your behavior. You may realize you can now do, think, or say things you could not do, think, or say before, and that you could do them again!

To focus on the positives — the Quantum Leaps you have jumped — begin a page in your logbook entitled "Quantum Leaps I Have Jumped" and write a beginning list of fifteen leaps you've taken since beginning your weight-loss program. Take time to write the list a little each day. Write the blank numbers on a page so you'll keep thinking about it. The "Quantum Leaps I Have Jumped" page gives you space to write your Direct Quantum Leaps and Ancillary Quantum Leaps. At the end of the exercise, you'll have a list of at least fifteen ways you are thinking and acting differently than you were before your Program. But don't stop there! Fill up the pages with additional numbers, and when that page is filled, start a new page and keep writing your Quantum Leaps.

One Quantum Leap might be that you leave the table before you finish all the food on your plate. Another might be that you brush your teeth instead of pouring your usual cup of coffee at four o'clock. An important Quantum Leap is to realize that you made all these small changes, and it's all okay.

A Quantum Leap might be that you're wearing clothes you haven't fit into in years. Maybe you're traveling with your scale — something you're doing now that you were not doing before exposure to The Program. One woman exuberantly wrote, "I love fitting into my ski pants with no problem. I love that I can go into any store and try on anything again. I enjoyed trying new food at a Thai restaurant. I left over more than half of my food. An old bathing suit that has always been too small now is slightly big. I love feeling more in control. Water is my go to."

Why do I ask you to write these things down?

Scripta manent, verba volant.

What is written remains, what is spoken vanishes into air.

By capturing each Quantum Leap in writing, when you review your notes, you'll be reminded that you did these things once, and it was okay. It's fine. It's wonderful. It's doable. It's great.

To help you get started, I've listed some other people's Quantum Leaps. I encourage you to capture some of these for your own list. Conversely, if you happen across a Quantum Leap on this list that you're not yet doing, but you would like to do, you might enter it on a newly created "Needs Work" page.

Some examples of Quantum Leaps include:
- I eat only when I'm hungry. That's awesome.
- I am more in control and less out of control. Yes.
- No popcorn during the movie, and nobody died.
- Not opening and closing the refrigerator door.
- The scale is my friend. I love getting on it.
- Not stuffed after eating, and that feels good.
- More 20-Minute Meals than not.
- I can tie my shoelaces without causing internal injury.
- Separating food and emotion.
- No nibbling between meals and it's okay.
- Sleep has improved.
- Less indigestion and heartburn. So good.
- My energy level has improved.
- I leave food over and it's fine.
- My golf swing has improved. That's amazing.

- I'm smaller and don't need as much as I used to need.
- I didn't gain weight after Thanksgiving. That's better than okay.

Additionally, reading your Quantum Leaps aloud after writing will allow you to understand them on a deeper level. Acknowledge and enjoy every improvement and accomplishment throughout your Program journey.

Finally, you want to quantify each of your Quantum Leaps by ending with positive phrases such as: "… and it was okay," "… it was awesome," "… it was amazing," "… it was wonderful." In this way, when you're reviewing your notes and you bump into "I left food over at the barbecue, and it was okay," you will know that since it was okay once, you'll be fine doing it again. If you don't acknowledge that leaving food over is okay (in writing), then the next time you review that page, you'll come across "left food over" and be thinking, "poor me." Each time you write and review your Quantum Leaps, you'll be reminded that since you did these things once, you lived to tell the tale, and you weigh less, calmed down, and life goes on. You won't remember any of it anyway.

Muriel C: I have started brushing my teeth during the day to discourage mid-afternoon eating. I like doing this. Recently, I've been under the weather, and it has slowed me down from reaching my goal. I really want to get to my goal. I've got twenty-five pounds to go.

Caryl: You mentioned in your note that you are brushing your teeth during the day to discourage mid-afternoon eating, and you like doing it. That's a new Quantum Leap for you! Those are the things you want to keep practicing so they become and remain automatic. As you go onward and downward, you will encounter many food offerings. Some of these have long ago established patterns of frequency and portion.

In *INC.* March 2010, Catarina Fake wrote, "I read books and articles, and I take a lot of notes. I put stickies in passages I find interesting, and later I write them into my notes, because that reinforces them in my memory. And I'll make a point of going back and rereading them. Otherwise, it's like cramming for a test in high school where you don't retain any of the material."

Sadie H.: I was out a long time. I was really hungry. I took a deep breath, thought about what I was going to eat, bought a small portion of tuna — my portion — took a few bites slowly, sat on a bench in Sag Harbor, and was surprisingly fine till dinner. I felt very present. I never would have ordered that amount of food before, and yet it was the perfect amount. This is definitely a Quantum Leap for me! I'm discovering new things about myself and that I am okay and feeling great with these changes.

Henry W. was twenty years old and a student. He used to be very athletic in high school, but now with his lifestyle changes, he was finding less time to exercise. Henry was always munching on something while sitting at the computer. He was becoming more aware of this.

Henry: I thought about eating after dinner last night, but I got up and went to study instead. Then I got some water with ice and drank it instead of eating. Before bed, to make sure I was organized, I went around and put things together, including my logbook. It made me feel in control and happy.

Caryl: This is why you're down another two pounds after a major holiday — approximately two-thirds to your goal. Be proud. You've done this. All these actions are called Quantum Leaps. By acknowledging your achievements, they live longer in your head and heart. You can read and re-read the efforts and accomplishments. When you internalize the information, it becomes the new way. Eventually, it will be automatic. Be proud. That's a nice Quantum Leap.

Lora J.: I am almost finished reading your book, and there have been some serious Quantum Leaps:

1. Happy to drink warm water all day at work instead of coffee, coffee, and more coffee. It has made a huge difference in my clarity, focus, and mood.

2. I love getting used to smaller portions. It sounds so obvious, but it has never been reality for me. I have tried other methods so many times, always looking up those zero point foods to binge on.

3. I am becoming much more diverse and even adventurous in my meal choices. I am a vegetarian and am trying to deal with that as well as variety and getting enough protein.

4. I am weighing myself twice daily, and I now jump on the scale in the morning because I know what the scale will say based on what I weighed the night before. I love weighing twice a day.

Caryl: Wow! It does look like there are many Quantum Leaps. Continue to work on other parts of the Program, stay conscious of your achievements, and applaud all the baby steps. They will become Quantum Leaps.

Carrie C.: It's been a few weeks, but I wanted you to know I haven't dropped off the face of the earth. I'm still here — still learning — and still changing habits.

Today was a really good day. Thanksgiving has always been a day to stuff myself, but I made a different choice this year, and I feel so good about it! I wanted to tell you about it since this is something major for me.

We went over to some friends' house with a small group of people. Ahead of time, I worked it out with our hosts that I would help in the kitchen since the wife needed to be out with the guests. So I helped her husband (the cook) in the kitchen, served the guests, brought food in and out, served coffee, filled water glasses, removed dishes from the table, and then did all the clean-up in the kitchen (ran two loads of dishes in the dishwasher, cleaned countertops and sink, and even mopped the floor). So for most of the evening, my focus was on helping others and tending to their needs, rather than on stuffing myself! And it was very gratifying!

When it was time for me to sit down and eat, I put small amounts of my favorite foods on my plate (didn't even come close to filling my plate) and skipped the other items. Of several things, I only served myself a one or two bite amount, knowing I just wanted a taste — not a whole serving. Same with the pie. When it was time for dessert, I served myself two bites of mincemeat (I've never tried it before) and about three bites of pumpkin pie.

Here's what I thought was neat: I didn't feel deprived at all. In fact, I felt very comfortable and satisfied, yet not even close to full or stuffed. I can remember being sore after eating some Thanksgiving dinners because I would eat so much! Not this time.

Now (midnight), I'm very comfortable and feel ready for bed. I'm still amazed that this was Thanksgiving, and that I was able to eat so much less than I used to eat. I felt in control, focusing on small amounts of my favorite foods and skipping everything else. And yet I felt so satisfied. My attention was on the people, not on the food. What a nice difference!

Caryl: Do I say, "Wow!" or "Nice job!"? I'm so happy for you and proud of you! Your whole letter seems to reflect The Program. The calmness, thoughtfulness, and pro-activity is terrific.

You planned ahead, stayed active and focused, portioned your meal for the smaller you, and in the end, you acknowledged how great you felt. Amazing Quantum Leaps! I almost don't want to know anything else because this is such a powerful place to end. So Happy Thanksgiving, my dear. You're doing just great. But don't get cocky. As comedian George Carlin said, "Just 'cause you got the monkey off your back doesn't mean the circus has left town."

THE NECESSITY OF A POSITIVE STORY

"Tell me a positive story," I said into the phone. Larry B. was calling, as instructed, with his morning weight and positive story, the usual once a week assignment for participants of The Program. It was a few days after his first meeting. "I am very discouraged," he groaned. "My weight went up from two days ago." "That doesn't sound like a positive story," I teased.

A positive story is to acknowledge something you're doing now that you weren't doing before you began your weight-loss program. Even if you didn't think it was going to be okay (part of the Addiction Thinking you've practiced and perfected for decades), the Program thinking is that if you are a little more mindful and awake when around food, you're most likely going to make choices better aligned with reaching your weight goal. This is a positive story.

I explained to Larry B. that losing weight was not the only positive story. A positive story could be that the bowl of soup was enjoyable, satisfying, and enough. Small steps need to be acknowledged, so you can begin practicing the telling of positive stories. This becomes your truth. He finally said, "I think I got it. I had wonton soup in a Chinese restaurant and it was enough. I didn't think it would be enough, but it was."

By acknowledging that a bowl of soup was enough, Larry was beginning the shift in his thinking that would accumulate and become weight loss. If he were to have a bowl of soup just once a week for lunch and once a week at dinner, that would be 104 times a year when soup was enough. Sometimes he could add a salad, or sometimes he might have a piece of bread, or sometimes the bowl of soup by itself would be the perfect amount.

Addiction Thinking has been repeating the words "It isn't going to be enough" since childhood. No one ever stopped to test the amount of food to see whether it actually wasn't enough. And what if it weren't? Most of you can get additional food in a short period of time. There's always a Fourth Meal. Keep food in your office.

There was one man I encouraged week after week. Try to have soup one evening. Plan a one-item dinner of soup. Week after week he did not accomplish this. He kept telling me, "I'm a big guy. A bowl of soup isn't going to be enough."

"You're not burning off those extra dinner items," I reminded him. "Yes, I am," he insisted. "But the scale is not moving," I replied. Back and forth we went.

One evening, when we were nearing in on his ninth meeting, I retrieved from my answering machine a message from him. (We didn't yet have e-mails at that time.) It was from him and he said: "Okay. Okay. Okay. Okay. I had soup for dinner. It's 11:30 and I'm going to bed. And yes," he says laughing, "it was enough." I kept that message for a few weeks and the fun and satisfaction and laughter in his voice let me know he was succeeding.

On the day after Thanksgiving, Jen C. sat before me, staring bleakly. I could see she was trying hard to think of a positive story to tell me. She could not. I threw out suggestions: "You kept a log? Got on your scale twice a day? Ate breakfast?"

"No. No. No," she said.

Our meeting continued. Her notes were only partially copied. Pages were in disarray. The three-ring binder was not yet purchased. I tried another few times to get her to acknowledge a positive story. Nothing.

Since she was my last appointment of the day, we went together downstairs and to the street. We walked in the same direction, chitchatting, and I asked what she did for Thanksgiving. A big smile lit up her entire face when in amazement she answered, "I sent everyone home with food — there is not a crumb left except a few slices of turkey."

I stopped walking and looked at her. "That's a positive story. Go home and write about that on a page in your journey book entitled, 'Quantum Leaps I Have Jumped.'"

"I guess it is a positive story," she smiled. "I know I would have never done that before."

When you are so used to failing, you disregard your successes unless they are enormous. You often miss the buds of habits forming. They need to be watered and pushed into the sunlight to bloom. Acknowledge the smallest amount of change; the efforts accumulate. You'll see success everywhere.

When the artist Matisse was asked where he found flowers to paint in winter, he responded: "When you look for flowers, you find flowers."

Retrain your brain to look for the positive story, and you'll find the positive story.

Pam D. spent most of her time entertaining clients for breakfast, lunch, and dinner. Five years earlier, she had noticed that her weight was steadily increasing. The most she had ever weighed had been a year ago. She said all of her friends looked great in their clothes. She hated feeling self-conscious about the way she looked.

Pam D.: Slowly, but surely, I am progressing toward my magic number — I am now six pounds from my goal and love shopping. Also, my tailor loves you. I went to another store and the owner was very happy that I needed new clothes.

Caryl: Perseverance works. Nice job. The old way is decades old. The new way — relatively speaking is a little baby a few minutes old. Keep gaining awareness of all your new eating habits. Get comfortable doing them. You may reach your goal and then think you don't have to do whatever it took to reach your goal anymore. Yes, you do. Keep on keeping on. When you do your Program, it works. When you stop doing it (or any part of it), it stops working. Not at the beginning, but eventually. At the beginning, the weakening of the foundation of the Basics is not apparent. The house still appears to be standing strong, but eventually, it becomes unstable and collapses.

It's as if you drop a stitch over here and not drink enough water one day. Then you drop a stitch of eating only when you're hungry. You might drop a stitch of weighing twice daily because you were afraid of what the scale was going to say. Eventually, the sweater will unravel. When you don't want to do these simple assignments, you're in your addiction.

Clara M. had been following The Program for six months, and she had seen her life change. She was still losing weight, and she was still focused on her weight-loss goals.

Clara M.: I'm still losing weight a little at a time. All those little things you have me doing are paying off because they are now part of my life, and I'm still getting mileage out of them.

My positive story is that — drumroll — I am only two pounds from my target weight! It has been expensive (wardrobe-wise) as I went from size 12 to 10 to 8, and now my size 8 jeans are loose on me. I am really amazed at how much you changed my life without actually making any BIG, unrealistic changes in me. It has also been a windfall of tops for my sister and bottoms for my friends.

Caryl: I'm delighted to hear you are only two pounds from your goal. You see how all your efforts big and small accumulate?

I remember when I went down from one size to the next to the next, it was quite exciting. It's always helpful to lock in these things by going over your notes with a yellow highlighter or reading a chapter from your notes every couple of days as a reminder of all the things you're trying to juggle. I am so happy to hear of your update. I'd love to know when you nail the goal. I put a big arrow on each person's page when he or she reaches his or her goal. When I go through the files and see those arrows, it always makes me smile.

Andrea A. was a thirty-five-year-old medical student and stay-at-home mom who had been turning to food for comfort after taking care of kids all day. She realized she needed to get her food addiction under control. The food she used to comfort herself often involved massive amounts of all kinds of meat. She was challenging herself to have red meat only once a week as suggested and to add poultry and fish for a wider variety of nutrients. She also wanted to be more creative with All-Vegetable Meals.

Andrea A.: A positive story is that I'm even looking for meals without protein. In the past, vegetables were a side dish, not a main course. But I'm enjoying them, and if I have soup at night, I'm almost guaranteed a weight loss the next day. I never would have thought of any of these things before. I think I'm starting to piece it all together now. And it is all okay.

MORE POSITIVE STORIES

Some positive stories that arrive in my e-mail inbox stand alone. They may have been sent by someone who read my first book, *Conquer Your Food Addiction,* or an article I'd written for the Internet, or one of the participants who've gone through The Program. Maybe they heard me speak. Every example shows the new way of thinking: The Program way. Each person expresses excitement not only about accomplishing a new way of thinking and a new weight, but discovering new ways to cope with the ups and downs of life without using food. Against great odds, so many are conquering their inappropriate use of food. They are aware and proud of what they have achieved. These are indeed the most Positive of Stories.

Laurie R.: Bet you didn't expect to hear from me again so soon. Well, something happened today that I would like to share with you. As I was dropping my youngest daughter off at her math tutor and the door was closing, she told me she wasn't hungry anymore and she stuffed a chocolate chip cookie into my hand. The elevator door had just closed. So here I am waiting for the elevator with this freshly baked, moist, delicious-looking cookie. Well, I start thinking of my strategies to cope: I take a nice deep breath. What wafts up to my nose? The aroma of the cookie I am holding. So I continue to go through my "Caryl Repertoire." Was I thinking of eating this cookie two minutes before she gave it to me? Most definitely no. Okay. Let's move on. But my Addict Pea Brain keeps annoying me and I start thinking, "It's only a cookie. What difference is that going to make?"

But I've learned that if there are too many exceptions, you are left only with the exceptions and no rules. If you put it in your mouth, you ate it, and it all adds up. The elevator is still not here. I finally decided that if I don't eat that cookie, I will e-mail you and that will be my goal — to be able to e-mail you with my success story. When the elevator finally arrives, the elevator man has changed his clothes, which explains the delay. Once I get out of the building, I make it to the garbage can on the corner and I throw away that cookie — and it was fine. Success!!! And now I get to e-mail you this positive story.

Caryl: You can feel the joy. This was her Mt. Everest.

Morton T.: I'm fifty-seven years old, and as long as I can remember, I've always had to shop in a big and tall man's shop.

Now that I've lost sixty pounds, all my clothes are too big to be altered. When I went back to the big and tall man's shop to buy new clothes, they told me I couldn't shop there anymore. They didn't have anything for me. For the first time since graduate school, I am shopping in a real store. This is pretty emotional. I'm enjoying shopping. Every place I go has my size. I even bought my first pair of jeans.

Even though I've lost all this weight, I'm still using my Program Voice when it comes to food, especially during special occasions. I often review my old notes because I know how powerful food addiction is.

Lucy M.: I'm still losing weight. I reached a real landmark: When in a plane, I don't have to use the seat-belt extension anymore. This is such a happy day for me. I'd have to travel with one because some planes don't have enough to give out. I don't need one anymore. Hooray for me!

Ronnie L.: I was just trying out a repatterning technique: instead of going into the pantry to get some more candy, I went in the bathtub with your book. I read about the woman with cerebral palsy who finished the marathon, and it made me realize I don't want to give up! I am in training and there will be ups and downs, but I will reach my goal of _____ pounds. Tomorrow, I am going to buy a large thermos so I will have my hot water with me at work, and when I get home, I won't have to go into the kitchen to get my hot water. Thanks for the tools.

Patsy C.: Skipped coffee and dessert today. Having more soup lunches or dinners and finding them satisfying. I think my cravings are diminishing. It's still a challenge when visiting the grandkids (just returned from two different sets of kids). Fortunately, no pizza dinners! I was able to suggest an alternative that proved an excellent choice for everyone. Then the ice cream birthday cake arrived. I took a deep breath and relived a moment of addict's remorse from when I felt terrible after giving into a mid-day No-Meal Meal. I took control of the situation this time. Next time I have to get there before the regret, which is what I did tonight when everyone else ordered dessert. Saying no felt great!

Paul J.: Positive story from this weekend: Went to an Italian restaurant with friends on Saturday night (same friends I went out with to the Greek restaurant a few weeks ago when I over-ate). Long story short, I ordered an entrée, told the folks I'd pick at some of the appetizers, ate some of the appetizers — a taste here, a taste there — and had water with my glass of wine. So you're wondering where the "positive story" part is? By the time the appetizer plates were cleared and before the entrées were brought out, I realized, "Wait a minute; I'm not really hungry anymore. I'm a smaller guy now." That's the positive part — real-izing I didn't need to eat the entrée because I was no longer really hungry. When they did bring the entrée out, I took two forkfuls, set my fork down, drank some water, enjoyed the rest of the con-versation, and watched my dinner-mates totally stuff themselves to the point of exploding. All the while, I heard your voice in my head saying, "It's not the last supper; it's just another meal. And it all counts." Not trying to be perfect anymore — who is? But I am so much better and thoughtful than I was. And since last month, I'm down sixteen pounds.

George R.: When we met on Friday, I shared my concerns about eating/drinking plans for a fundraiser event I was attend-ing that evening. I've been there in previous years, and it is a very social event with tons of drinking as part of the conversation with people from around the country coming to New York. There is also lots of good catered food. My greatest fear was knowing that it is customary to drink beer and talk, and that each year I could easily down four to six beers throughout the evening and load up on food throughout the night. When I left your office, you challenged me to come up with a strategy to break that cycle and come up with other coping strategies. I honestly had no idea what I was going to do.

And then it hit me! Instead of taking a subway or cab downtown to the event, I decided to drive my own car. Even though I knew I'd have to shell out $30 for parking, I figured, "Late on Friday night on Wall Street I'm not going to find a cab anyway, so I might as well have my own car with me, and if I have my own car — I won't drink. And if I don't drink, I'll be mindful enough not to overeat."

Long story short, I drove down there, had water (and a ginger ale as my stomach was upset from lunch), had a small plate of shrimp and veal, and that was it! And later that evening, when my friend dragged me over to the dessert table, I not only didn't eat a single dessert — I just wasn't hungry — but told my friend he was eating because he was sexually frustrated, and instead, he should work on that issue directly. Later that evening, I introduced him to a lovely woman standing next to us. She was cracking up at our whole conversation.

I found my coping strategy in advance by driving, I didn't drink beer, ate just enough, and helped my friend out, and to top it off — the parking only cost me $15. All in all, it was a great evening.

Edgar A.: First and foremost: I reached my second weight-loss goal this morning. Why the new goal? I've lost an even fifty pounds since six months ago. It's truly second nature now. I'm really not conscious about obeying the rules; they really have become new habits — and far healthier ones.

Meredith C. was a bit of a perfectionist, set high goals, and was disappointed if she did not achieve them. Meredith was noticing her weight loss one pound at a time. She told me her weight on this morning was one pound less than last week.

Meredith C.: One thing I learned is that one pound is an accomplishment. I know in the past I wanted to lose three pounds a week. If I didn't, I was a failure. Now I've realized that if I keep my eye on the ball, so to speak, and be patient, the one pound adds up.

Georgia L.: My husband had neck surgery this week so a pretty stressful week that I would have normally eaten through the stress. I did not! I also brought lunches/dinners to the hospital for myself.

One more. I weighed 145 pounds today. I ordered a size 6 pants online from a contemporary retailer and they fit!!! Online yet! I didn't have to try them on and had confidence that they were going to fit. Yay me.

Sean J.: Early morning weight is down. I'm feeling good about my progress so far this week. I feel much less hungry and have not had any cravings in the last few days. Had a business dinner last night and felt great skipping a free pasta dish as I really was not even hungry.

Charlene D.: New clothes make me feel thin. I didn't realize how fat I really was. I figure that I lost about 10 percent of my body weight. Thanks to you, I ordered food from a caterer for Thanksgiving as I know I can't resist eating my own cooking the entire time I'm cooking.

Pearl: For a welcome change, I am filled with positive stories. Weight this morning is on target. I have achieved more Skipping and Scattering, two no-dessert days, a decreased number of meal items, and am feeling more in control, lighter, and happier than when I saw you a few days ago. I succeeded at attending two dinners where I managed to hold my own in spite of what others were having for their meals.

Caryl: It does take a bit of time for all the efforts to accumulate enough to be seen and felt. You have positive stories pouring forth. You are aware. You know they are important enough to share. Begin a page entitled "Quantum Leaps I Have Jumped" and write down those things and date it. Then when you're down, you'll review how far you've come and realize how much you have done and how good you feel. Remember the three words you used to describe yourself: more in control, lighter, and happier. Wonderful mindfulness when you say you succeeded at being at two dinners where you managed to hold your own. It's relatively new, yet you held your own.

Can you imagine how practice and repetition can really make this automatic? Keep doing them and after a while the new way will not only feel better and have such wonderful benefits in self-esteem and waist size, but the old way will be less compelling. Many participants tell me they think their palate is changing. They are craving vegetables and soups. Me too.

Sheila I. was a thirty-one-year-old single woman who worked as a party planner. She and her fiancé often ate out for dinner several times a week. Every day she ate lunch away from her home and office. She had seen the creeping weight become galloping weight. She'd been doing The Program for a few weeks and wanted to relay a positive story.

Sheila I.: I am finally getting comfortable having developed a Home Base — a safe harbor. I now have a few local restaurants as clients for the spice company where I work. So they are totally thrilled when I come in for lunch and couldn't care less whether I'm by myself or with someone else. They prepare my food exactly the way I tell them to. It took a while for me to get comfortable asking for things I want. I used to think I needed to eat to please others — fiancé, my mother, the waiter. I don't do that anymore. It's empowering.

Caryl: Asking for what you want — what a concept. Enjoy your lunches. Because Americans eat in restaurants as a matter of convenience, think of a restaurant's kitchen as an extension of your own. You can order exactly what you want, prepared exactly the way you want it, the only difference is that others have done all the work. They even clean up afterwards. Enjoy that aspect, too.

Lorissa J.: Thank you for this wonderful book! I am a fifty-year-old woman and have been fighting food addiction for most of my life. I purchased your book three months ago (am on my third reading) and have been faithfully following assignments with phenomenal results. I am definitely on my way to permanently changing destructive food habits. I have lost eighteen pounds in the process, but more importantly, I have been eroding a lifetime of ritualized eating behaviors and replacing them with wonderful new habits.

Everything has improved. After several attempts, I finally found a logbook I like, so I re-wrote everything one more time. It was amazing how I'd read something two, six, ten times before I realized how I could improve my behavior. There's so much to work on: one-item dinners, soup meals, even getting on the scale at night. I'm now calmer around food, and like you say, "It's only food."

The next story comes from one of the editors of this book. She says: This is great. I don't think new participants realize how helpful it is to have to, write in, and re-read a logbook. I remember I was very resistant to it at first, thinking I had better things to do with my time. I eventually realized how much writing the assignments down and re-reading them helped my progress!

Caryl: You learn by writing, reading, speaking, and hearing. The Program attempts to have you repeat those actions. Reading is helpful but reading aloud reaches your subconscious even more deeply.

Sounds as if you all need to hit the Quantum Leaps list with all of these wonderful thoughts. It is still a bit fragile compared to the decades you reinforced the old behavior. When you write them down, you relive them. Your brain doesn't know whether it is real or a memory. Then you write it down. Your brain thinks you've taken the actions again. Then you review the "Quantum Leaps I Have Jumped" list and your brain thinks you've done it again.

Some habits take two minutes to form. Some habits take two hours, two weeks, two months, two years to change. And some take two decades to lock in. Work on each of these things. You can do it a little bit each day.

Sahara H. was a twenty-eight-year-old comedian. She traveled often and performed in various cities. She often received complimentary meals and drinks after her act.

Sahara H.: I performed in Mexico over Thanksgiving. Every night, dinner was a buffet. Every night, I planned in advance what I was going to have, from the number of items and Fillers to determining whether my meal would be Protein or No-Protein. I brought my scale — I always do that. It keeps me honest.

I don't feel bloated after eating anymore. It's a good feeling. I still have some things that need work, but it's getting better than what I used to do, which was eating the same food night after night. The Program keeps me on a good rhythm. I always feel better and happier when I am present. Thank you for the gift of this program.

Peter J.: So this morning I weighed exactly sixteen pounds less in one month since starting! I keep telling my wife, "That's as much as a bowling ball!"

Tina E: Today I saw my favorite sandwich at a place near school, and instead of eating the bread, I put the bread on the side and ate the things inside. I realized it was even more delicious without all that bread. It tasted like the true taste of the food.

Caryl: Terrific observation. Nice job.

Carla K.: I reached my goal. Thank you. Thank you. I can't believe it. I'm so happy!

Caryl: It's a good time to go back and see how far you've come! You're a different person now than you were two months ago. Now, the words will have a different meaning.

Patsy M.: Positive story: Rethought the Friday night Margarita, stayed in and took a bath, and read an indulgent, home make-over magazine, and felt very noble. Staying with the Program and looking forward to our Tuesday meeting.

Caryl: All good things. You took care of yourself in a really positive way: stayed in, took a bath, read something enjoyable, felt noble, and it was okay. It was fine. Good things happened. You took care of yourself.

Patsy M.: Tonight at 5:30 p.m., I resisted the temptation to eat the dinner I was serving my kids. Instead, I waited until 6:30 p.m. and ate an appetizer for dinner with a friend at a Mexican restaurant. I enjoyed it, savored it, and tried hard to recognize the difference between eating consciously and unconsciously. It's small, but it counts for me. It's all about building belief and confidence in myself.

Caryl: Excellent reflection. And the moment passed. That's important to acknowledge. You waited when your children were being fed, ate an appetizer for dinner, and it was okay.

ACKNOWLEDGE NEWLY FORMED HABITS

Newly formed habits need to be acknowledged. When I weaned myself off caffeine, I realized I was a calm person rather than the hyper-nervous one I thought myself to be. I'd been in denial about caffeine having an effect on me. Many participants recall how caffeine used to be part of a meal and that clarity has returned with a caffeine-free system. Some men and women tell me how much, for the first time, they're enjoying oatmeal. Soup is a new, big favorite for a lot of participants of The Program. Many times, participants are surprised to admit how enjoyable and satisfying their entire meal is. What are some of your newly formed habits? Start a positive story section in your book. Add as much paper as necessary.

_____

_____

_____

_____

_____

_____

Winona M.: I'm working hard on a twenty-minute breakfast and giving myself the time to sit quietly — no TV, no news — and savor it. I now find that the mornings I get up late and rush through breakfast are not at all satisfactory to me. I am beginning to appreciate this way of eating you teach. My breakfasts every day this week have been Twenty-Minute Meals, which I have thoroughly enjoyed.

Caryl: Good. The Twenty-Minute Meal is worth achieving. I like it, too. You'll find the more you do it, the more you want to achieve it. The old way doesn't feel good anymore. Nice. Do whatever it takes to maintain slow eating. I often read the morning newspaper when I eat breakfast.

Erena A.: I had a No-Meal Meal of onion rings at a party I attended last night and didn't throw in the towel for the whole evening. I went home and had chicken and Brussels sprouts. It definitely made the difference on the scale this morning. Previously,

I would have just kept eating onion rings and anything else at the party. I didn't feel pressured by all the food and the people eating around me. In the past, I would have been miserable throughout the whole party. But this time, I felt great!

Caryl: This is a positive story on two levels. The first is that you did what you did. The second is that you knew it was a positive story and gave it more shelf life by sharing it with me. Eventually, you'll put that story on your Quantum Leaps list. Nice job.

Geneen C.: I feel like I have been making a tremendous amount of progress and understand it is unrealistic to think I will change everything overnight. I am doing much better than I would have, even though I might not have done everything. Last night, I met my friend before dinner and had water while she had wine — big step! Also, I had coffee at lunch yesterday instead of at breakfast — a baby step! But at least I'm going in the right direction, and it shows.

Caryl: You are doing better. That is what the review is about. It reminds you how far you've come, what you've accomplished in this journey. Keep up the good work. Not only did you do these things, but you knew they were acts of progress. You acknowledged that all your efforts are adding up. Remember these things when you may be in new challenging eating circumstances.

Gia V.: I went to one social event that had free refreshments and I didn't even bother looking at the food table, definitely a first for me. Also, I was handed a drink by the host at another event and actually walked off and threw it out. Another first, and it was all okay. I felt so good and in control.

Caryl: You feel so good and in control. Yesss!

Eileen M.: I attended a trade show for the wine industry. I knew there would be a ridiculous amount of wine and appetizers to sample, which can be very tempting, and for food and drink-challenged people like me, ultimately detrimental. I had been to these types of shows before, and always woke up with a hangover the next day, in addition to feeling stuffed from eating way more of the hors d'oeuvres that were served at the event than I should have. This year, I planned ahead.

My plan was to go, stay for a short period of time, sample only the wines that I knew pertained to my job, and to spit the samples, instead of swallowing, a common thing to do at wine trade tastings, although not everyone does. I knew there would be appetizers, but I ate a late lunch that day so I would not be overly hungry at 5:00, when the event started. I arrived at the hotel ballroom, ready to proceed with my plan, and the first thing I saw was food, food, and more food. Wall to wall food. I was suddenly overwhelmed. And shaky.

How could I not partake in this extravaganza? I can't get this at home! And it's all FREE! As soon as I heard my Addict Pea Brain talking (and making SENSE!), I turned around, walked out of the ballroom, and hightailed it to the ladies room, where I took a deep breath, and talked myself down from the ledge.

I reminded myself that there was not one food in that room that I had not tried before, and not one that I most likely wouldn't encounter again. I reminded myself that I was not hungry and wanted to weigh _____ pounds. I took another deep breath, looked at my outfit in the mirror, reminding myself that I still wanted it to fit me the next day. When I calmed down, I marched back to the ballroom, armed and ready. I walked past the food tables, did a quick loop around the room to ascertain which wines I wanted to sample (as I would have done with the food offerings in a buffet line), and followed my plan.

Instead of trying to "speed drink," like I might have in the past, to taste as many wines as I could, I went leisurely from exhibitor to exhibitor, talking to the winemakers and asking lots of questions. I had such a good time meeting people in the industry and learning about their wines that I forgot about the food. I was ready to leave halfway through the show. I went home, and had dinner with my husband — the dinner we had planned ahead to have that night. I was sober, not stuffed, and had stuck to my plan. It was a great feeling!

Caryl: When you read Eileen's beginning, middle, and wonderful ending of her trade show encounter, she mentions it was the abundance of the foods that grabbed her attention. That may be part of it.

In the past when she worked for a wine company and she would go to those trade shows and eat and drink (with the other salespeople), she learned and repeated all the rituals. Her subconscious recorded every drink and every taste of everything.

Years later, she walks into that old situation and her entrenched patterns took hold, the muscle memory came to life, and she had a desire to eat even though she had not done that in decades. The moment of discomfort was when her Addict Brain was trying to take hold of the Program Brain and Eileen repatterned in a dozen ways. Until the moment passed.

It was the moment when she felt that anxiety that she left the scene of the crime and went to the ladies room to calm herself down. All those repatterning techniques she'd been using kicked in. She left the area: physical repatterning. She talked to herself: mental repatterning. She looked in the mirror. She recommitted to her goal. She calmed herself down. She used all the things she practiced when she didn't need them. They all bubbled up when she did need them.

A great win!

ONCE YOU'VE REACHED YOUR GOAL

Once you've reached your goal, additional goals need to be set and boundaries need to be defined for the smaller person you've become.

You want to learn how to live as a thinner person no matter what the situation or circumstance. A good first step is to remain vigilant. Stay awake, aware, conscious, and mindfully present by keeping a detailed log. No "I blew it," or words to that effect. Even if you did go off your Program, I'll bet you still did better than you might have. You need to remind yourself of that, too.

It's important to learn how to add food back into your food plan so that you won't continue losing weight. If the scale keeps going down, it's almost a residual effect of all you have been doing. But if it goes down by itself, it can also go up by itself.

You've almost finished this book, but your weight-loss journey to the new you is just beginning. Before you continue your journey, let me review some other Program tips and give you my answers to many of the frequently asked questions I receive that I may not have covered elsewhere in the book. However, if you have questions about anything that is not covered here, feel free to contact me via e-mail at Caryl@ConquerFood.com.

QUESTIONS & ANSWERS WITH CARYL ABOUT YOUR PROGRAM

This is a compilation of frequently asked questions that Participants have asked in the past regarding food items, planning meals, and other Program-related topics. These questions are personal, some are random, but they do a good job at shedding more light on what The Program is all about. I know these answers have helped Participants in the past, and I hope they help you as well!

FOOD QUESTIONS

Question: Why no finger foods?

Caryl: Any bite on the run, even a raw carrot, is totally mindless. You're not aware of what or how much you're eating. It doesn't register. Quite often you're eating more food than you need just to free your hands.

Food on a plate eaten with utensils is memorable. You want to look at it as you cut and spear and bring the food to your mouth.

Question: Why can't I drink diet soda? Can I drink it if I choose it as a beverage (one of the BBDA) with my meal?

Caryl: Does the choice of bread/beverage/dessert/alcohol include Diet Soda? No, it does not. Regular soda is fine, but no diet products. When not at meal time, drink flat water, either hot or cold.

Regarding the No Diet Soda edict: Diet products give you a false sense of accomplishment. If you're drinking all of these things because they are low in calories and you remain stuffed and full, then when you eat something that is not as low in calories, your body expects to achieve that same full, bloated, and stuffed feeling.

Reaching your goal is about being loose in your clothes, not stuffed. Soda contains a lot of sodium as well — the carbonation process requires it. Sodium may contribute to retention of water. If you drink all that soda, you might have difficulty consuming 8-10 glasses of water each day in addition to the soda, let alone the food you need for nutrition.

Question: Where does cheese fit in and what about pizza?

Caryl: Cheese is a High-End Protein, which means it is high in fat, cholesterol, and sodium. It's fine to have red meat once every 7-10 days. Or you could have cheese in lieu of the red meat, though red meat has other positives that cheese does not. I think of cheese as coagulated fat. It is the kind of fat that accumulates in the arteries.

Pizza is bread *and* cheese, a High-End Protein — two items. It should be eaten on a plate with a knife and fork, sometimes with a side salad, sometimes without, depending on where the food/fuel needs to take you. If you're eating pizza for dinner and going to sleep an hour later, I would treat it as a two-item meal (bread and cheese). If you're having it at lunch and plan on going back to work afterwards, then you might (or not) add another item, such as a grilled veggie combo of onions, peppers, and mushrooms to the pizza. That would make it a three item meal.

You might choose a salad, to make a three-item meal as well. The question is: How far does the fuel need to take you?

Sometimes I'll order the grilled vegetable pizza and only eat the vegetables on the top. I'm not a big bread eater anymore, but friends like it so I adapt.

Question: Where does yogurt fit in?

Caryl: If yogurt has fruit, it's dessert. If it's plain yogurt, mix a dollop with the milk you're putting into your cereal. You can mix it with salad dressing. Put a tablespoon on a portion of vegetables.

Always spoon onto food or onto a plate. Take all foods out of the containers. The point is, always put food on flat plates. It gives you a more accurate viewpoint on what (and how much) you're eating.

Question: Where does avocado fit in?

Caryl: Avocado is a salad-like component. Like everything, have a few slices with a salad on occasion. Sometimes I have avocado and tomato. Another time I might have carrots and chick peas. Variety is a keynote.

Question: Your Suggested Meal Plan form did not mention juices, though I realize you probably consider them fruit. Would they fall under the dessert category?

Caryl: Yes. Cookies, candy, pie, and cake, as well as the less obvious items such as fruit, fruit *juice*, jam jelly, syrup, honey, nuts, seeds, potato chips, popcorn, and nachos are all desserts on The Program.

Questions: What do you recommend for fiber?

Caryl: Whole grains, hot cereals, and cold cereals daily except when you are having your twice-a-week egg breakfasts. All-Vegetable Meals, with dark (chewy and crunchy) vegetables; maybe shmushy veggies such as eggplant, squash, zucchini, and spinach (among others); side salads with a wide variety of ingredients (cucumber, lettuces, yellow/red/green peppers, celery, radish). Beans, quinoa, and other whole grains have needed fiber. And water, water, water.

Volume is not the goal here, but a wide variety of foods. Oil (olive oil or vegetable oil) in some of the meals also helps fibrous foods to be moved through the system. And, again, water.

Question: Is it okay to chew gum? I find that sugarless gum after a meal takes my mind off eating.

Caryl: No. Gum is not okay to chew. It is not changing the habit of putting something into your mouth when you're not hungry. You are just exchanging food for gum and mindlessly chewing. Eating diet foods is the same thing. You're just exchanging higher calorie food for lower calorie food. You still feel deprived because you're still not getting what you want.

Try brushing your teeth. Swishing your mouth with mouthwash is also very helpful. When repatterning, use a combination of physical things such as brushing your teeth, taking a deep breath, or doing neck and arm stretches. Distract yourself by repeating helpful affirmations. When the kitchen is closed, your mouth should be closed, except for water, of course. Henry Ford said, "Whether you think you can or you think you can't — you're right."

Are you one of the people who sets yourself up to fail so you can later say, "See, I told you"? No matter what I do, nothing works.

A few weeks from now, you might find yourself in a stressful situation with no gum available, so you'll say, "Yes" to that breath mint someone offers. It'll be a hop, skip, and a belt-notch away from a breath mint to Life Savers, which might turn into thin mints and then chocolate. Remember, overeating is very progressive. The frequency of how often you need something increases. Portion size increases, too. So no, gum is not okay to chew to take your mind off eating.

Question: Would a vegetable/bean soup count as a protein? I like lentil soup or soup containing white beans. What about vegetarian chili? If I eat it with a baked potato or a salad, is it also a protein?

Caryl: When I talk about protein, I am referring to animal protein such as poultry/fish/veal and occasionally beef. If you only eat poultry or fish, try to choose the widest variety of fish and fowl, as well as many different types of seasonings, food temperatures, and preparations. This way, you won't be eating the same thing every day, which contributes to mindlessness.

You ask whether you can eat a baked potato with chili. If the chili contains beans (a starch) and the baked potato is a starch, you need to avoid eating those two items together (an old habit). Have the potato on one day with a vegetable and have the beans on another day with a salad. It's helpful to break up these old food combos.

Question: What about pastas, noodles, and breads? I know those are high in carbohydrates and big no-nos on a lot of weight-loss programs.

Caryl: Pastas, and noodles, are starches on this Program, and you need to make sure you get a wide variety; that means including less obvious, but very nutritious starches. For example, all kinds of beans, potatoes, yams, and corn are three starches that come from the ground and have more nutrition than the processed pastas/breads.

Question: I am a vegetarian. Is tofu a good source of protein for The Program?

Caryl: The only food items considered protein on The Program are animal proteins such as chicken, fish, veal, beef, or steak. Tofu can be used in a vegetable meal. That said, if you are a vegetarian, then use tofu, and seitan, as your protein meals in lieu of chicken, fish, or veal. If you eat eggs or fish, switch those off

302   FOOD ADDICTION: PROBLEMS AND SOLUTIONS

with the tofu. The important point here is you must have protein every day. A whole egg has many amino acids and other nutrients that might not be available in tofu.

Question: Does tabbouleh count as an All-Vegetable Meal? I am slowly decreasing my animal meat intake and increasing the variety of vegetables in my food consumption. I'm trying to find some easier and tastier All-Vegetable Meals.

Caryl: Yes, tabbouleh counts as an All-Vegetable Meal. An All-Vegetable Meal is a meal without animal protein. The usual ingredients in tabbouleh include bulgur (a type of wheat), tomatoes, cucumbers, parsley, mint, onion, and garlic — seasoned with natural spices and oils. It is a healthy All-Vegetable Meal. Remember that no matter what you're eating, the portion needs to be consistent with all your other portions.

Salad/soup/vegetables fit into the definition of a meal without protein. Your food portion, whether protein or no-protein, solid or liquid, should reflect your new portion for the new smaller person you are.

If you are a vegetarian, then Tofu, seitan, or tabbouleh can be used as a protein meal, and meals without those can be considered All Vegetable.

All other people need animal Protein.

PROGRAM METHOD QUESTIONS

Question: Last night I went to bed starving! I was that hungry. Am I supposed to be that hungry?

Caryl: No. You're not supposed to be hungry, let alone starving. It takes a few days until you'll know how much food is enough. If you are hungry enough to commit to twenty minutes with food on a plate while using utensils, have a Fourth Meal.

Or perhaps you're not having an animal Protein by Lunch.

A Fourth Meal is one item of food such as an egg, a cup of cereal or soup, one or two slices of turkey or tuna on a plate eaten with utensils, usually eaten between lunch and dinner if lunch didn't contain enough food to take you energy-wise to dinner. It is also eaten slowly (for twenty minutes), and should be treated as a Meal.

Question: I know you like to use the phrase *going off The Program.* I'm *only snacking* before major exercise. Is that still considered *going off The Program*?

Caryl: Snacking? Snacking? A snack is a word that the snack-food industry created because it didn't know what to call high calorie, low-nutritional crap.

Being on The Program is about nourishing your body with food on a plate and eating it with utensils, whether in or out of your home. If it tastes good or looks good or smells good, that's a bonus. It is still not a reason to overeat or eat when you're not hungry enough to commit to a meal. Instead, count it as a one-item meal or a Fourth Meal and give it nutritional value and time.

Question: I'm reading and reviewing the sheets from meeting #2. Am I supposed to copy all the information from all the sheets from meeting #2 into my notebook? I know that sounds like a dumb question coming from a forty-one-year-old, but nowhere on the documents did it say, "Rewrite."

Caryl: There are no dumb questions, only unasked questions. Yes, rewrite everything I give to you into your book so it will be your program, in your handwriting, with your notes.

Question: Rewrite, or just review?

Caryl: A double-header. Rewrite *and* review. It is a daily reminder of the things you're trying to accomplish. Since there are so many things grabbing your attention, even when you read, it takes a while until you remember what you read, internalize what you read, and are able to juggle all the different and varied components.

You do get benefit by taking notes. But the bigger benefit is by reviewing your own notes.

Question: On the last page of your first book, before the acknowledgments, it says now go back to the beginning and begin again. Why do you say that?

Caryl: When you read things the first time, you're not always ready to receive the information. That's part of the "resistance to change" component. You choose to work on all the things that look doable. But now, if you're doing this Program from start to finish, and getting a good result, you can go back to the beginning and pick up the things you resisted at the start. You are a different person, and you will receive the information differently than you did a few months ago.

Two stories: One was my dermatologist removed something from my face. Normally, he'd put some ointment on it and send me home. But this time he gave me a small box containing four small jars. They were labeled 1, 2, 3 & 4. There was a little booklet in the box. I read it and it said put on the cream from jar 1. Put on jar 2 and so on.

The next day (to be sure) I read the booklet again. Put on the cream from jar 1. From jar 2 and so on.

The third day (to be really sure) I read the booklet, but this time it said put on the cream from jar 1 and wash it off before putting on the cream from jar 2.

Who knows why I didn't see the washing off part. Maybe the phone rang. Or someone asked a question. Or I was distracted by something else. So you don't know what you don't know.

I told this story to a participant who told me he had been ordering the same sandwich every day at lunch for months. And after meeting two, he decided to deconstruct the sandwich as I had suggested. He laughed when he was telling me the story; the turkey sandwich he had eaten day after day for months had contained avocado and he had never realized it.

MEAL PLANNING QUESTIONS

Question: Would it make a huge difference if instead of having four-ounce portions, I had three-ounce portions and added an additional three-ounce portion? (I am presently having four four-ounce items a day). My idea is this: 1) breakfast = one item, 2) lunch = two three-ounce portions, and 3) dinner = two three-ounce portions.

Caryl: This is a perfect example of an addict pushing the envelope. The reason the answer is no is because the 3-ounce portion will become a 4-ounce and then 5-ounce portions. The number of times a day you eat will escalate as well. That's how you got in trouble in the first place.

You need around 4-5 ounces of animal protein each day. It accumulates from all the foods you eat. It's okay to add an extra item if needed, but scatter that item so it appears sometimes at breakfast, sometimes at lunch, and other times at dinner. It's a Fourth Meal, a lesser portion of a Protein or No-Protein meal, and is used only when you're hungry enough to commit to a meal.

As you work The Program more and more, you'll need a Fourth Meal less and less often. If extra food is always in the dinner meal, you'll start to gain back the lost weight.

Always see how you feel each day before adding food. Sometimes you need a bite or two more, and sometimes you don't. When you weigh your goal weight, there are so many variables. Lots of variety is important and nothing is etched in stone.

Question: Are the Suggested Meal Plans just to keep variety, or is it important to have seven All-Vegetable or Soup Meals a week for lunch and dinner? When you say in the book that I can switch, does that mean I should pick from the three, let's say, dinners for that day?

Caryl: The plans are to encourage a wide variety of all foods. That said, it is important to have an All-Vegetable Meal at lunch and dinner, a Soup Meal at lunch and dinner, and an Egg Meal at lunch or dinner so you have a No-Protein (Soup/All-Vegetable/Egg) Meal once a day at lunch and dinner, and a Protein at the other meals. Planning should have three All Vegetable/Soup meals at Lunch, and four All Vegetable/Soup at Dinner.

(For those who choose not to eat an egg more than the two at breakfast, choose one additional Soup or All-Vegetable meal at lunch or dinner.)

Protein once a day is sufficient for most people, and on a few days, you might be having an egg protein in addition to the chicken/fish/veal protein you've chosen. It's sort of a *bonus* protein.

To answer your question, the Suggested Meal Plan is to achieve a Soup, an All-Vegetable, and Egg Meal once a day at lunch and dinner, and to ingest the widest variety of foods from each category. You can switch chicken, fish, and veal depending on your likes and dislikes. Some people don't eat veal. Others don't like fish. Get a variety of spices and use a variety of preparations. Sometimes hot and sometimes cold. Spicy or not.

PROGRAM REMINDERS TO FEED THE PROGRAM BRAIN

The following are reminders of things that have proved to work for the behaviorally addicted.

PROGRAM REMINDER #1

So you want to lose some weight. Get a three-ring binder and rewrite any of the suggestions or comments, tips, and tactics that you feel will help you with your goal. Create a title page. It might say, for example, "The Journey of Jane D." Set an official goal. "I want to weigh _____ pounds because: (write about the benefits that will accrue physically, mentally, emotionally, fashionably, sexually, socially, healthfully, and financially)." Among other things, one man wanted to feel comfortable no matter where he was. I wanted to be more in control around food when with others. Another woman wanted everything in the closet to fit.

PROGRAM REMINDER #2

Weigh yourself once in the morning and once in the evening and write it in your book. Using the scale at both ends of the day is to remind you there are rewards and consequences for every food choice you make throughout the day. Take the time to buy a scale you can throw in your suitcase. You want to learn how your body works. How much is your a.m./p.m. differential? Two pounds or less is a nice goal. If you have a bowl of soup for dinner you're almost guaranteed a weight loss the following day.

PROGRAM REMINDER #3

Write down everything you eat in your food log. *If it's not water, it's food. Write it down.* That includes soda, salad, sorbet, celery, every shred, every crumb you pick off your child's plate, and every morsel of food you taste while preparing food. Also, include the bite of dessert you took from a relative's plate, the swallow from a friend's soda, and every cup of coffee or tea you drink. If it's too much trouble, that's resistance to change. You're in your addiction.

PROGRAM REMINDER #4

Before consuming any food, ask, *"Am I hungry, or what?"* If hungry, put all food on a flat plate and eat with utensils (knife, fork, spoon). Try to make each meal last for twenty minutes or more.

When New York City's Mayor Bill de Blasio came to office, the thought that he was eating pizza with utensils, as if he had committed a food faux pas, was front page news. Participants called to inquire whether the mayor had been through The Program. He had not.

PROGRAM REMINDER #5

1. Every bite should be the size of a nickel. Not a shoe or a pickle but a nickel.

2. Put utensils down between bites of food and sips of beverage.

3. Sip water between bites of food and sips of beverage.

4. Make sure mouth is empty before inserting more food.

Repeat 1-4 above.

When you eat too quickly, you'll always eat more than you need. Slow down. It's a Meal not a Marathon. It took weeks of concentrated effort to achieve my new status: Slowest Fork on the Block.

PROGRAM REMINDER #6

Once a day, at lunch or dinner, have a Soup Meal, an All-Vegetable Meal, or an Egg Meal.

By pre-circling your calendar and planning ahead, you are more apt to find these items across a crowded menu.

PROGRAM REMINDER #7

Choose (or not), *Bread or Beverage or Dessert or Alcohol — one of four or none.* Put these items (or not) into breakfast and lunch as well as dinner.

Program Reminder #8

Tally the Number of each Filler in a seven-day period.

A Filler is a food that fills you up but doesn't nourish your body. Fillers are the obvious bread, beverage, dessert, and alcohol (BBDA). But you also want to tally the number of salads and starches that are often eaten because they appear to be free. When you tally the BBDA, see whether anything is consumed more than four times a week.

Program Reminder #9

Whether fish and steak, or coffee and cake, all items need to be *Skipped and Scattered*. If you have an item today, Skip a day before ordering it again. If you have an item at breakfast, Scatter the meal when you order it again, perhaps at lunch the day after tomorrow.

Program Reminder #10

Have a consistent number of items and sips of water at each meal and each day to establish an eating rhythm. One and two item Breakfasts, Lunches, and Dinner. Three, Four, Five, or Six items each day. If you're eating slowly enough, this will be enough physically. It takes a while to make it enough emotionally.

Program Reminder #11

Breakfast food/fuel should take you to lunch.

Lunch food/fuel should take you to dinner.

Dinner food/fuel need only take you to Bedtime.

You only need enough fuel at bedtime to keep your heart and lungs working. The burning of the stored fat will do that fine.

Program Reminder #12

Eat Forward rather than Backwards.

Program Reminder #13

If not hungry and thinking of food, pick a few *Repatterning Techniques* (things to do instead of eating) from each of the following categories:

- Physical (stand in place, move, change location)
- Mental (think: "I want to weigh _____ pounds. I can do it. The moment will pass whether I eat or not. I won't remember any of this later anyway.)
- Verbal ("No thanks; I'm fine. No thanks, but you go ahead. No thanks; I'm not hungry.")
- Refreshing (brush teeth, take a nap, get a massage, take a shower/bath, play music that soothes)
- Use a combination of physical, mental, verbal, and refreshing techniques.

Your goal is to keep doing something until the moment passes. It always does.

Program Reminder #14

Each day, *include a wide variety of foods* such as Hot Cereal (i.e., Oatmeal, Wheatena, Cream of Wheat), Grits, Cold Cereals (i.e., Miniature Shredded Wheat, Grape Nuts), or egg for breakfast.

In order to get the widest variety of nutrients, it's helpful if you choose a wide variety of foods, seasonings, temperature, and preparation over the course of a week. Although you need protein and water daily, many vitamins and minerals are stored for later use if not used immediately. It is not necessary to squeeze every food category into every meal every single day.

Choose a wide assortment of food, which includes variety of content, preparation, temperature, and seasoning as well. This will keep you conscious of the exact moment you are no longer hungry. In addition to protein once a day, you should also look for Soup Meals and All-Vegetable Meals (meals without protein), and/or an occasional Egg Meal such as a broccoli or mushroom omelet at lunch and dinner as well as at breakfast (on different days, of course). Note: If you have a cholesterol problem, consider egg whites. For all others, eat the whole egg.

PROGRAM REMINDER #15

Drink 8-10 eight-ounce glasses of water each day, in addition to all other beverages.

PROGRAM REMINDER #16

Package foods such as chicken, chopped meat, and turkey burgers, steak, and fish into single 4-ounce portion sizes, upon arriving home. Then freeze. If you bring home prepared food such as Chinese takeout, serve yourself first; then portion it into individual packages and freeze leftovers before sitting down to eat. In that way, when you walk back into the kitchen, you won't be thinking, "It's only broccoli. It's only shrimp." You'll be thinking that if you eat the leftovers, you'll be consuming an entire second meal. And besides. It's already been in the freezer for a half hour.

PROGRAM REMINDER #17

Think this thought throughout the day, as needed: *I want to weigh _____ pounds.*

Twenty minutes into your meal is a good time to put down utensils and ask that question: *Am I still hungry?*

PROGRAM REMINDER #18

Holiday, travel, rain, loneliness, stress, or boredom does not mean second portions tonight. Find another hobby. *Create new strategies to replace the old.*

Program Reminder #19

Buy a la carte, not a *prix fixe* meal where you'd feel compelled to eat everything because it was paid for. Perhaps substitute one or two appetizers as a main course if you know dinner is to be late. The later you eat, the fewer number of items you need.

Program Reminder #20

Don't wait to eat until you're famished, starved, or ravenous. And even if you are, you still only need enough food/fuel to take you from where you are to where you are going to be for your next meal, or in the evening, your bedtime. Slow down. Bad planning? You still only need enough fuel to take you a few hours of sedentary time.

Program Reminder #21

Leave one bite of food over each day or one bite each meal, if possible. One bite at each meal is over a thousand bites at the end of the year.

Program Reminder #22

Review your notes daily. If this is not happening, make an appointment with yourself to do it. Rewriting the assignments and reviewing notes helps you to internalize the information. A few lines, a few minutes each day. All efforts add up. You might read them until you come to something that needs work. Put a paper clip on the page and work on that one item. Achieve that and pick another item to work on the next day. Always pick up each day where you left off the day before.

Program Reminder #23

Overeating is overeating. *Watch portion size of salads, vegetables, and beverages*, as well as desserts, breads, alcohol, and Hi-End

Protein. A portion is the size of a deck of cards, not the deck on a boat.

PROGRAM REMINDER #24

Cheer yourself on rather than beating yourself up. Maintain a positive attitude and you will get positive results.

PROGRAM REMINDER #25

There is no such thing as: little, crumb, small, just, tiny, or trivial. *If you swallowed it, you ate it, and it all adds up.*

PROGRAM REMINDER #26

You cannot lose any significant amount of weight with exercise. It might even backfire. You might be thinking that you can eat more because you did an extra leg lift. If you like to exercise then it's good for your head and heart. Are you one of those people who underestimates what you eat and overestimates how much activity you did?

No matter your preference, whether to join in group sports or actually use a gym membership or to pursue running, hiking, or biking alone, you need to move, <u>get up, and walk.</u> Make several trips to serve a meal or clean a table. Walk up and down stairs instead of using elevators or escalators. Walk up and down the escalator. Even one flight of stairs a day is 365 flights you've walked by the year's end. In New York, it's easy. It might be more challenging in other places.

There was an article in *The New York Times* about a woman who lived in a five-floor walk-up for years. The first year she moved into an elevator building, she gained ten pounds. Any effort is better than none.

REVIEW

If you've started your program, kept a log, got on the scale twice daily, took nickel-sized bites of food among other things, then this is a good time to see what works and what needs work. Use Review Number One.

If you're not ready to review, you can read each statement slowly and thoughtfully without checking whether you're doing something or not. Most of the Review numbers are statements; as if it is already so. So just read the statements. Not every one of you will be ready to review at the same time. It's all fine.

Once you've been doing some of the suggestions and have started your Program, use Review Number One about a week or two after you've begun your Program.

Be kind to yourself. It takes a little bit of time to organize the materials and to incorporate these concepts into your eating. The more you read the materials, the more sense it will make.

WHY REVIEW?

There's a statistic floating around that says you forget 60% of what you read an hour later. Is that you?

When reading this book it is helpful if you highlight passages you want to remember. Regularly reading the highlighted material, helps you to remember what you've read in the long term.

A review reminds you of something easily overlooked or something you forgot. It is best to read a little each day while being mindful and thoughtful rather than racing through the material only to forget what you read.

There are two kinds of reviews.

The first is when you read the highlighted passages. You're reading what <u>you think</u> is important. That is important. These are the things you feel comfortable changing. That's great.

Of course there may be *resistance to change* when you choose to do one assignment over another. If you're still losing weight you might even think you got away with not doing this or that.

The 2nd kind of review is a little more formal. It covers the things <u>I think</u> are important.

I think it's important to review at least once a week to find out what works and what needs work. The results change daily as new habits take hold.

All reviews can be used again and again. The Review Number Three is the most comprehensive. Review Number Four allows you a numeric component. You're trying to get your score to be as close to 100 as possible. You'll have time to improve your score if you review on a regular basis.

Be kind to yourself. While reviewing, make sure to give yourself credit for improving, working on something, repatterning, moving you or it, changing location, drinking water, modifying behavior, trying, and attempting, while proactively conquering your own food addiction. Give yourself credit for every attempt, try, endeavor, undertaking, effort, adjustment, change, start, or step you take toward weighing _____ pounds.

REVIEW NUMBER ONE   DATE: _____

1. How much did you weigh when you began your Program?   _____
2. How much did you weigh this morning?   _____
3. Weight difference plus or minus?   _____

	More Often than Not	Could Do Better	Seldom Accomplish
4. I keep a log of food consumed.	_____	_____	_____
5. I review assignments a little each day.	_____	_____	_____
6. I weigh daily (a.m. and p.m.).	_____	_____	_____
7. I plan ahead the foods I'm going to eat.	_____	_____	_____
8. Before eating, I ask: *Am I hungry, Or what?*	_____	_____	_____
9. I always put food on a plate and eat with utensils.	_____	_____	_____
10. I take nickel-sized bites.	_____	_____	_____
11. I put utensils down between bites of food and sips of beverage.	_____	_____	_____
12. I sip water between bites of food and sips of beverage.	_____	_____	_____
13. I create a relaxing 20-minute meal.	_____	_____	_____
14. I choose bread or beverage or dessert or alcohol, one of four or none.	_____	_____	_____
15. I Skip and Scatter same category foods.	_____	_____	_____
16. When eating, I choose food from the middle of the Meal Parameters List before choosing items from the top or bottom of the list.	_____	_____	_____
17. I drink 8-10 glasses of water each day.	_____	_____	_____
18. Breakfast contains a variety of Hot cereals, Cold cereals, or egg.	_____	_____	_____

	More Often than Not	Could Do Better	Seldom Accomplish
19. I eat a wide variety of Soups, All Vegetable, or Egg meals once a day at lunch or dinner.	_____	_____	_____
20. I circle on my Food Log four Soups and All Vegetable Dinners, and three Soup and All Vegetable Lunches.	_____	_____	_____
21. I feed a smaller person and buy, order, prepare, serve, and eat less food.	_____	_____	_____
22. If not hungry, but thinking of eating, I take as many steps (thought, word, action) as necessary to help the moment pass.	_____	_____	_____
23. My challenging moments are less frequent, shorter in duration and diminished in quantity of food.	_____	_____	_____
24. I review the *Could do Better* (and *Seldom Accomplish*) items and each day pick one or two items to prioritize.	_____	_____	_____
25. I can do it.	_____	_____	_____

REVIEW NUMBER TWO   DATE: _____

1. How much did you weigh when you began your Program?   _____

2. How much did you weigh this morning?   _____

3. Weight difference plus or minus?   _____

	More Often than Not	Could Do Better	Seldom Accomplish
4. I transferred all notes into one convenient log book, computer, or cell phone.	_____	_____	_____
5. I keep a detailed food log.	_____	_____	_____
6. I weigh twice daily (a.m. and p.m.)	_____	_____	_____
7. I review daily my assignments, goals, things I'd like to accomplish.	_____	_____	_____
8. Before consuming any food I ask: *Am I hungry, or what?*	_____	_____	_____
9. If hungry, I put food on a plate and eat with utensils.	_____	_____	_____
10. If hungry I take nickel sized bites to create a relaxing 20 minute meal.	_____	_____	_____
11. I make sure my mouth is empty before inserting more food.	_____	_____	_____
12. Mid-meal, I ask: *Am I still hungry, or what?*	_____	_____	_____
13. I choose bread or beverage or dessert or alcohol, one of four or none.	_____	_____	_____
14. I Skip and Scatter same category foods.	_____	_____	_____
15. I choose food from the middle of the Meal Parameters list before choosing items from the top or bottom of the list.	_____	_____	_____
16. I sip, not gulp, 8-10 glasses of water daily.	_____	_____	_____
17. I choose a wide variety of Hot Cereals, Cold Cereals, or an Egg for breakfast.	_____	_____	_____

	More Often than Not	Could Do Better	Seldom Accomplish
18. I choose an All-Vegetable meal, a Soup meal, or an Egg meal, at least once a day at lunch or dinner.	_____	_____	_____
19. I circle on my food log, Soup, All-Vegetable, and Egg Lunches and Dinners.	_____	_____	_____
20. I seek a wide variety of foods, vegetables, seasonings, and preparations.	_____	_____	_____
21. I keep a daily tally of my Fillers.	_____	_____	_____
22. Fillers are scattered every other day, and are decreasing in frequency.	_____	_____	_____
23. I have some one item breakfasts and occasionally it's two.	_____	_____	_____
24. I choose one, two, and occasionally a three item lunch.	_____	_____	_____
25. I choose one, two, and occasionally a three item dinner.	_____	_____	_____
26. I choose a four item meal when it is New Year's Eve and my Birthday on the same day.	_____	_____	_____
27. I consume 4/5/6 items or fewer each day.	_____	_____	_____
28. I buy, order, and prepare less food.	_____	_____	_____
29. I leave over, throw out, or freeze leftover food, if appropriate.	_____	_____	_____
30. If not hungry, and thinking of food, I think, speak, or move until the moment passes.	_____	_____	_____
31. My challenging moments are less frequent, shorter in duration, and diminished in volume and ferocity.	_____	_____	_____
32. I do many things to relieve stress, tension, and boredom rather than using food.	_____	_____	_____
33. No matter what I have done, I get back on The Program at the very next meal.	_____	_____	_____

	More Often than Not	Could Do Better	Seldom Accomplish
34. Every food choice I make reflects my ultimate weight-loss goal.	_____	_____	_____
35. I am feeding a smaller person.	_____	_____	_____
36. I can do it.	_____	_____	_____

When reading the items checked in the Could do Better or the Seldom Accomplish columns, pick one or two things you could prioritize today. Tomorrow read again and pick another. And so on.

REVIEW NUMBER THREE   DATE: _____

1. How much did you weigh when you began your Program?   _____
2. How much did you weigh this morning?   _____
3. Weight difference plus or minus?   _____

	More Often than Not	Could Do Better	Seldom Accomplish
4. I transferred all notes into one convenient log book, computer, or cell phone.	_____	_____	_____
5. I keep a detailed food log.	_____	_____	_____
6. I weigh twice daily (a.m. and p.m.)	_____	_____	_____
7. I review a little bit of my logbook daily; Assignments, goals, and things I'd like to accomplish.	_____	_____	_____
8. I anticipate my day and plan (in advance) the content and Number of Items for each meal.	_____	_____	_____
9. Before consuming any food I ask: *Am I hungry, or what?*	_____	_____	_____
10. If hungry, I put food on a plate and eat with utensils.	_____	_____	_____
11. If hungry I take nickel sized bites to create a relaxing 20 minute meal.	_____	_____	_____
12. I put utensils down between bites of food and sips of beverage.	_____	_____	_____
13. I sip water between bites of food and sips of beverage.	_____	_____	_____
14. I make sure my mouth is empty before inserting more food.	_____	_____	_____
15. I choose bread or beverage or dessert or alcohol, one of four or none.	_____	_____	_____
16. I Skip and Scatter same category foods.	_____	_____	_____
17. I choose food from the middle of the Meal Parameters list before choosing items from the top or bottom of the list.	_____	_____	_____

	More Often than Not	Could Do Better	Seldom Accomplish
18. I sip (not gulp) 8-10 glasses of water each day.			
19. If it's not water, it's food. Write it down.			
20. I choose a wide variety of Hot Cereal, Cold Cereal, or an Egg for breakfast.			
21. I choose an All-Vegetable meal, a Soup meal, or an Egg meal, at least once a day at lunch or dinner.			
22. I circle on my food log, Soup, All-Vegetable, and Egg Lunches and Dinners.			
23. I seek a wide variety of foods, vegetables, seasonings, and preparations.			
24. I keep a daily tally of my Fillers.			
25. Fillers are scattered every other day, and are decreasing in frequency.			
26. I have some one item breakfasts, occasionally it's two items.			
27. I choose one, two, and occasionally a three item lunch.			
28. I plan one, two, and occasionally a three item dinner.			
29. I choose a four item meal when it is New Year's Eve and my Birthday on the same day.			
30. I know that "occasionally" means once or twice a week.			
31. I consume 4/5/6 (or fewer) items each day.			
32. My portion size is four ounces; the size of a deck of cards, not the deck of a boat.			
33. The portion size of coffee, tea, and soda is a cup (8 ounces) or less.			
34. The portion size of a glass of wine is 5 ounces.			

	More Often than Not	Could Do Better	Seldom Accomplish
35. I buy, order, and prepare less food.	_____	_____	_____
36. I leave at least one bite of food on the plate at every meal, more than a thousand bites by the end of the year.	_____	_____	_____
37. I leave over, throw out, or freeze leftover food, if appropriate.	_____	_____	_____
38. I feed the smaller person I am becoming and want to be.	_____	_____	_____
39. If not hungry, and thinking of food, I think, speak, or move until the moment passes. I find new ways to cope with the ups and downs of life.	_____	_____	_____
40. Every food choice I make reflects my ultimate weight-loss goal.	_____	_____	_____
41. My challenging moments are less frequent, shorter in duration, and diminished in volume and ferocity.	_____	_____	_____
42. No matter what I have done, I get back on The Program at the very next meal.	_____	_____	_____
43. I do many things to relieve stress, tension, and boredom rather than using food.	_____	_____	_____
44. I am feeding a smaller person.	_____	_____	_____
45. I can do it.	_____	_____	_____

It is helpful to re-write the review pages into your own log book. You learn by reading, writing, speaking and hearing.

When reading the Could do Better or the Seldom Accomplish, prioritize two or three things. The next day pick another few. Continue to embrace and polish each assignment so they all become part of your life and comfortable. Remind yourself that you want to weigh _____ pounds.

REVIEW NUMBER FOUR   DATE: _____

1. How much did you weigh when you began your Program?   _____

2. How much did you weigh this morning?   _____

3. Weight difference plus or minus?   _____

RATE YOUR PROGRESS

4 = Part of your life and comfortable
3 = Aware and trying
2 = Improving but could do better
1 = Holding on to old habits

Be kind to yourself.

1. I am aware of food, weight, and measurements daily.   _____

2. I slow down, put food on a plate, and take nickel-sized bites when eating.   _____

3. I get a variety of Cereals, All-Vegetable meals, Soup meals.   _____

4. I sip (not gulp) 8-10 glasses of water, hot or cold, daily.   _____

5. I eat only when hungry.   _____

6. I stop eating when no longer hungry.   _____

7. I plan, in advance bread or beverage or dessert or alcohol,
one of four or none.   _____

8. Whether salad or steak, coffee or cake, I Skip and Scatter all
categories of foods.   _____

9. I use a Suggested Meal Plan each day.   _____

10. I know the Meal Parameters and Guidelines, and use them.   _____

11. I count Fillers each day and total Fillers each week.   _____

12. I eat one and two item meals with 4/5/6/items daily.   _____

13. I choose a uniform portion size of all items.   _____

14. I leave over one bite at every meal, over a thousand bites by the
end of the year.   _____

15. I acknowledge all strong new habits as they become more comfortable.   _____

16. I am aware of habits that *need work*.   _____

17. I remember the reasons I want to reach my weight-loss goal.   _____

18. I remember the reasons I want to be thinner.   _____

19. I remember the negatives of overeating.   _____

20. I remember the negatives of being overweight.   _____

21. I enjoy the positives of eating the right amount for me.   _____

22. I enjoy the positives of being a smaller person.   _____

23. I am aware of new habits being formed, and old ones disappearing.   _____

24. I review my notes a little each day and adjust actions accordingly.   _____

25. I keep on keeping on, and never stop trying.   _____

Out of a possible 100 points, your total is: _____.

Use this form once a month. It'll give you time to improve. As always, it's a reminder of things you've accomplished and things you want to accomplish.

AFTERWORD

Throughout this book, I used a variety of e-mail exchanges that covered the gamut of problems from food addiction to compulsive eating. There's a lot of new information to digest. And of course, the only way to internalize this information is to continue your quest to weigh _____ pounds. By reading the notes you realize the value of logging and mindfulness. I'm hoping you find comfort, connection, understanding, and advice from some of the exchanges. At the very least, you've hopefully realized there are many who succeed. You can too.

Do not be fooled by the seemingly simplistic structure of The Program. There are hundreds of pieces to making it succeed. Each ritual has been attached to another, and then another sized habit. The Program has dissected and unraveled the problems and solutions of food addiction. Food was, after all, just produce a few moments ago. You need to remind yourself of that, too.

Part of addiction is resistance to change. At the start of your program, you might have been more resistant than you are now that you've lost weight. But you are a different person now than you were when you began reading this book. Go back to the beginning and begin reading again. You will most likely be even more ready to receive information than when you read the same information a few weeks or months earlier. It'll seem as if you'd never read it before.

Let me hear an I Can Do It!

It has been my pleasure to share with you, and it would be my pleasure to hear from you. Email me at Caryl@ConquerFood.com or visit me at www.ConquerFood.com and let me hear your questions, comments, Quantum Leaps and Positive Stories.

THANK YOU . . .

Thanks to all the participants of The Caryl Ehrlich Program who shared their stories about conquering food addiction. Thanks to people from all over the United States (and the world) including doctors, lawyers, financial planners, clergy, opera singers, and people who sing in the choir for participating in The Program and for sending your friends and co-workers. A special thanks to Northwestern Mutual for referring so many people to The Program. And to all the manuscript readers for reading various incarnations of the book you are reading.

Thanks to all the participants of The Program who said I could use their names, pseudonyms, initials only, and no-names at all. People said yes or no and then changed their minds. And because I respect everyone's anonymity, I decided to not use anyone's name. But from the bottom of my heart, thank you all for reading, commenting, laughing, arguing, and agreeing with all you've learned by telling me positive stories about a meal or a food encounter that came out better than what you imagined, and also telling me what has tripped you up. I appreciate every comment and funny story made on behalf of a better book.

Thank you to Ilene Style for your many editing suggestions and stories of your own journey. Thanks to Susan Kim for her calm demeanor while moving chapters around, cleaning up forms, and then moving them back when I changed my mind again. Thank you to Tyler Tichelaar who did a good job in editing my sentences and making other suggestions that made everything read better, and tighter. Thanks to Susan Friedmann, owner of Aviva Publishing, for her guidance every step of the way to help make this beautiful book possible.

I couldn't have done it without all of you.

Onward and downward,
Caryl Ehrlich

Send Questions or comments to:
Caryl@ConquerFood.com

The Beginning

OTHER BOOKS BY CARYL EHRLICH

Conquer Your Food Addiction: The Ehrlich 8-Step Program for Permanent Weight Loss

ABOUT THE AUTHOR

Caryl Ehrlich has had an extraordinary record of success with The Caryl Ehrlich Program, a behavioral approach to permanent weight loss for food addicts.

She has maintained The Caryl Ehrlich Program – one of the longest running programs of its kind – for over thirty-six years, supporting it at different times as host of a successful radio show on WMCA. She additionally had a cable show for many years. Caryl lives and teaches her weight loss methods in NYC and all over the world by phone.

www.ingramcontent.com/pod-product-compliance
Lightning Source LLC
Chambersburg PA
CBHW060246100426
42742CB00011B/1652

*9 7 8 1 9 4 0 9 8 4 8 7 2 *